Flagship Captain

A ship under ground

This hillside opening in Hawaii is the entrance to a vast underground complex that was among the U.S. military's most guarded secrets when I commanded it in the early 1960s.

During these years it was, for all practical purposes, the flagship for the Commander-in-Chief of America's military forces in the Pacific – an area of responsibility spanning two-thirds of the earth's surface.

By the time this photograph was taken in the early 2000s, it had become an installation of the National Security Agency (NSA).

Flagship Captain

The Cold War Navy
at Sea, Ashore, and Underground

George P. Sotos
Captain, USN (Ret.)

Mt. Vernon, Virginia ▪ Mt. Vernon Book Systems

2021

Printing 1.0

Copyright © 2021 by George P. Sotos. All Rights Reserved. No part of this book may be reproduced in any form by any means (electronic, mechanical, xerographic, photonic, quantum, or other) or held in any information storage and retrieval system without written permission from the copyright holder.

Mt. Vernon Book Systems
P.O. Box 21
Mt. Vernon, VA 22121

Visit us at: `www.sotos.navy` or `www.mtvernonbook.com`

Printing 1.0
Please email comments to: `mail@mtvernonbook.com`
Kindly include the printing number.

Printed in the United States of America

This book was produced using Macintosh computers, Scrivener, and the TeXShop front-end for the TeX and LaTeX typesetting system. TeX is a trademark of the American Mathematical Society. TeXShop is by Richard Koch and Dirk Olmes, and includes work by Gerben Wierda.

ISBN 978-1-7365399-0-3   (softcover)

Also by the author:

Plateau of Chains

Living with the Torpedo

Contents

List of Figures	ix
Introduction	13
1 Kunia	17
2 Nuclear War Command and Control	25
3 The Real Thing	37
4 A Dumb Decision	55
5 Back to School	67
6 The Berlin Crisis	77
7 Learn by Doing	93
8 Land the Landing Force	105
9 Boot Camp	121
10 More Boots – The Korean War	141
11 Collision	157
12 Destroyer Command	167

Contents

13	This One's Greek	177
14	Self Discipline – Navy Style	199
15	War College	205
16	The Pacific DEW Line	213
17	Carry Out Your Orders	221
18	Birth of a Command Center	227
19	Kunia II	239
20	Nuclear War Readiness	245
21	Man Overboard	255
22	At The Top	267
23	The Joint Chiefs of Staff	273
24	Loyalty Is a Two-Way Street	291
A	Photo Credits	300
B	Bibliography	302
Index		304

List of Figures

A ship under ground ii
Another view of the entrance to the Kunia complex 12
Above the Kunia complex 16
Admiral Harry Felt 21
The "big board" in SAC war room 24
Communications room 30
Communications room 31
Entrance to an underground center 36
USS *Gary* (DE 326) 54
Ships mothballed in Green Cove Springs 56
USS *Tolovana* (AO 64) 61
Line School classmates 66
USS *Colonial* (LSD 18) 71
LSD well deck 72
One of many airplanes for Berlin 76
Unusual orders to command the *Colonial* 78
LSDs and aviation 81
Well-deck of present-day LSD 82
LSD amphibious operations 92
The almost-collision 94
Maneuver diagram 95
Maneuver diagram – what actually transpired 97
Well deck from above 104
Welcome aboard 120
Recruit fire training 123
Realistic fire training 124

Esprit de corps	140
USS *Tolovana* giving fuel	156
USS *Harlan R. Dickson* underway	166
Dickson on the cover	176
Formal reception in the *Dickson* wardroom	181
Our Greek hosts on the island of Rhodes	184
Greek barge, adrift	187
Recruits at Great Lakes	198
US Naval War College	204
War game in the electronic era	209
Pacific Barrier segment of the DEW Line	212
A corner of Pearl Harbor, 1959	220
Desks and displays in SAC war room	226
Organization of Kunia (FOCCPAC) war rooms	228
If no news, send rumors	235
Map of Oahu	238
Writing about secret matters	244
Tolovana vs. aircraft carrier	254
Tolovana in profile	256
The Pentagon	266
National Military Command System	272
Joint Staff organization	275
Combatant Commands	276
Defense Communications Agency, circa 1965	277
Spreading the word about computers at the highest levels	290
Age vs. teaching	297
A goodbye from DODCI and the Navy	298
About the author	305

These memoirs are dedicated to my wonderful family:

Georgette (Gina) Sotos

John G. Sotos, MD
Colonel, California Air National Guard

George A. Sotos, MD

Figure 12: **Another view of the entrance to the Kunia complex.** The view here is from the direction opposite that of the Frontispiece. The entrance to the Kunia tunnel is in the lower left of the top photo, buried in the hillside just above the "H" that marks the helipad. In this 2008 photograph the pineapple fields of the 1950s and 1960s, which had been at the left and bottom of the photograph, are gone.

Introduction

Command – especially command at sea – is one of the toughest, yet most desirable, jobs to which a naval officer can aspire. It is a job that requires unbreakable mutual bonds of trust and confidence between the captain and the entire crew. This is especially true on a flagship, where the captain's immediate superior is riding his ship and expects a level of mission support second to none.

But, as in every society, a small number (less than 2% in my experience) of people are careless and can rupture that bond. The well-publicized, deadly collisions in 2017 between merchant ships and the destroyers *Fitzgerald* and *McCain*, as well as the reprehensible conduct of a group of senior officers in the Seventh Fleet (2018) are examples of the impact of such ruptures.

High quality leadership – the type that influences subordinates to strive for and achieve a personal level of self-discipline that accommodates responsibility and accountability and drives these individuals to improve every aspect of his or her life – can eliminate these ruptures. But strangely, it remains the Navy's most insidious flaw and one of its greatest challenges.

This book recounts the many faces of the leadership challenge I confronted during an adventurous and unusual Navy career that spanned much of the Cold War and two hot wars.

Of the many ways to present information to readers, I have chosen to use dialog liberally, given that spoken words are the cornerstone of a Navy officer's life aboard ship and on shore –

Introduction

or were, until the advent of email. Although perfect recall of decades-old conversation is, of course, not possible, the tenor and tone of the conversations are accurate, as are any operational or technical matters discussed.

I am indebted to my smart and pretty wife of 62 years who had the patience to listen to my sea stories and encouraged me to record them. Thank you, Gina. To be truthful, though, without the guidance and help of my multi-talented son John, this memoir would have never advanced beyond the stage of a rough manuscript. Thank you, John.

Orthographic Notes

There is no standard spelling for the syncope of "forecastle." This book uses *foc'stle*.

Military ranks are not capitalized, unless they directly precede a personal name.

Some personal names have been changed. These are not real names: Pierson p. 28 / Hines p. 33 / Torelli p. 33 / Martin p. 81 / Ryan p. 85 / Smith p. 107 / Clark p. 158 / Jones p. 190 / Broffman p. 199 / Piccion p. 213 / Thelon p. 214 / Harmon p. 214 / Warren p. 264.

Figure 16: **Above the Kunia complex.** The left half of this 2008 satellite photograph shows the site of the Kunia complex. Probably taken on a weekend (parking lot is empty), the bulk of the complex is under the farm fields. The right half of the photo shows an area of Wheeler Army Airfield. The proximity is no coincidence – Kunia started its life as an aircraft assembly plant.

Chapter 1

Kunia

For three years at the height of the Cold War – including the unbearably tense week when nuclear fire came close to incinerating human civilization on earth – I commanded the most unique and, arguably, one of the most important, military facilities in the world.

It was, of course, secret. Located deep under a hilly pineapple field on the Hawaiian island of Oahu, and guarded by single-minded Marine sentries, its formal name was the Fleet Operational Control Center Pacific (FOCCPAC). We, however, universally referred to it as "Kunia," the name of the small town nearby. (Pronounced kuh-NEE-uh.)

An installation of this size and mission could not be completely secret, but let me give you an idea of how focused on secrecy we were: One day I received a call from the chief of the sentries, who said, "Sir, there's a reporter crawling around the pineapple field. Do you want us to shoot him?"

When military planners and fiction writers write about waging a nuclear war, it is no exaggeration to say that critical phases of such a war would, for over half of the earth, have been waged from the Kunia complex. The Pentagon, just outside Washington, DC, would certainly be reduced to rubble in the first minutes of such a war – just one hijacked plane proved that on Sept. 11, 2001. Although the Pentagon has an underground

1. KUNIA

command center, it has long been considered useless in a nuclear war.[1]

Kunia, on the other hand, was designed to ride out and survive an attack with the nuclear weapons of the time. The top military commanders safely inside would continue to fight the war.

Kunia started its life during World War II, shortly after the attack on Pearl Harbor, as a tunnel for aircraft assembly. (Other nicknames for the complex included "The Tunnel" and "The Hole.") It wasn't really a tunnel. Rather, it started as a three-story hangar-like structure with a large open bay and reinforced concrete walls, all covered by dirt. Later, it served as a map-making facility and an ammunition depot before beginning in 1958 its transformation into a military command center.[2] I arrived there the following year.

Compared to the massive Pentagon (5 floors, 2 basements, 3.7+ million square feet of office space), Kunia was much smaller. It had 250,000 square feet of office space on three floors of hardened concrete. It was connected to the outside world by two quarter-mile long tunnels (one for entrance, the other for air intake), each high and wide enough to accommodate two large trucks abreast. With its hardened concrete ceiling ten feet below the pineapple field, Kunia was designed to withstand the explosive force of a 15-kiloton atom bomb (about equal to the one used on Hiroshima). It was also designed to be a command center focused on continuity of command, having a very large communications center, one of the largest computer systems in the military, and many other advanced technological systems.

Our fully buried center was designed for up to 700 people. It had nine separate war rooms; two completely independent television systems that fed into almost every room in the build-

---

[1] A billion-dollar "deep underground command center," 3500 feet below ground, with high-speed elevators to the Pentagon and State Department, was considered in the 1960s but never built. Graff, page 174; Schlosser, page 274.

[2] Bamford, page 313. Also: Oahu *Star-Bulletin*, April 24, 1960 (Figure 235).

ing; two large modern television studios; a 150-seat theater; and a vast temperature-controlled computer room with wiring below a raised floor. The room housed two of the largest Control Data computers in the nation. We also had a two story communications and relay center destined to be the largest in the Pacific; a massive internal air tube message delivery system that went from the communications center to every key office and war room in the building; an independent internal water supply that drew water direct from its own private protected well; a modern sewage disposal system; three huge generators which furnished uninterrupted power throughout the building; an air intake tunnel that could direct all incoming air through two giant biologic and chemical filters; a large modern cafeteria; a dispensary; an emergency food supply to feed 400 people for four months; sleeping accommodations for hundreds; and armed Marines on 24-hour guard duty above, at the entrance, and inside the facility.

When I walked into the Kunia complex for the first time on December 10, 1959 to take command, I had no instructions on what to do. That would not change over the three years I served there ... with the exception of three crisp sentences. But those sentences were the best set of orders I ever received, and they got us all through the time when the world nearly ended – when I became perhaps the only American military commander ever to formally set DEFCON 1 in anticipation of a nuclear war.

• • • •

My official title was commanding officer, Fleet Operational Control Center Pacific (FOCCPAC). The FOCCPAC housed the emergency war rooms of Commander in Chief Pacific (CINCPAC) and eight of his major Pacific commanders, as well as a number of additional intelligence offices. (Figure 228 lists the rooms.) Four-star Admiral Harry Felt was CINCPAC during my tenure at Kunia (Figure 21). During any war involving the United States, Admiral Felt would have been the military commander for all operations in the Pacific area, including those of the Army and Air Force.

1. KUNIA

Kunia had a four-fold mission:[3]

1. Provide and maintain the hardened Kunia facility.

2. Provide continuous support and assistance to the war rooms of CINCPAC and to major commanders on the island of Oahu in the execution of their command and control operations during an attack on the U.S. *(The war rooms are listed in Figure 228.)*

3. Maintain instant readiness of the computer based operational data supporting CINPAC's nuclear weapon mission in the Pacific.

4. Maintain and operate, around the clock, a major communications center and relay.

For obvious reasons the number of emergency and alternate command centers like mine was closely held, secret information until 2017.[4] In 1962, as far as I knew, there were only three other large underground command centers like mine. One was in western Maryland, at Fort Ritchie (Camp David), for use by the President and the Joint Chiefs of Staff. The second was outside Omaha, Nebraska, for the Strategic Air Command (SAC), and the third was the North American Air Defense Command (NORAD), located in the bowels of Cheyenne Mountain, which looms 3000 feet above Colorado Springs, Colorado.[5]

Mine was not the biggest center, nor was it the safest, since our 9-foot thick concrete ceiling on the third floor was only about ten feet below the pineapples. However, except for the SAC center it was the most efficient, best organized, best

---

[3] These missions were not assigned to us. We developed and inserted them in all our relevant policy statements, publications, and correspondence.

[4] See Graff in bibliography.

[5] There were a large number of relocation sites – some underground – but they were not as deeply involved in support of command and control of nuclear war operations. Graff describes more than 16 of them.

Figure 21: **Admiral Harry Felt.** He was CINCPAC – Commander In Chief of the Pacific region for all the military services. Others have described him as "smart, short, and irascible" [Rust, page 209]. I found him hard-working and serious.

---

equipped, and most flexible. I say this with some confidence, since I visited and toured the other centers.

Why then, was the FOCCPAC at Kunia so operationally effective? The principal reason was the guidance I received from Admiral Felt.

Kunia was his emergency command center. The war rooms and subsidiary offices were for his subordinate commanders, from all services in the Pacific, plus other key organizations such as SAC, the CIA, and various intelligence commands. All had people from their operations staff in my building on a permanent basis.

I only met with Admiral Felt four or five times in my entire three year tour at Kunia.

At my first meeting, when I was quite new and bewildered by the still uncompleted building, and by the complexity of the command center, and by my sudden role at a high command

1. Kunia

level, he asked me how I was getting along.

I told him that there was no precedent for the command center: no organization manual, no standard instructions, no guidance of any type, nothing in the way of policies which could be implemented in the building or on an intra/inter-service level.

He didn't smile. But I could see that he knew all about my predicament and my problems.

He said, "Captain, you are the skipper of a flagship here. Run this place just as you would a flagship." Then, before I could say anything, he added, "Every Flag Officer who has a staff in Kunia is on your flagship – treat him as you would on a flagship. Make a courtesy call on each one and let him know you are his flag Captain ready to help him. Do you understand?"

"Yes sir," I responded as the light turned on in my brain. I had been the flag skipper for Commander Destroyer Flotilla Six in the Sixth Fleet, and so I knew well a flag skipper's role.

That was the only guidance I received from Admiral Felt in my entire tour at Kunia. But it was crystal clear.

It was the only guidance I received from any one.

Figure 24: **The "big board" in SAC war room.** No internal pictures were taken of any part of Kunia while I was there. This photograph was taken in the command center of the Strategic Air Command in Omaha, Nebraska. Our briefing room stage was about the same size. However, our presentation boards were about one-third the height of those shown here, and we had a large television screen, measuring about 8 feet by 8 feet.

Chapter 2

Nuclear War Command and Control

What does a nuclear command center look like? If you have visions of early-1960s war rooms from movies like *Dr. Strangelove*, you are actually not that far off.

In addition to the nine separate war rooms, the communications center, engineering plant, and other features mentioned in the previous chapter, Kunia had a large, specially-designed room that was a combination small auditorium, conference center and joint war room.[1]

It had a large stage that ran the width of the fifty-foot room. The stage itself had a depth of about forty feet, but the fourteen-foot ceiling made it look much larger. At the back of the stage, behind black curtains, were work rooms where different groups of display and computer experts worked with the war room staffs to prepare the visual aids. These ranged from sixteen-by-four foot maps on plywood boards to large television monitors and overhead projectors.

In front of and below the stage there was a large, mahogany, oval conference table with chairs for fifteen people. All the

---

[1] In military parlance, "joint" means "more than one military service." The Army, Navy, and Air Force all had staff at Kunia, making it joint.

2. Nuclear War Command and Control

chairs except one were on one side facing the stage. The exception: a rotating chair at the head of the table was for CINCPAC.[2]

To the right of each chair, level with the table but slanted upward so it could be seen easily, was a video monitor that could receive television pictures from any of the nine war rooms, the major television networks, the White House, and messages from the communications center. If all of this sounds routine, remember this was 1959.

Behind the large conference table, in the back of the room, was the "gallery," so named because it was the seating area used by the staffs of the flag officers who sat at the conference table. With the floor sloping upward, the people in the rear of the ten-row gallery could see and hear quite well.

The seat in the gallery's first row, closest to the CINCPAC, belonged to his senior War Room watch officer, a Navy captain. My seat was next to him.

Directly above my seat, but extending out toward the stage, almost above CINCPAC's chair at the table, was a small one-man balcony. During exercises, my operations officer occupied it.

At those times, he had a script in his hand and was busy talking, but no one on the floor below him could hear his voice. He was wearing a headset with one earpiece that connected him directly to CINCPAC, every war room, the television control center, the computer room, the intelligence center, the display work rooms, and the communications center.

With his uncovered ear he was expected to hear, and when relevant, respond to everything said below him by CINCPAC and the others at the table. It took excellent timing and superb coordination between the different war rooms and my operations officer to make it work. And because of exhaustive training, which I witnessed, I knew it worked damn well.

It was, indeed, a most unusual set-up. Just think, there were nine separate flag officer war rooms scattered throughout the

---

[2] Recall that CINCPAC is short for Commander in Chief Pacific, a major Unified Command commanded by a four star admiral.

building. Each had a separate mission that included support of CINCPAC. The staff in each war room listened in on the meeting. They not only provided information when requested, they frequently volunteered information that might be relevant to what they were hearing. The entire operation was designed to provide formal briefings and immediate answers to questions from CINCPAC or from any of the flag officers at the table.

Obviously, we never fought a nuclear war during my time at Kunia. But we did rehearse and train extensively. In fact, war drills and training for all participants was a large part of our daily operations.

As mentioned earlier, Kunia was an emergency command center to which the major commands would relocate for continuity of command and control during nuclear war. Essentially, this translated to two staffing and readiness levels: peace-time and war-time. The peace-time level included DEFCONs 5, 4, 3 and 2. The war-time level corresponded to DEFCON 1.

Generally, readiness training emphasized three major areas:

1. Training required for the FOCCPAC staff in Kunia. This included wide varieties of newly-developed punched-card, computer and automated techniques that reduced large masses of target data and target damage assessments to easily handled, accurate analysis and displays to support decision-making.

2. Training required by each major command to insure a smooth relocation of war room staffs to Kunia when so ordered.

3. Combined training of the nine war rooms, FOCCPAC, and all Kunia tenants under DEFCON 1. This included at least twice-yearly all-hands participation in 2-to-3-day-long communication and operational worldwide nuclear war exercises.

2. Nuclear War Command and Control

The DEFCON 1 combat exercises were meant to be realistic. Thus, our experience during those exercises provides the best guide to how nuclear war would actually have been fought in the Pacific in 1962. Here, then, is an annotated recounting. It would happen like this...

Attached to a small metal box that is welded to a large steel pole in the middle of our communications relay center, the usually-quiet nuclear war alarm suddenly springs to life with an ear splitting ring. Bathed 24/7 in a bright light, the box was a permanent companion to all the technicians in the room who operated the clicking teletypes.

"Call the captain!" shouted Commander Gil Clark, the communications officer, as he came running out of his office and headed for the box. Everyone in the room stopped what they were doing and watched intently as Clark pulled a switch shutting off the alarm, dug into his pocket for a small key, and quickly opened the door to one of the box's two compartments.

Reaching in, he pulled out a large sealed manila envelope and held it tightly unopened, until, breathing heavily after running down the stairs from my second floor office, where I had been notified by phone, I unlocked the door to the other compartment, reached in and retrieved another manila envelope.

An essential element of our "go" message procedures – which I approved – included locating the metal box in an exposed, visible location under 24/7 surveillance by multiple responsible personnel in the room who knew that only Clark and I were authorized to open the box. There were no other keys. Both Clark and myself were expected to be in Kunia when needed, unless otherwise arranged.

In a few seconds we were both tearing open our envelopes as Pierson, the radioman who had received the flash message on his teletype and sounded the alarm, was standing beside us holding a message that had been originated by the President.

Addressed to all the major commands in the U.S. military, the message read: EXECUTE WAR PLAN 76. REPEAT EXECUTE

WAR PLAN 76. The message also included several authentication words.

These would not be the exact words of the message. Plus, during exercises the message text would have multiple statements saying THIS IS A DRILL, THIS IS A DRILL, THIS IS AN EXERCISE. In the present scenario, War Plan 76 is a hypothetical order from the President to the military leaders to carry out (execute) the pre-specified steps named in plan 76.

The readiness of the military leaders to carry out such an order is largely their responsibility, although an order for increased DEFCON levels may come from the President, as happened during the Cuban Missile Crisis. In the scenario here, military leadership had already assessed the threat level as critical and the armed forces, including Kunia, were already in DEFCON 1 readiness. Given the way we were organized and operated, we were always just a few hours from readiness for DEFCON 1.

Clark and I opened the envelopes we had retrieved from the metal box and removed a piece of paper from inside. To see if the authentication words in the envelopes matched the words in the President's message, we each read out loud the authentication words. We saw immediately that the words matched. Clark said, "The message is authenticated. Do you agree, Captain Sotos?"

"I agree it is a match. The nuclear war go message is authenticated," I responded.

We both again reached into our envelopes and we both removed one small section of folded pre-punched paper tape. (See Figure 30.) We handed the tapes to Pierson, as Clark ordered him to relay the "go" message to all the addressees.

At Kunia, relaying messages was a two-step process. It meant, first, using a teletype machine with a paper-tape converter to copy the words of an incoming message to a new paper tape then, second, taking that tape to another machine that was configured to send messages to a specific communication center thousands of miles away. These teletypes were connected by underground wires that ran from our building to a radio transmitting site with tall towers that was about eleven miles away.

2. Nuclear War Command and Control

Figure 30: **Communications room.** No photographs inside Kunia were taken or allowed, but these images of a Navy communications center on Guam in the 1960s suggests what our communications room looked like.   **LEFT:** For each of the first 8 or 9 weeks after I started my inspections of the communications relay center, I saw a large room about three times this size, with about twice the number of men shown here. They were all busy reading the incoming messages which created a punched paper tape along with the printed message. At the end of each message the attendant would tear off the paper tape, move to a different machine determined by the address in the message and hang it on a nearby nail to await its turn to be transmitted on that particular machine. (The man in the foreground is holding paper tape in his hands.) Despite its large size, it was a very noisy, crowded, and, to me, confusing scene. But it turned out I was wrong. The men, even as they were stringing wires, reading the traffic and relaying it as required, knew exactly what they were doing and were working toward a more efficient operation.   **RIGHT:** About six months after I started my inspections of the communications relay center and started to monitor the workload, I noticed some solid changes. Even as the workload kept increasing the relay center became quite orderly (though still noisy) and much better organized. The delay between receipt and retransmittal (relay) of messages shortened. The degree of improvement they made in six month's time can be illustrated by the more controlled atmosphere in this picture. From the compliments that came our way from the communications office (J6) of CINCPAC and the Fleet Headquarters, I couldn't have been happier with the competence and professional character of my communications officer – Commander Gil Clark. The equipment in this picture is much newer, smaller, more automated and requires far fewer people than ours did.

Figure 31: **Communications room.** This is not the Kunia communications room – it was too secret to ever be photographed. However, this photograph of an Army communications center in the 1960s does illustrate the approximate size of the Kunia communications room. Our teletypes were laid out in two long rows of about 20 machines each. Each teletype sat at about waist height, on a metal frame about 6 inches from the adjacent one. The equipment in this Army room is one or two models newer than the equipment we had in Kunia, but reels for paper tape are still being used.

Because of the constant, large workload of routine messages, the technicians would hang the paper tapes on a large nail near the outgoing machine to await their turn. The number of messages (paper tapes) hanging on these nails was a good indicator of the speed of our relay process.

Pierson quickly ran to his teletype, and made paper tape copies of the tapes we gave him. He then walked to each relevant transmitting teletype and handed a tape to the operator who promptly inserted it into his machine, ahead of all the tapes

2. Nuclear War Command and Control

still hanging on the nails. In this way, the "go" message was distributed to all Pacific Commands including, of course, all the war rooms and commands within the Kunia facility.

It was all completed within minutes.

About a half hour after receiving and relaying the "go" message, we started to receive reports of the damage caused by our missiles and aircraft strikes.[3] These reports would come into our communications center, where copies would be relayed to the addressed force commander, each war room, and the computer center. In the computer center the data would be extracted, converted into punch cards and paper tape, then entered into computers. The computer software would identify the targets in our "Damage Assessment Program" files then, based on the amount of damage reported, would decide whether that particular target was a candidate for a second strike. At subsequent intervals the computer program would identify all second-strike candidates and place them in a designated file for a briefing.

In those early days of automation most of the data entry into computers was by keyboard, punch card, or paper tape. These are labor intensive tasks and they were performed mostly by my staff for the war rooms that used the computers. Also, most of the tasks associated with the creation of the displays used for the briefings were accomplished by my staff. In the development of our electronic displays my electronic technicians received a great deal of help from our local SAC group in Kunia.

---

[3] I don't believe the half hour interval between our relay of the go message and the damage reports was meant as an estimate of the time it would take in an actual missile exchange. Also, the reader should be aware that we studied work-arounds to compensate for the interference with communications caused by the electromagnetic pulse associated with nuclear explosions. For example, we had considered installing and burying wires that would connect Kunia to nearby underseas cables. That idea went down the drain when Kunia became no longer safe from the larger and more powerful hydrogen bombs. With hundreds of times the explosive power of Little Boy (the 15-kiloton atom bomb dropped on Hiroshima), the hydrogen bomb made underground command centers like Kunia obsolete.

Status and decision briefings were scheduled by the CINCPAC war room. Preparation for the briefings, supervised by the CINCPAC and Fleet war room officers, was a key task which involved my people, especially those who designed and built the large PACOM map displays[4] that were moved in and out on overhead rails.

About 20 minutes before the briefing to CINCPAC was to start, people started to take their seats. Five minutes before the start-time, all attendees, including the flag officers, were seated. For each flag officer three or four staff officers sat in the gallery, along with me and several of my staff.

As CINCPAC (Admiral Felt) arrived, my chief master at arms announced "Attention on deck." Everyone in the now-quiet room rose and then sat, as, all business, the admiral sat down and glanced at his senior war room officer, Captain Hines, seated in the gallery next to me. Hines motioned to my operations officer who was sitting on the small balcony just above us.

Immediately, an officer walked to the middle of the stage, introduced himself as Commander Torelli, the CINCPAC briefing officer, and stated that he would provide an update on three topics: the damages and casualties within the PACOM area caused by the enemy's nuclear attack, the enemy's damage and casualties within the PACOM area resulting from our response to that attack, and the targets recommended for the PACOM second-strike force.

As Torelli finished his introductory words, all the main lights in the huge room went dark, except for low level floor lighting and the stage area.

At the same time, a 16-by-4 foot map display, showing the entire PACOM area, rolled slowly on overhead rails to the center of the stage. At the top right of the display was a large clock-face that showed the time of the information being reported.

---

[4] PACOM is the acronym for "Pacific Command," an area about half of the earth, under the command responsibility of CINCPAC. In May 2018 the name was changed to U.S. Indo-Pacific Command. So, instead of CINCPAC, one now speaks of CDRUSINDOPACOM – a mouthful.

2. Nuclear War Command and Control

With a hand-held button-switch that was connected to the display board, Torelli turned on a number of small, sharp, bright, steady, red lights which appeared at many different geographical locations on the map.

"These steady red lights show those U.S. and Allied targets that have been hit," said Torelli. He then paused to let his listeners examine the map.

The display boards and much of the equipment used for briefings was designed and built by our own staff. The lighting on each board was responsive to the holes in IBM punch cards that were produced by the computer after it had processed relevant information received from subordinates throughout the Pacific area.

Torelli pressed another button. Blinking red lights, about one third the number of the steady red lights, appeared on the map. "These blinking red lights," he said, "are U.S. and Allied targets that we believe have been hit, but for which we have not received any reports."

In a few moments Torelli pressed a third button, adding a large number of steady white lights to the blinking and steady red lights. "These steady white lights are enemy sites that we estimate we have hit," he said, and paused.

After two more button-presses, blue lights appeared in the enemy geographical area, along with a greater number of steady green lights in our own geographical area. "These blue lights are surviving enemy sites which we propose to hit with our second-strike forces available at the sites shown by the steady green lights.[5] The CINCPAC war room is in the process of assigning these targets now."

The briefing continued for about thirty more minutes, with questions posed by the flag officers and answers provided by Torelli and the war rooms, before CINCPAC ended it.

---

[5]The subject matter and thrust of Commander Torelli's briefings are generally accurate. However, details, such as the colors of the lights used to communicate information about events in the PACOM area, may not be 100% accurate.

That was the only briefing we had for the flag officers. But for the war rooms and the computer room staff, the damage assessment and re-targeting efforts continued full tilt.

The exercise officially terminated after about 72 hours. We then set DEFCON 5 and smoothly reverted to our peace-time routine.

But our peace-time routine didn't last very long!

Much to my amazement, just a few months later, on October 14, 1962, I found myself in the same situation, only this time it was not a world wide nuclear war exercise.

It was the real thing!

Figure 36: **Entrance to an underground center.** Photographs of the Kunia entrance tunnel were prohibited for security reasons. In 1963 NORAD (the North American Aerospace Defense Command) built a command center underneath North Bay, Ontario, Canada. This photo shows the 17-ton blast door at its entrance, reached through an underground tunnel of several hundred yards. See Figure 235.

Chapter 3

The Real Thing

It was October 14, 1962, and my tour at Kunia was coming to an end. My new orders assigned me to take command of the USS *Tolovana*, a large fleet oiler that operated with the Seventh Fleet in the Pacific. I was somewhat surprised, since this new command of a deep-draft ship meant that I was still in the competition for promotion. When first ordered to Kunia I was convinced it was a second-team billet that would take me out of the competition for promotion to the next level. I suspect, however, it was Admiral Felt's focus on the Kunia command center that kept me in the running. In any event, I guess I owed an apology to Captain Baumburger (the Captain detailer) for resisting when he sent me to Kunia.

In a way my new orders were good news for all the members of my staff since they indicated the Navy had a high regard for what was being done there.

There's no doubt, however, that the Kunia assignment was not just exceptionally challenging, but also at the front door of a wide range of new technological developments that enhanced the professional career of almost everyone assigned. Not only did everyone on the staff develop a working relationship with computers, communications, television, and the operation of war rooms, but they also became acquainted with a subject still distant from the vocabulary of most Navy people: readiness for

3. THE REAL THING

nuclear war.

On a personal level I knew that the rest of my career would probably be connected with the use of computers at the higher command levels. That particular insight arrived when a Captain Trickey from the Office of the Chief of Naval Operations (CNO) came out to Kunia to interview me as his replacement. He headed a key research and development division in the office of the CNO at the Pentagon. I thought his visit was a little strange, since I had just received the *Tolovana* orders. Of course he knew about those orders, but was, nevertheless, lining up his replacement.

Trickey told me that, among other challenges, his office was responsible for research and development in command and control. That was then a new concept referring to the use, at higher levels, of systems analysis, information technology, software development, computers, electronic warfare, communications, and other technology – just as we were doing at Kunia. After talking for some time he offered me the job. I was flattered and quite impressed. I knew that my wife, Georgette, would love Washington, D.C. and, without any hesitation, told him I would be happy to have the job.

"OK," he said. "I'll recommend you as my replacement and you will probably get orders when your tour on the *Tolovana* is up."

As you will read later, I did indeed get the job after I finished my one-year tour on the *Tolovana*. However, before I describe that part of my career, there is still more to relate about my experience as the commanding officer of the FOCCPAC at Kunia.

We had steadily increased involvement with, and support of, all the war rooms in Kunia, including our Air Force tenants, who continued to help us with our training. In return, we provided the Air Force tenants with as much free computer time as they wished plus around-the-clock use of all our equipment. Yes, FOCCPAC kept busy and everything was running smoothly. We all pretty well knew what we had to do, and we kept busy doing it. However, it was clear from the increasing number of visitors we received that the rest of the Navy was largely in the dark about our particular installation.

In spite of our high security level, groups with the appropriate clearance were showing up and asking all types of questions. To accommodate all these visitors we developed a standard tour and briefing, but we prohibited note-taking and did not hand out written materials. For many of these visitors it was the first time they had seen how computers were being used to support operational requirements.

It was the uniqueness of our operational support that puzzled our visitors. Let me explain. If you were observing the operation of the CINCPAC war room during a world wide nuclear war exercise, you would see 35 to 40 people performing tasks at various desks and work spaces. About 20 of those people – all experts in optimizing the use of punch card equipment, computers, computer keyboards, software, teletypes, and other specialized Kunia equipment – would be from my organization (FOCCPAC). However, they worked for the war room boss, who was usually a senior Navy captain or colonel from a flag officer's operations staff. The FOCCPAC personnel in the war room were responsive to his leadership and folded so nicely into his operation that they appeared to be permanent members of that team. And the same concept of support and work integration was true for the other war rooms, too, albeit with with lower levels of support for the smaller war rooms which had limited nuclear war missions.

In those early days, when very few people knew how to use computers and automated support, my organization was able to support multiple war rooms – because that is all that we did. And without our support they simply would not be using the automation capabilities which are really essential for command and control in nuclear warfare.

One of our visitors in mid-1962 was Admiral George Anderson, the Chief of Naval Operations (CNO) – the highest-ranking officer in the Navy. I escorted him on a private tour for about an

3. THE REAL THING

hour, just the two of us. Of course it was a big nerve-wracking surprise for me, but he was very friendly, curious, asked a lot of questions, and surprised me with the knowledge he already had about Kunia and my FOCCPAC command. He seemed especially interested in the really excellent working relationships that we had developed with the other military services working in Kunia.

Along with the steady growth of automation in the war rooms, the headquarters staff of each war room started to take advantage of our capabilities. We were still the Navy's only substantial computer-based organization in Hawaii. The operations division at Pacific Fleet headquarters outside Kunia, in particular, steadily increased its use of our support and we developed a number of automated procedures that not only saved them time and effort, but gave them new operational capabilities. For example, we completed a "Contact Correlation Program" that would, in just a few seconds, provide good information about every ship within a specified radius of a particular spot in the Pacific Ocean. The Commander Hawaiian Sea Frontier used this for air-sea rescue incidents, as did the Pacific Fleet commander, for planning and implementation of war-time control of shipping as well as other uses. One of these other uses was a program designed and written for the Pacific Commander of the Navy's Service Forces (Logistics) by my supply officer, Lieutenant Quinn Morrison. Upon request it would provide, in seconds, the total amount of fuel oil afloat in the Pacific at that instant, as well as its location.[1]

---

[1] It is important to recognize those who developed most of the initial basic software systems we used at Kunia. A project team from the David Taylor Model Basin (in Maryland), led by Dr. Ruth Davis, worked very hard to write the basic software for the "Sea Surveillance System," a then-unprecedented, large and very complex software capability. Funded and guided by some very intelligent and forward-thinking individuals in the office of the CNO, well before Kunia was ready, it became the foundation for many of the applications we subsequently developed. Similarly, a foundational system to support command and control during nuclear war was developed and provided to us by a project team headed by IBM. Almost all of our initial growing

Matching the activity in our computer center, our communications center kept getting larger, busier, and more useful, especially for the CINCPAC and the Fleet Commander's communications divisions. Before I left Kunia we were the control center for pickup of astronauts in the Mercury program who landed in the Pacific after their space flights. And I understand that, several years after I left Kunia, it had become the control center in the Pacific for the new global positioning satellites.

But the most troubling part of my entire tour at Kunia happened the week before I was scheduled to turn over command of FOCCPAC to Captain Frank Quinn. It started October 14, 1962, when an Air Force reconnaissance plane detected Soviet missile launchers being installed in Cuba.

This was a crisis in every sense of the word. The missiles were just 90 miles from Key West, Florida, with their nuclear warheads pointing right at the U.S. Our communications traffic at FOCCPAC increased abruptly and substantially, a sign of the resulting uproar in the nation's military.

My reactions and experiences during the Cuban Missile Crisis can be divided into three areas: first, as a senior naval officer thinking strategically, second, as the FOCCPAC commander operating tactically, and third, as a human being facing the prospect of some very difficult decisions.

Strategic Considerations

After learning of the missiles, the President quickly established a group called the EXCOMM to collect facts, study the situation, and provide him with recommended responses to this surprising Soviet aggression. By October 18, after almost around-the-clock meetings and discussion, the EXCOMM had

---

pains were involved with learning these systems and adapting them to our new large computers to provide operational support to the war rooms at Kunia.

3. The Real Thing

settled on three options for the President: an invasion of Cuba, an air strike on Cuba, or a quarantine (blockade) of Cuba.[2]

Although this confrontation with the Soviet Union was unexpected, neither it nor the idea of a naval blockade was surprising. Naval blockades are an ancient concept of warfare, and U.S. military leaders had been war-gaming operations against the Soviets ever since the end of World War II.

In fact, three years earlier, as a student at the Naval War College in Newport, Rhode Island, I had wrestled with a similar problem during a major class war game (see page 208). Acting on the other side – in the role of the chief of staff for Soviet long-range air transportation – I had voted during a serious deliberation of our Decision Council to pre-emptively strike the Blue team (United States) with nuclear weapons, even though we were winning the limited conflict then in progress.

Why did I vote for a nuclear strike? It was a difficult decision, but all the members of our Council were convinced that Blue, who was suffering significant casualties in the game, would never accept defeat and that they would initiate the use of nuclear weapons when they realized that defeat was inevitable. The fact that Blue had a history of using nuclear weapon (at Hiroshima and Nagasaki) made our decision easier. As soon as we made the decision to pre-empt Blue and initiate a nuclear strike, the game ended.

Before that game I had never put myself in the shoes of a senior Soviet officer. Now, I found myself doing exactly that, thinking about the large number of Soviet ships heading toward Cuba, including six of their submarines, and the possible paths to a nuclear exchange.

A blockade is not a simple or a predictable tactic to enforce. The American blockade would be against cargo ships. The presence of armed, submerged Soviet submarines indicated an intent to resist the blockade and had to be considered a threat to the blockading destroyers. I was comfortable making this type

---

[2] Bibliography: Sorenson. Blockade was first discussed on Oct. 16.

of analysis, having had considerable combat experience against submarines.[3]

Making matters worse, the blockading destroyers and the submerged Soviet submarines could not communicate with one another. If communications are not perfect between a submerged submarine and a surface ship, both captains are literally on their own. For example, if a destroyer gains underwater contact on a submarine, the submarine commander is aware of it immediately and, like it or not, when that happens both ships are in a lethal risk situation. If either makes a movement involving the use of explosives, even if the explosives are small and are intended as only a signal, he invites the other to respond in some way. Without communications there is no way either ship captain can be certain of the other's intentions, and so must assume the worst. It would be like two professional gunslingers facing each other at lethal range with their guns holstered.

If the captain of a destroyer thinks his ship is in danger, he invariably will take any action he considers necessary to protect it, no matter his orders of engagement. I knew that almost any action by a blockading destroyer, even one as basic as gaining and holding underwater sonar contact, could easily be misinterpreted as an act of war by the commander of a submerged submarine – an interpretation which could prompt him to fire a torpedo at the ship holding underwater contact on him.

At the same time, my experience as a destroyer captain told me that if the submarines escorting the Soviet surface ships remain submerged in the vicinity of the blockading destroyers, those submarines would, in fact, be inviting an attack. Putting myself in the shoes of those blockading destroyer captains, I knew that, no matter what their orders were, they simply could not afford to let a submerged Soviet submarine get near them.

---

[3] For 40 months – from April 1942 until World War II ended in August 1945, including 20 months at the Key West sound-school as a lead instructor in anti-submarine warfare (ASW) at sea – I was immersed in ASW. See my earlier book, *Living with the Torpedo*.

3. THE REAL THING

In other words, trying to blockade an armed, submerged submarine with whom there is no communication is a risky, aggressive act that literally invites a war-like response. And as far as I could understand, that is exactly what we were doing.

Compounding this, my personal assessment was that the Soviets would not back down in the face of a blockade. At the same time I knew that we would not back down. I was convinced that there was little or no chance for avoiding a horrible war that would bring Hiroshima-like devastation to Chicago, Washington, Norfolk, New York, and other cities.[4]

Tactical Considerations in FOCCPAC

Twenty years earlier I had literally stumbled my way through the first year of our nation's lack of readiness for World War II. Now I was in a similar spot. Only this time it was for a different type of war.

A nuclear war!

But now I was no longer a stumbling green ensign. I was an experienced Navy captain running the emergency command center that housed the war rooms of Commander-in-Chief Pacific and all his top commanders. In my capacity as the commanding officer of FOCCPAC I wanted to make sure that everything under my command was ready for nuclear war.

---

[4]And I was right! Our anti-submarine units – destroyers and helicopters – detected three of the six Soviet submarines that were in the blockade area and tracked them in an effort to force them to the surface. In the process, they set off explosives that were supposed to be a signal for the submarines to surface. However, Captain Valentin Savitsky of the Soviet submarine B-59 interpreted the explosives as a sign that war had started. He decided to launch a torpedo that had a 15-kiloton nuclear warhead – the same as the Hiroshima bomb. He was prevented from doing so by his flotilla commander, Captain Vasili Arkhipov who was aboard. Unquestionably, had he fired his nuclear torpedo it would have started a nuclear war. Captain Arkhipov, now deceased, has since deservedly been recognized as the man who saved the world. Bibliography: Watson. Also: Wikipedia "Soviet submarine B-59."

So, on my own authority I ordered my people to set DEFCON 1, placing the entire command center on a war footing, which included the following actions:

- We started our three big 1250 KW generators and used them to supply power throughout the building;

- We closed the huge door at the input end of our long air intake tunnel and forced incoming air through a set of chemical filters;

- Water for all purposes was obtained through our own private wells;

- We started using our own private sanitation system;

- Our large, well-stocked cafeteria was placed on 24-hour operation;

- Sleeping accommodations were readied for all off duty personnel;

- All entrance doors were secured and anyone, exclusive of flag officers, desiring to enter or leave had to get permission from me or my executive officer (my second in command);

- We readied our communications center and computer center to handle, assess, and display the anticipated incoming post-strike information in order to recommend second-strike targets;

- Our two building-wide television systems were integrated with the communication center, the nine war rooms, the main conference center and other selected rooms.

- We were fully staffed, and there was no need to call anyone from home.

3. THE REAL THING

In other words, we were no longer dependent on outside support for anything.

It may be confusing to the reader that I, as the commanding officer of FOCCPAC, had authority to set DEFCON 1 without consulting my boss, CINCPAC, who was nearby. I did consider consulting him but decided that, as his Flagship Captain, he would expect me to take any actions I considered warranted by the circumstances, without bothering him, as long as those actions did not adversely impinge his mission in any way. The latter half of the previous sentence may not appear in any formal naval instructions or policies, especially as relates to the commanding officer of an emergency nuclear command center, but that was not an obstacle. I had no second thoughts. There were so few such command centers in 1962 that the differences among them were far greater than the similarities. I suspect it is still true today.[5]

We had practiced setting different DEFCON readiness conditions many times in war drills and, while we did notify the war rooms, the actions were of the type that didn't involve any battle staffs. While they complied with the internal instructions, such as berthing, exit, and entrance controls, that was the only impact on them. Anyone not in our engineering plant would probably not notice other changes. Nevertheless, it placed our installation at the maximum level of material readiness. Our DEFCON 1 staffing required assigning specialized personnel to the war rooms and that too was accomplished quietly to avoid any publicity.

---

[5]Our national policies concerning actions to take during a general nuclear war remain vague and virtually unpublished among the nation's civilians as well as the nation's military. Graff (see bibliography) well describes how hopelessly vulnerable and uninformed are the people of our nation, probably including the military. This is not because of unawareness of this problem – the military and even some pockets of the civil population are certainly aware of this situation. Instead, the core of the problem is that no reasonable courses of action exist to ameliorate the devastating horrors caused by explosions of hydrogen bombs.

The flag officers who relocated to Kunia were not especially conspicuous. Some would leave Kunia for short intervals, but most remained in their war rooms or in a large group of office and berthing rooms on the second floor known as "Flag Island." The FOCCPAC personnel, myself included, remained at Kunia for three nights straight. This did not unduly alarm our families, as we had stayed there for at least three days during our worldwide exercises.

At the only meeting for all the flag officers called by Admiral Felt, all but one showed up. General Emmett O'Donnell, the Pacific Air Force Commander, was represented by a senior colonel. The agenda, developed by the CINCPAC senior war room officer, included a short update on the probability of a blockade and the number and location of Soviet ships heading for Cuba. Then, prompted by a question from one of the flag officers at the table, a member of the Commander Anti-submarine Forces war room led a short discussion about the capabilities of the Soviet submarines escorting their surface ships. There was no mention of the possibility the subs might be carrying torpedoes with nuclear warheads. The latest television news covering the blockade was then shown on our large monitor for about 15 minutes. The meeting was over in 45 minutes. I had the impression it was intended as an organizational get-together type meeting. There was no discussion on what might happen if the Soviet submarines did attack or any readiness actions for the possibility of a nuclear war.

I could have inserted my concerns about nuclear war readiness in the agenda for that meeting but I didn't. As the commanding officer of FOCCPAC the responsibility for Kunia's nuclear war readiness was mine. Except for making sure our tenants had the required staffing in their war rooms should a nuclear war start, there really wasn't any other Kunia readiness actions required of any of them.

Overall, in DEFCON 1, we made sure that all designated FOCCPAC people were on watch in their respective war rooms, ready to provide the required data preparation, computer sup-

3. The Real Thing

port, and other assigned tasks. The actions I took during the Missile Crisis to protect the people in Kunia were those any commanding officer would have taken.

Human Decisions

The question that bothered me the most at Kunia was a rare one for a naval commander ashore.

Because of its specialized construction, I had been told that Kunia would survive the explosion of an atom bomb. At that time, the warheads aboard Soviet missiles had an explosive force of about 15 to 20 kilotons, a blast that Kunia could reportedly withstand, barring a direct hit. (The more powerful hydrogen bomb changed all that.)

So, if a nuclear attack occurred on Hawaii, we would be alive and well in our "tunnel," and completely isolated from the destruction in rest of the world. But what would be my obligation for the safety of the nearby local civilian population, including our dependents, living in the vicinity of my command center? More personally, I had a wife and two young sons living only a few miles away.

Curiously, there was a complete absence of any requests to extend the safety of our well protected underground command center to others. There wasn't a peep from my boss, nearby residents, my subordinates, the media, my family, or anyone on that subject. It was as though everyone was so certain that war would not start, that survivability simply never entered their minds.[6]

While that made my job easier, I attributed the absence of such pressure to the failure of the media, civil government leaders, and even the military to inform the public adequately about the terrible conditions that might envelope them. I must admit that I could have done more to make sure that my subordinates were well aware of the chaos that would result outside Kunia if there was indeed a nuclear war. But, frankly, because the only

---

[6]This is particularly ironic in light of the scare in Hawaii when a missile attack alert was mistakenly issued in 2018.

information I could impart was that of hopelessness, I simply kept my mouth shut.

Did I alert my wife to the dangers I saw ahead?

No, I didn't.

Had I done so, I knew she would insist on some immediate actions to protect our children. As you will read below, I did have a desperate last-resort plan – a course of actions that, if divulged in advance, I felt would risk a serious loss of discipline inside Kunia.

I wrestled with the question for a long time, alone. There was no one to consult. Even if I had access to the policies followed in the government's other bomb-proof centers, I would not have wanted to see them. I knew generally what their policies would be on this question and I didn't want to be bound by them. For example, at the Strategic Air Command's command center during this same crisis, it was later reported that the SAC commander, General Power, would permit his staff just one phone call to say a final goodbye to their families – but could not say the reason for the call.[7]

Formally, I had set a policy earlier that only people contributing to our mission would be granted the protection and safety of our underground building. I had also issued written orders that, once we had set DEFCON 1, only the executive officer or myself could authorize an exit or an entrance. But, if nuclear war started, I knew that I could not ignore the exposed plight of the civilians in the Kunia area.

So, without confiding in anyone, I had made up my mind that once I was sure that enemy missiles were on the way, I would risk internal chaos by rescinding that policy. I figured that we had a window of about an hour between the time we learned of the launch of Soviet missiles and the arrival and explosion of an atom bomb in Hawaii. We would send transportation to pick up all our dependents, and squeeze into the building as many

---

[7] See Galinsky in bibliography.

3. The Real Thing

nearby people as it would safely hold before locking the doors. I estimated we could squeeze in about 3500 more people.[8]

Wind-Up

Although the flag officers themselves relocated to Kunia during the Missile Crisis, I thought it was strange that none of the major commanders relocated their full war rooms to Kunia. Instead, events continued to be monitored from their regular headquarters war rooms that were 8 to 11 miles away. While the regular headquarters war rooms and the emergency ones in Kunia kept in close contact, those at Kunia were relatively quiet.

It was obvious that none of the major commanders anticipated a further deterioration in the crisis and, therefore, there was no reason to relocate the war rooms to Kunia. I disagreed with that position, but the decision not to relocate was certainly that of each major commander.

When I realized there would be no relocation of the war rooms, I nevertheless maintained FOCCPAC's condition one material readiness. However, we reduced our augmentation personnel in the war rooms.

This lessening of readiness in Kunia meant that we could proceed with my change of command ceremony, which took place on October 21, 1962. In front of most of my staff, I made a short talk complimenting them on changing a large, empty building into an amazing futuristic command center using only their own imagination, hard work, and talent.

The ceremony was completed against the backdrop of the Missile Crisis and, after thanking them all, I was on my way. Of

---

[8] At the time, I was unaware that a September 1961 episode of the popular television series, *The Twilight Zone*, had dramatized a similar situation. In that now-famous episode, called "The Shelter," a yellow alert turns a friendly neighborhood group of families against the one family that has built a bomb shelter and retreated into it. That story was fiction, but the dilemma was quite real for me, and a hundred times larger. Although it was almost 60 years ago that I had these concerns about the vulnerability of the American people in a nuclear war, the situation is now apparently the same or even worse, according to Graff (see bibliography).

course I passed on all the relevant information to my successor, Captain Frank Quinn.

On October 22, the day after I departed Kunia, President Kennedy spoke to the nation about the Crisis, ordering the military to set DEFCON 3 and the Navy to quarantine (blockade) Cuba. Of course, much like at Kunia, most of the military was already at an advanced DEFCON readiness condition.[9]

Admiral Felt was kind enough to send me the letter shown in Figure 244. Also, since he knew I was returning to the mainland United States for a lengthy leave before going to my ship, he asked if I would stop in Monterey, California, at the Navy Postgraduate School, to lecture about our operational use of computers at the strategic command level. It seems he was told that, while the school had an excellent course on computers, they had trouble finding real-life examples of effective operational use of computers at the strategic level – which is what we were doing for him. Of course I was happy to do it.

On October 28 the crisis was over.

My earlier statement that a U.S. blockade would lead to a nuclear war between the Soviets and the U.S. because the Soviets would never back down was almost correct. Thankfully, it turned out to be wrong because the Soviets did back down. They agreed to remove the missiles and their military aircraft from Cuba. We in turn agreed to remove the Jupiter missiles we had installed in Turkey at the Soviet border.

---

[9]While it seemed that the missile crisis occurred suddenly, it had actually been building up more gradually. For example, a present-day Russian source describes a Soviet operation that included 85 cargo ships making 180 trips to Cuba, covered by 2 cruisers, 4 destroyers and 11 submarines of the Soviet Navy, and involving 50,000 people. (Source: sputniknews.com, in bibliography.) By July 1, 1962, U.S. intelligence knew the Soviets had delivered to Cuba 160 tanks, 770 field artillery pieces, 8 anti-tank guns, 580 anti-aircraft guns, 36 fighter aircraft, 24 helicopters, and 3,800 military vehicles. (Source: Clift.) On August 29 a CIA U-2 plane photographed anti-aircraft missile sites in Cuba, but did not see offensive missile sites. Shortly thereafter, U-2 flights were suspended until October 14 because of weather and because mainland China had shot down a Taiwanese U-2 in September. (Source: Walker.)

3. The Real Thing

Was it just good luck for us that they backed down? I am sure that most people believe it was good luck. I thought so.

It turns out, however, that in such a crisis good luck is another set of words for good leadership. And from my perspective, history will recognize President Kennedy's exceptional leadership in deciding upon a blockade, the riskiest course of action, and Admiral George Anderson's exceptionally confident leadership in getting it done – actually implementing a blockade that included stopping at least three submerged Soviet submarines armed with and authorized to use nuclear torpedoes.

It was good fortune for all peoples of the world that so seemingly unsolvable a crisis was steered by two such American leaders, and that Chairman Khrushchev of the Soviet Union had the good sense and guts to back down. We were lucky that the leaders of both nations had some common sense.[10]

When I left Kunia I knew that I would never have another Navy job like it. The best part was that, in my entire three years there, I did not have a real boss. Together with an eager, curious, intelligent staff, we wrote our own mission and found ways to implement it to the satisfaction of CINCPAC.

Yes, we made mistakes – a lot of them. But no one jumped on us about the mistakes we made. We learned well from them. And in the process we discovered that we had become experts in an area that was brand new, not only to the Navy, but the entire nation.

And for some reason my luck in this regard continued. That is, I went on to new types of complicated jobs that involved the introduction and use of automated technology at the national level and worked for flag officers who told me what had to be done and then let me do it without a lot of detailed supervision.

Of course, the mistakes didn't go away entirely....

---

[10]Khrushchev, page 483.

Figure 54: **USS *Gary* (DE 326).** My second command. *Gary* was her commissioned name. Following US Navy tradition, ships named after Navy personnel carry only the last name of the person honored – in this case, Seaman 2nd Class Thomas J. Gary, who died at Pearl Harbor. However, in January 1945 the ship was renamed *Thomas J. Gary* so the Navy could name a planned – but never-built – light cruiser after the city of Gary, Indiana.

Chapter 4

A Dumb Decision

It was late afternoon on September 3, 1946, when the tug that was towing us, about eighty feet ahead, started turning from a southerly to westerly course. He was trying desperately to enter the St. John's river entrance, which was protected on our right (its northern side) by a long breakwater of massive concrete blocks.

A thirty knot wind and four foot waves were clearly making it tough for the tug as it struggled to get us turned to the channel course,

The turn was agonizingly slow. We could see and feel the wind, just forward of our port beam, trying to blow us onto the breakwater.

We saw the heavy tow wire come up rapidly out of the water, as it responded to the increasingly heavier strain.

Suddenly, the cable broke!

When a cable breaks under that kind of strain, the loose ends can snap back and cut right through a man like a big sharp knife. Thankfully no one was in the way.

But we did see one end of the tow wire hanging straight down from the tug's stern, and the other end hanging loosely from our bow down into the water.

We had no power and were adrift in a 30 knot wind. We were about 80 feet from the massive concrete blocks! All we could do

4. A Dumb Decision

Figure 56: **Ships mothballed in Green Cove Springs.**

was watch helplessly from the protection of our pilot house.

That's when the nakedness of our plight hit me. I was the commanding officer of a commissioned naval ship, with all the responsibilities of command. Yet, I had absolutely no control over the ship itself or any of its emergency capabilities. I could not even drop an anchor to stop our movement toward the concrete breakwater.

Not only did I feel helpless, I felt very stupid for allowing myself to get in such a pickle.

How did I get into such a dangerous spot? Well, it all started innocently enough.

I was pleasantly surprised on June 15, 1946, to receive orders that directed me to assume command of the USS *Gary* (DE 326) and take the ship through a scheduled overhaul at the Charleston, South Carolina shipyard, prior to mothballing at Green Cove Springs, Florida. (See Figure 56.)

Command of a DE, like the *Gary* was still a big deal for me. In Charleston, I relieved Lieutenant Commander Russell Crenshaw, USN, and supervised the three month overhaul process. Things started out nicely. The yard workmen knew their jobs and all we had to do was to make sure they didn't miss anything.

On the lighter side, we were near a nine hole golf course that kept me busy. And the night life wasn't too bad, but I soon tired of frequenting the local bars. Not married at the time, for me there was a shortage of girls. I just couldn't meet any.

After giving it some thought, I decided to go where the girls were. I enrolled in an evening secretarial school.

I couldn't believe my luck. The first night in class I counted 23 girls – most of them quite friendly and very good looking. I was the only male in the class.

My euphoria disappeared, however, after the first class was over and we descended the stairs into the street.

There was a line of guys and every girl in the class had some one waiting for her. I stuck it out twice a week for three weeks, but despite making friends, I never dated one of my classmates. For me, that's when Charleston, South Carolina, lost its reputation as a good liberty port for sailors.

The work of overhauling the ship started to lose its glow as well. We kept losing personnel as the sailors completed their service and the Navy continued to downsize. Despite protests to my local boss in the chain of command, I received no replacements. Of course I understood his predicament. He simply did not have any replacements to give.

For my part, even though the *Gary* was headed for the mothball fleet, I knew I was responsible for the quality of the overhaul and the safety of a commissioned naval ship and her crew. I also knew that if anything happened, despite the official nature of my crew's depletion, I would be held accountable.

It may seem a waste to invest so much time, money and energy into a ship that may never again be needed. But that really wasn't my decision. What I did know, however, was that good readiness demanded that it be operationally ready if and when needed.

4. A Dumb Decision

To bring matters to a head, I wrote a letter addressed to the Chief of Naval Operations (CNO) through my chain of command. In the letter I advised him that I could no longer assume the responsibilities of a commanding officer of a commissioned United States naval ship because of unacceptable personnel shortages. This may sound like a routine letter but I challenge the reader to find a similar letter anywhere in the U.S. Navy literature.

About three days after I mailed the letter to the CNO, through my immediate superior, nineteen Chief Petty Officers came aboard reporting for duty. They solved my immediate personnel problem and I never heard from the CNO. My guess is that my letter was never forwarded to him. Or if it was, that my immediate boss had included an endorsement that he had taken care of the problem.

Naval procedure required that he send me a copy of his endorsement. But he didn't. And since my problem was resolved I forgot about it. I did notice, however, that relations with my boss turned ice cold after I sent the letter.

While I solved that problem, I foolishly overlooked another more serious one at the end of our overhaul.

A civilian tug, the *Nancy Moran*, was assigned to tow us to Green Cove Springs. We had no propulsion power – deliberately. Everything on the ship had been sealed up and moth-balled, including our anchors. All we had running was one generator which supported our mess hall and the ship's lighting system. In other words it was no longer a ship over which I, as the captain, had any control whatsoever. It was simply a tow under the complete control of the tug, And for anyone who has ever been towed at sea, it is clear that even the tug has no other control than to move the ship forward or not at all.

I was no rookie. I had over four years of responsible war time sea duty behind me, and the *Gary* was my second command. How could I have been so careless as to allow such a tow – especially in waters whose weather I knew well and never trusted? I guess the absence of hostilities had me in a dream world.

The few hundred miles tow from the Charleston Navy Shipyard, south to Green Cove Springs, Florida, should have been a sight-seeing breeze. While slow, it should be a nice cruise, I thought. All we had to do was sit there and enjoy the scenery as the tug did all the work.

That's the way it started. But I knew now that I had really blown it. I was in command of a sealed-up, completely helpless commissioned ship with 50 men aboard.

The wind, now full on our port beam, was blowing us right toward those huge rocks! I was certain we were going to hit them. I was also sure that jutting rocks would pierce the side and under-bottom of the ship, fill us with water, and set us on the bottom. Frustration gripped me as I realized that even our boat and life rafts were all sealed up and useless to us. There was nothing we could do in any way to save ourselves if we hit those rocks, which were coming closer and closer. Even our life jackets were stowed away securely, waiting for the next war.

Frantically, we ran out to the foc'stle and started yelling at the tug. With the parted, long tow wire hanging down from his stern dangerously close to fouling his propellors, I knew his maneuvering was limited. Thank God he was a real professional.

He quickly closed us and I thought he was trying to get on our starboard side, between the ship and the rocks, to keep us from hitting them.

But no.

At the last minute, just touching us on the port bow he got another line over to us. In seconds we pulled it through the bullnose (bullnose is the opening on the main deck at the most forward part of the ship – used for the bow line) and secured it on a foc'stle bollard (foot-high round metal blocks welded to the deck). Then the tug skipper skillfully controlled the strain on the new line and slowly, very slowly, managed to pull our bow away from the rocks and make slow headway into the channel.

Twenty feet more and we would have hit the concrete rocks.

I don't recall how long it took before we got into a lee where the wind subsided and the danger had passed, but it seemed for-

4. A Dumb Decision

ever.

A couple of hours later, as a still nervous, but far wiser and tougher naval officer, I supervised mooring the *Gary* at her final resting place, alongside a dock.

This experience was one of the most important and unforgettable lessons of my entire naval career. Here is the lesson:

Never, never under any circumstances leave port unless the power to maneuver and control the ship is completely available. If it isn't – don't move the ship! And don't listen to or trust anyone who orders you otherwise. When the safety of your ship is involved, reserve the final decision for yourself. Trust no one to assume that responsibility for you!

That particular experience influenced many future decisions I had to make concerning ship safety.

For example, fifteen years later in 1961, when I had just assumed command of a fleet oiler USS *Tolovana* (AO 64), we were moored to an oil pier in Yokosuka, Japan. Having just completely unloaded all our cargo oil, the ship was empty. An empty fleet tanker alongside a pier is an amazing sight. About 600 feet long, its hull alone, not counting the mast or the bridge superstructure, towers massively a good 50 to 60 feet in the air. (See Figure 61.)

As luck would have it, a local storm warning advised that winds of 30 to 40 knots were coming. I immediately became very worried that the powerful winds blowing against our exceptionally large expanse of exposed steel would part our lines and blow the ship onto the land that was about 100 feet away.

Making my luck even worse, the high wind warning was delivered just after I received an invitation for lunch from the commander of the Seventh Fleet, Admiral Thomas Moorer (later, 1970-74, Chairman of the Joint Chiefs of Staff). His flagship was anchored there in Yokosuka, and he had invited all the skippers of ships present to have lunch with him.

I had never met the admiral who was now my boss. Career-wise this luncheon was a golden opportunity to be known to

Figure 61: **USS *Tolovana*(AO 64).** A large fleet oiler used to refuel carriers and other large ships of the Seventh Fleet, it is almost fully loaded with fuel in the left photograph, as evidenced by its depth in the water. When empty (right image), it would ride about 28 feet higher. The vertical black structures in the left photo are hoses. Figure 156 shows how they were used.

---

him. It was, indeed, a big deal for me! However, I didn't hesitate.

I contacted his aide, who seemed surprised when I told him I would not be attending the luncheon. We both knew it was not a career enhancing move on my part. But when it came to bad weather I had become a bit of a worry wart. I learned later that of eight ships there in the harbor, I was the only skipper who did not attend the luncheon.

Not only did I remain aboard the Tolovana, I ordered my crew to add a number of additional lines to hold us against the pier. I also directed that they disconnect our anchor chain from the anchor and run it through the bull nose to the pier to augment the forward mooring lines. Some of my older sailors grumbled about the extra work, but I think they learned something when they saw the chain share the strain.

The wind did hit us hard and strained every line we had out,

4. A Dumb Decision

including the anchor chain. It was a short wind storm, less than an hour. But several ships, whose captains were attending the luncheon, dragged anchor and had a harrowing time. I was glad I ordered the extra lines and the chain, and was proud of myself. We had the most exposed ship in the harbor and rode it out nicely.

It's not easy for a new captain with an experienced crew, as I was at the time, to make the unusual decisions I did, especially with the anchor chain. There's no doubt that the *Gary* experience hardened me to the necessity of making such decisions.

With the tow completed, the *Gary* was now secure in her Green Cove Springs moth ball fleet berth. After a few days, I turned over command to my exec, a young lieutenant junior grade, who would never have cause to move the ship. I reported to the local commander of the reserve fleet who put me to work at the boring job of inspecting the quality of the preservation work on the DEs.

The objective of my inspections was to insure proper custody and control of valuable equipment and proper sealing of the ships in readiness for the next war.

Most of us doing these inspections knew, in a sense, that our work seemed almost ludicrous.

I thought, "Why in the world are we spending such enormous sums to mothball all these ships? Hell, no one in the world is even close to posing a threat where these ships might ever again be needed."

Though I questioned the wisdom of the concept, I felt the planning was pretty good. The St. Johns was a fresh water river that was easy on a ship's bottom, when compared to the rust and deterioration caused by salt water in the oceans. Upwards of 600 ships were to be berthed in Green Cove Springs. In any terms, that's a lot of ships to be parked in one place!

Subsequent world events proved me wrong. The concept wasn't so laughable after all.

Just four years later, in June 1950, North Korea invaded South Korea and we were back at war. At the same time we sent some military advisors to South Vietnam. (But we didn't really go to war in South Vietnam until 1964.)

About the time the Korean war started, the U.S. had a total of 2,777 ships of all types in its reserve fleet, 850 of them at Green cove Springs. During the Korean and Vietnam wars, about 1,619 ships of all types were reactivated from the moth-ball fleets including, of course, a large number of DEs.

And strangely, as you will read later, in 1958 I found myself as squadron commander of nine DEs that had been taken out of the reserve fleet and converted into destroyer escort radar (DER) ships. Even stranger, one of the DEs I helped moth ball was the USS *Haverfield* (DE 393). In 1944 it was the flagship for our wartime DE squadron. Just 14 years later, in 1958, it was my DER squadron flagship for operations in the mid-Pacific air-sea early warning barrier.[1]

The sinister part of my tour at Green Cove Springs was the excessive exposure I (and others) had to asbestos – day in and day out. The mothballing material apparently contained a lot of the asbestos that was later learned to cause mesothelioma – a deadly cancer for which the industry was forced to establish a multi-billion dollar trust fund to compensate victims or their survivors. Thankfully I never had to make any such claim.

The good part of the job at Green Cove Springs was that I could get away and play baseball with the local Navy team. I played one full season, did a lot of nearby traveling with the team and was part of a winning group. In fact, we won 19 straight games and thought we were so good that we accepted an exhibition game with a class "A" minor league team.

That turned out to be one more mistake. It was a night game.

---

[1] Even the *Gary* made it out of mothballs, in 1956. She was converted to a radar ship (DER 326), as shown in Figure 220, and served in the U.S. Navy until 1973, when she was sold to Tunisia and became the *President Bourgiba* – the largest ship in the Tunisian Navy. In 1992 she suffered a fire that rendered her non-operational, after a service life that approached 50 years. Her mast holds a place of honor in the Tunisian city of Bizerte. See bibliography: GlobalSecurity.com, LaVerde.

4. A Dumb Decision

We had never played under lights and it showed. I played third base and made so many errors I lost count.

We lost by a lop-sided score. That was the last time I ever played organized baseball. It never did make up for the five years of no baseball during the war – a loss of little consequence when considering the alternative – but it did help me re-live my student days at the University of Chicago, where I played on the varsity team.

When not playing ball, I spent a lot of time visiting the tourist sites and the nearby bars of northern Florida. A close friend, with whom I spent a lot of time, was a fellow naval officer, William (Butch) Vaughn.

Butch, a lieutenant commander, as was I, actually made my off time in Florida a memorable experience. An exceptionally good looking and charming guy, I never saw a girl that did not like him. The nice thing about that was all his girlfriends liked to double date – and I was Butch's best friend.

Butch even managed to cast his spell over the nurses that cared for him in the naval hospital at Jacksonville, Florida.

He had suffered an eye injury during the war. A piece of something got in his eye during a gunnery practice and caused him some serious problems that kept him in the hospital for a couple of weeks. He wasn't sick, he just wore a patch over his eye most of the time. A restless guy, he was all over the hospital helping the nurses.

One day when I was visiting I asked him, "Just what do you do all day?"

"Oh, I help the nurses."

"What does that mean?"

"I give penicillin shots and things like that."

"You're pulling my leg. They wouldn't let you do that even if you knew how to do it."

A penicillin shot was still a big deal in those days and I doubted they would let him do it.

He took exception to my remark and told me he would demonstrate his authority and ability to give those shots by giving me one. For some stupid reason, even though I didn't need a shot, he talked me into it. Such was Butch's magic.

He left for a few minutes and came back with the needle and a related package. He told me to bend over and gave me a shot.

I had to admit then that he knew how to administer a shot. I learned later that what he did was on his own. No nurse even knew about it.

It appears that I was as foolhardy in those days as he was.

Another nice thing about my duty at Green Cove Springs was the ease with which one could get leave, and that's what I did. I was soon on my way back home for a three week stay in Chicago.

Figure 66: **Line School classmates.** The line school was a ten month course. Most reserve officers who transferred to the regular Navy after World War II attended this course. I am in the second row, at far right.

Chapter 5

Back to School

"Lean against this wall somewhat casually and ogle her. Do it quietly and without drawing attention to yourself. But we want the audience to know that you are undressing her with your eyes."

That's what the director told me to do, and that's what I did.

It was easy because she really had a figure and was quite pretty.

It was about three months after I returned from leave, having been accepted into the regular Navy and ordered to attend a 10-month school at Newport, Rhode island.

Looking for something different to do besides attend classes, I applied for a part in a play put on by the students.

The director of the play, a professional who auditioned and selected me for the part, explained that I was a soldier, home on leave, who was attending a party with his brother. Not well acquainted with the other guests, I was told to wander around the party scene until I saw a quiet young lady in the background. Struck by her figure and natural good looks, I was to lean against a wall and spend all my time looking at her.

The director had arranged the scene so that, even as I lounged against a wall off to the side and had no lines to say, the audience knew and appreciated what I was doing. And that's

5. Back to School

how this young lady soon becomes the center of attention and no longer a "Wallflower," which was the name of the play.

That's all I did. But even with no lines, all my classmates attending the play learned who I was. I never again saw the girl I ogled. But I did see her husband who was a classmate. For some reason, even though he and I shared something in common, we never became friends.

The director must have liked the way I did my part because four months later, after auditioning me again, he gave me a pretty good part in another class play. I forget the title of that play, but I'll never forget the opening scene of the second act.

As the curtain went up, I was sitting on a big black couch facing the audience. I was supposed to start the scene by saying something to Reeba, the girl sitting on my right.

During the rehearsals I had trouble remembering my lines. And when that curtain went up and I was looking at the sea of faces, I forgot my lines completely!

With the curtain up, the entire stage was deathly quiet and I was just sitting there with a frantic look on my face. It was obvious to everyone that I had forgotten my lines.

After what seemed forever, someone backstage whispered my opening lines to me. But the whisper carried across the stage and into the audience.

I suddenly came to life and shouted "Reeba." But as I went on into the rest of my lines, I was drowned out by a roar of laughter from the audience that wouldn't stop. With intermittent help from backstage, I finally got through the scene. But the play had really come to life. Every time I said something there would be a loud burst of laughter. It was supposed to be a comedy. But the audience was laughing at the wrong times – mostly at whatever I did.

For a couple weeks after the play, a lot of my classmates called me Reeba.

The director of the play complimented me on my "timing." I don't know if he realized my timing was caused by my inability to remember all my lines. In any event, he made me feel that if I wanted, I had a future in the theater.

All my classmates, like myself, were naval officers who had applied for and been accepted into the regular Navy. The class plays were part of the recreational aspects of the school program. The 10-month long course was established to bring the new regular naval officers up-to-date on all things Navy.

It was strange arriving at the school in Newport, Rhode Island. All of my previous duty assignments had been on ships. Being a student in such a lengthy program was quite different, yet I relished the difference.

The school curriculum covered engineering, ordnance, naval customs and traditions, plus other subjects related to a naval career. Fortunately, I was current in almost all the subjects and the 10-month course was a pleasant review for me.

It was 1947. All my classmates were veterans of WWII. Most had extensive combat experience, so we had a lot in common. About one-third were naval aviators.

The objective of the course was to provide us with some aspects of naval education that we might have missed, since none of us were Naval Academy graduates. As a result, we went over some very basic material that was new to a few, but really old stuff to most of us. I thought the students knew more than the instructors when discussions of the different types of naval operations came up.

In many ways, it was a relaxing time where we could review from an academic perspective much of what we had experienced during the war.

In the years after graduation, I kept meeting classmates in different jobs all over the world, including as captains of aircraft carriers, flag officer billets (admirals), and other key commands.

At the end of the school year, we all received orders to our new duty stations. My orders were to be executive officer of the landing ship dock, USS *Colonial* (LSD 18). This was a new and unusual type of ship assigned to the amphibious forces.

5. Back to School

I managed to get a picture of the ship and was surprised at what I saw (Figure 71). It was a huge ship with its after three-quarters consisting of what looked like an outsize olympic swimming pool, called a well deck. Designed to carry large landing craft, the well deck ran forward from the stern about 350 feet to a point just below the bridge. Except for the 50 or so feet under the bridge, the entire high-sided well deck was exposed to the sea. (See Figure 72.)

By pumping sea water into the huge tank compartments under the well deck and tilting down a big gate at the stern (the very end of the ship), the ship would sink about eight feet, opening the entire well deck to the sea. Landing craft of many different sizes could then simply drive in or out. These craft, when loaded with Marines and their fighting equipment, including tanks, could be quickly discharged from the ship without anyone aboard even getting their feet wet, to ultimately land on a hostile beach.

When the landing craft returned empty or with wounded Marines, they would simply drive into the well deck to unload. When all landing craft had returned, the ship would pump the water out of the tanks to bring the well deck above sea level, emptying the well deck of water and grounding the boats.

It was an amazingly new and interesting sea-going concept and I was really excited about my new job. But before I left for Norfolk, where the ship was home ported, I had a visitor.

He identified himself as Lieutenant Commander (LCdr) John Paterson, a fellow graduating student.

"Are you the guy who has orders to the *Colonial*?"

"Yes, that's me," I answered happily.

"Well, I was the first commanding officer of that ship and I have some information to pass on to you. Are you interested?"

"Sure am."

John, a former merchant marine officer, sat down and pulled a sheet of paper out of his brief case. I could see that he had made a rough sketch of the *Colonial* and its huge well deck.

Figure 71: **USS *Colonial* (LSD 18).** Shown here in July 1949, the *Colonial* was 457 feet long, with a 72-foot beam (width), and displaced 9110 tons fully loaded. Its well deck, not visible here, could carry landing craft of any size, and a variety of outsized cargo. Able to land its 200+ embarked Marines, with their tanks and all other equipment, without even getting their feet wet, the LSD was (and is) a remarkable component of the amphibious forces. The Korean War demonstrated this: *Colonial* was known as "The Galloping Ghost of the Korean Coast" and her captain received a decoration for the ship's effectiveness.

"What do you know about your new ship? You know it's a new design and that it is one of the first in its class," he said without waiting for my answer.

I nodded affirmatively and he continued.

"A few months before the war ended we loaded up at Norfolk and headed for the Pacific. About fifty miles southeast of Cape Hatteras, in the early evening, we ran into some really bad weather. It was rougher than any weather we had ever been in before. Well, after a lot of pounding, my people told me that we

5. BACK TO SCHOOL

Figure 72: **LSD well deck.** An LSD's well deck occupied 75% of its length. The gate at the stern, when lowered, allowed water to enter the well deck, which, in turn, allowed vessels to sail in. Because LSDs were built primarily to support amphibious operations, "landing ships" commonly used the well deck, hence the term "landing ship dock." This is HMS *Highway*, built for the Royal Navy, a ship in the same class as the *Colonial*.

---

had a major problem in the well deck. Some of the cargo had come loose, and it was too dangerous to send men into the well deck to secure it.

"I went down and took a look. Not only had some wooden boats broken loose, they were now shattered and small pieces had clogged the scuppers (drains) on the sides of the well deck. Big waves were bringing in water that now had no way to drain back out to the sea. The drainage had stopped and the well was filling with water. To make matters worse, as the water rose the huge chains used to secure the cargo to the bottom of the well deck simply snapped and all the cargo was loose. The whole massive dangerous mess was sloshing and banging against the well deck walls.

"I slowed to 5 knots and set the smoothest course I could. But that didn't help much. No matter what course and speed I selected, the ship kept rolling from one side to the other. All the cargo, which consisted mainly of landing craft, was breaking up. The deck scuppers were plugged up solid and the waves were still mounting us and filling the well.

"After a while the weather subsided and I managed to keep the ship somewhat stable – but the water in the well deck kept rising. It overflowed the well deck and started to flood our engine room before we sealed it off.

"Then we lost power – all power!

"We were a dead ship, rolling around out there with the well deck full of water, smashed cargo bumping into the sides of the well deck, none of our big pumps working! I thought we were going to lose the ship, so I sent out distress messages. Believe it or not, we even started a bucket brigade to remove water from the well deck, but that was hopeless.

"We rolled around there, without any power throughout the ship for about four or five hours before a large tug boat came to our assistance. Using their pumps we started dewatering the well deck. Then later the tug towed us back to Norfolk. The next day an inspection revealed that we had some serious damage. The ship's back (its keel) was broken (severely bent by all the weight in the well) and our trip to the Pacific would be delayed for about four months.

"Of course I was shook up. I have spent a lot of time trying to figure out what I could have done to prevent what happened, and that's what I am going to explain to you now."

He paused and looked squarely into my eyes. "You see, George, the ship has a design deficiency.

"In the open sea during heavy weather you can't avoid the big waves that leave a lot of their water in the well deck. With the present design there simply isn't enough drainage to get rid of that water fast enough – even when the scuppers aren't blocked by damaged cargo. When that water rises in the well deck those heavy chains holding the cargo, snap like toothpicks. And any wooden cargo, like the boats we carry in there, smash against the sides and break up in no time at all. Then the scuppers become clogged and the water rises faster. It comes up over the sides of the well deck making it unsafe for anyone to be there.

5. Back to School

"We should not have lost power but we did! And that's what really hurt!"

He was talking pretty fast. Having never seen a Landing Ship Dock, I had a hard time visualizing what he was telling me – so I didn't ask any questions.

Then he told me what he should have done before he left port to avoid the near disaster.

"The well deck itself is the top of many tanks below it. We fill these tanks with water when we want to ballast down the ship so the landing craft can drive in and out.

"Each of these huge tanks has one or two manhole covers that are bolted down. When you walk in the well deck you can see these bolted down man-hole covers." He paused to draw a sketch.

"The thing to do is to remove at least half of these man-hole covers, replace them with a metal mesh material so debris can't get into the tanks. Then when the scuppers get plugged up, water will drain into the tanks and you can easily pump it out. It would mean a lot of extra work to remove the tank tops and replace them all the time. And you would have to keep the pumps manned all during any heavy weather to pump the water from the tanks. But that's the only way to keep the well deck reasonably dry and the cargo safe."

"Are the pumps powerful enough to remove that much water?" I asked.

"Hell, yes," he answered. "Believe it or not we had more pumping capacity than any of our submarines."

Then somewhat wistfully he repeated. "That's what I should have done. Our pumps could have easily handled it if the water had gone into the tanks. Yes, that's what I should have done."

I don't think he was disciplined for the damage to his ship.[1]

It was a very sobering visit for me, and I thanked him. He had done almost all the talking. I don't think he ever tried that procedure with the tank tops on the *Colonial* and I don't recall if

---
[1] An internet search records the storm damage on July 21, 1945.

he finally did take her to the Pacific. He wished me luck and left. I never saw him again.

I never followed up to see if the Navy ever issued a formal design change to fix this problem. I do notice, however, that there are few, if any, LSDs with exposed open well decks in operation today. On the other hand, there are many large ships with LSD hulls (and bigger) but none of them have exposed well decks.

LCdr Patterson's story took a lot of wind out of my sails, but it didn't last long. I remained anxious to get to my new ship, fully confident that whatever went wrong the Navy would have it fixed by the time I got there. But, thank God, I never forgot what he told me.

Figure 76: **One of many airplanes for Berlin.** German children watch a U.S. Air Force C-54 cargo plane coming in to land at Tempelhof Airport in Berlin during the crisis that threatened to starve the city in 1948. The response of the United States involved all three military services.

Chapter 6

The Berlin Crisis

Early in my naval career I learned that recurring world crises made a young officer's life far from routine. And just three years after WWII ended that pattern continued.

With orders to be its executive officer (second in command) in my hands, I walked happily aboard the USS *Colonial* (LSD 18) on July 10, 1948, and was promptly ushered into the captain's cabin.

"Welcome aboard George, glad to see you," said Captain Fahle, extending his hand. Then after offering me a cup of coffee and exchanging a few pleasantries he said, "I'll be leaving the ship tomorrow and you will be in command."

"Yes sir," I responded, a little surprised that he would be going on leave so soon after I came aboard.

Captain Fahle continued, "Bupers (the Navy bureau of personnel) will be issuing you orders today to take over immediately, so you better get started checking out the ship and signing off on the necessary papers." (Figure 78)

"Bupers!" I repeated without thinking. Then it hit me, "You are being detached?"

"That's right," said Fahle. "It's an emergency situation connected with serious problems in Berlin." He then told me that he was going to the staff of Commander Amphibious Forces, Atlantic Fleet, to help plan and carry out an evacuation of U.S. cit-

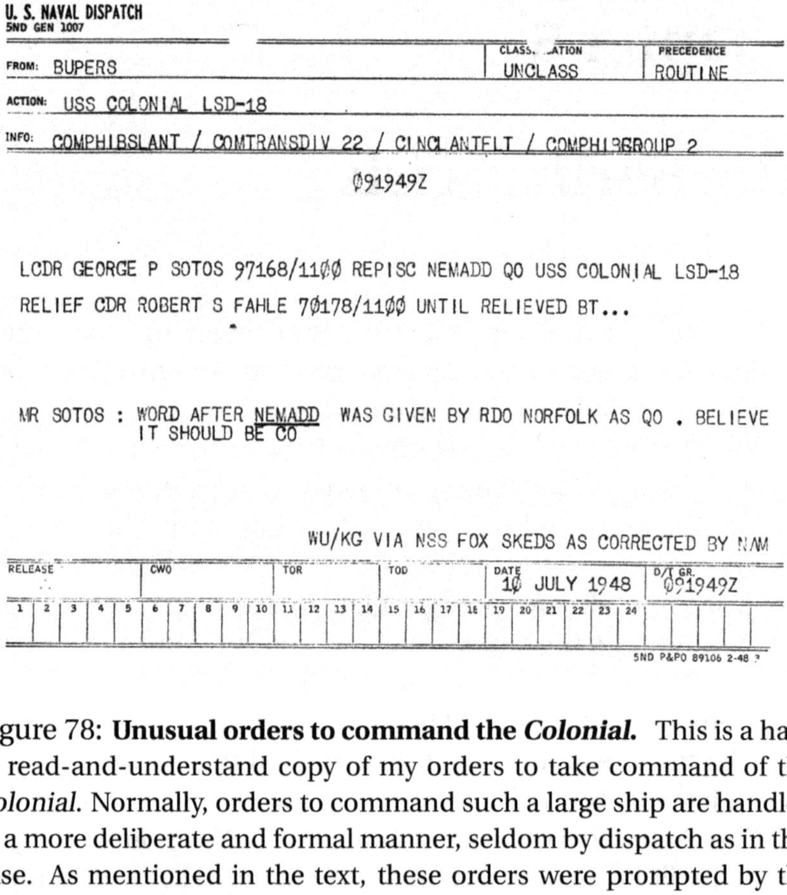

6. THE BERLIN CRISIS

```
U. S. NAVAL DISPATCH
5ND GEN 1007

FROM: BUPERS                              CLASS. _ATION      PRECEDENCE
                                          UNCLASS            ROUTINE
ACTION: USS COLONIAL LSD-18
INFO: COMPHIBSLANT / COMTRANSDIV 22 / CINCLANTFLT / COMPHIBGROUP 2
                        0919492

LCDR GEORGE P SOTOS 97168/1100 REPISC NEMADD QO USS COLONIAL LSD-18
RELIEF CDR ROBERT S FAHLE 70178/1100 UNTIL RELIEVED BT...


MR SOTOS : WORD AFTER NEMADD WAS GIVEN BY RDO NORFOLK AS QO . BELIEVE
           IT SHOULD BE CO


                    WU/KG VIA NSS FOX SKEDS AS CORRECTED BY NAM
RELEASE       CWO        TOR       TOD     DATE           D/T GR.
                                           10 JULY 1948   091949Z
 1  2  3  4  5  6  7  8  9 10 11 12 13 14 15 16 17 18 19 20 21 22 23 24
                                                          5ND P&PO 89106 2-48
```

Figure 78: **Unusual orders to command the *Colonial*.** This is a hard to read-and-understand copy of my orders to take command of the *Colonial*. Normally, orders to command such a large ship are handled in a more deliberate and formal manner, seldom by dispatch as in this case. As mentioned in the text, these orders were prompted by the events in Berlin, the urgency of which no doubt prompted the unusually terse orders shown here. The orders even include a significant typographical error.

izens from Berlin, if and when that became necessary. The admiral wanted him right away.

Of course I knew there were problems in Berlin. The city, a hundred miles inside the Soviet-controlled part of Germany was divided into the Soviet-controlled section (East Berlin) and the Allied-controlled section (West Berlin).

What I didn't know then was that 8,893 tons of supplies (food, coal, etc.) – mostly carried by rail – were required each day to support the two million people in West Berlin, and that the Soviets were threatening to institute a blockade that would stop that flow of supplies.

"Is it getting that bad?" I asked.

"Yes, I guess it is." Then he said something about the need to assemble all available naval units to prepare for a massive evacuation. He paused for a second and cautioned that it was closely held information and must be treated that way.

"Yes sir," I said, still not realizing what I was getting into.

"Bupers has gone over your record and since you are qualified for command, they will issue you orders to take temporary command of the *Colonial* until they can find a permanent replacement for me."

He continued. "The ship has been tied up here for the past six months. We have moved out into the stream once during that time to make sure the engines were still operational. Only fifty percent of the crew that is needed to operate the ship is now on board and there are no plans to fill those empty billets."

He saw my startled look. "Don't worry. You won't have to operate the ship. It will stay here in commission, but in a non-operational status. You won't have any mission. Just maintain it alongside the dock."

"Well, that's not so bad," I thought to myself. "Hell, I can do that."

He didn't say anything more. So I said, "I guess I better get started."

"Can you make your way around?"

6. THE BERLIN CRISIS

"Yes sir, I know what needs to be done." And indeed I did. My experience at Green Cove Springs, Florida, placing the WWII destroyer escorts out of commission and in the moth ball fleet, had insured that knowledge.

I was still somewhat in a daze about the ship itself. But that didn't last as I suddenly realized the lucky break I was getting. A big ship like this and no operating requirements! What could be sweeter. I'll have plenty of time to learn the ship at my own pace.

Except for the three week cruise I had on the battleship *Arkansas* when I was a 19 year old midshipman, the *Colonial* was easily the biggest ship I had been on. And now I was about to become her commander.

I knew even then that this LSD was not only a different type of ship, but one for the future. Quietly, but effectively, some gifted ship designers had managed to wrap all the lessons learned in WWII amphibious operations into the hull of this ship. Very high out of the water at the bow, she abruptly dropped to almost destroyer-level freeboard (the main deck's vertical distance from the water). The aft 350 feet formed the walls of the well deck.

One didn't have to be a student of amphibious warfare to appreciate the combat value of this new type of ship. I learned later, for example, that in the well deck we could carry fourteen 23-ton, 50-foot-long LCMs (landing craft mechanized) that each carried a medium tank and its Marines. And, that by ballasting down as we approached the landing area, we could launch all 14 in less than ten minutes. This was far more flexible and faster than the larger, more cumbersome transports that had to anchor and use cranes to lift tanks off their high decks. (See Figure 92 and Figure 104.)

It sounds like a very straightforward process, and after considerable experiences and many mistakes, I would later find that it was indeed straightforward. But it was also loaded with many variables that, if not attended to correctly, would cause serious problems.

I sent for Mr. Raab, the First Lieutenant. I introduced my-

Figure 81: **LSDs and aviation.** At left, the *Colonial* has its large "super deck" installed atop the well deck. The well deck had a total capacity of 960 tons and the super deck would hold an additional 230 tons of cargo or four helicopters. We never used the super deck during my two years on the *Colonial*. Right, an LSD brings a seaplane into its well deck. Considered as possible sea plane tenders, this concept was ultimately not adopted.

---

self and told him the news. I also told him he was temporarily promoted to executive officer as of right now.

Raab was no less surprised than I was, but I could also see he liked the idea of being Exec. He was a mustang officer (former enlisted) and I liked him right away. He didn't ask any questions after I told him I'd explain later the details to him and the other officers.

"Let's get started inspecting the ship. Captain Fahle wants to leave as soon as possible."

"Yes sir," he answered, "I'll get a Yeoman and we'll get started."

He was back in a few minutes with a sailor carrying a clipboard, whom he introduced as Yeoman First Class Martin.

Similar to an office manager, Martin had a copy of the relieving-of-command letter which Fahle had used just six months earlier when he had assumed command. I looked at it briefly and saw that he had listed a number of deficiencies, which Raab said still existed. Fahle had noted the dangerous

6. THE BERLIN CRISIS

Figure 82: **Well-deck of present-day LSD.** This photograph of USS *Portland* (LSD-37) shows a well deck that is largely covered, removing exposure to boarding seas. Hearing of the *Colonial*'s problem in boarding seas 50 years earlier was a surprise to the Captain and officers, who were perhaps a little relieved that the problem no longer exists.

---

shortage of experienced ship's company in almost every department of the ship. The shortages made it impossible to assure that the ship could be operated safely. He had also stated that much of the machinery, including operation of the huge ballast and deballasting pumps needed to fill and empty the well deck, was suspect – they had not been used operationally in the past eight months. Further, there were not enough men on board to operate them safely. I included all the deficiencies from Fahle's list in the list of deficiencies that I would compile.

The three of us spent the next four hours going over every compartment and piece of machinery on the ship. I added a few more minor deficiencies to the list, but it remained essentially the same as the one Fahle had used.

We both signed the necessary papers and, two days after I came aboard as the second-in-command, I was the commanding officer. Wow, I thought to myself. "Can't move up much faster than this at the ripe old age of 27." And you can imagine what my family thought when I wrote to them about it. They thought I would be an admiral in just a few more months!

I had just settled down to enjoying my new status when, early the second morning of my command, the radioman knocked on my door and handed me a message marked urgent.

The message from Commander Amphibious Forces, Atlantic Fleet read, "USS *Colonial* get underway soonest. Arrange for refueling and replenishment at Naval Operating Base, Norfolk, and, when ready in all respects for sea, report to Commander Underway Training, Norfolk to undergo operational readiness inspection (ORI) preparatory to full operational status."

I looked again at the message heading. Yes, it was from my boss, Commander Amphibious Forces Atlantic Fleet, an admiral. I knew my predecessor had joined his staff. But I also knew that whoever released that message for the admiral hadn't consulted with Fahle. Yes, Fahle was in the planning division but, hell, he and the admiral were in the same building and should be talking to each other.

I was disturbed, of course. Fahle had assured me the ship wouldn't move. Deep down though, I wasn't that shook up. I had been through ORI's before and, while they were hectic and very hard on everyone, they did help get the ship in shape and ready to operate at sea.

I sent for Raab. I knew how very valuable, well rounded and experienced an officer he was. And I was right. I leaned on him heavily in the months ahead.

I showed him the message and saw his jaw drop.

6. THE BERLIN CRISIS

"Captain, we don't have enough men to even get the ship underway let alone go through an ORI."

"I know Mr. Raab," I replied. "But we'll make a stab at it and see what happens." I was strangely confident that we could do it and I guess it showed.

"We're going to need more men right away, especially in the engineering department, before we can move," said Raab sharply, letting me know by the tone of his voice that he knew more about the ship than I did.

His strong response didn't bother me. I knew he was right and I had learned to appreciate forthright comments from experienced sailors.

"Yes, I know," I replied. "But let's get all the officers and chiefs together in the wardroom so we can go over what needs to be done."

"You want the chiefs, too?" Raab asked.

"Yes, I want to talk to them all at the same time. I haven't met them yet and I want to make sure they get the word on what's happening."

I then told Raab about the reason for Falhe's transfer. "And I guess they need us ready for the same reason."

"Aye, aye, Captain, I'll get them all in the wardroom and let you know when we are ready." I could see that he wasn't happy. Not only was he the new Exec, he had a new young skipper who had never even seen an LSD before, let alone commanded one. I knew if I were in his shoes I wouldn't be too happy either. But I also knew he would get it done.

Forty-five minutes later I addressed all the officers and chiefs of the *Colonial*. As I recall there were seven officers and eight experienced chief petty officers.

After introducing myself and shaking hands all around, I explained the reason for the meeting. I ended up by telling them I was confident we could do the ORI. I had been through several really tough ones in the past and suggested they had also. But I was wrong. I found out later that only two others had been through an ORI. One was Raab, the other was the Chief Machinist Mate, Pat Ryan.

I guess not knowing what was in store for them in the ORI tempered their reaction to my announcement. I told them I'd keep them informed and then let them go, while asking the officers to remain behind.

I was surprised at their age. Except for Raab they were all much younger than I expected. They reminded me of the fresh-caught young officers I was part of at the beginning of WWII. But even that didn't bother me too much, since I was aware of how fast and how responsibly these young officers could take hold of their jobs.

I wasn't disappointed. In ten days I sent a message to the Commander Underway Training, Norfolk, telling him that *Colonial* was reporting for duty. In that ten day period we not only refueled and replenished, we got underway and tested our anchor engines and the ballasting-and-deballasting system.

All was not roses. Starting with myself, I was almost floored by the ship-handling differences between the massive eight thousand ton LSD and my previous destroyer escort command. Our first time underway was a revelation for me. After we moved away from the pier in Newport News, where she had been berthed for the past eight months, the pilot headed her into the channel to the Naval Operating base which was nearby.

Peering ahead into the channel I told the pilot that the *Colonial* appeared too big and wide to fit in that channel. A fatherly type, the pilot laughed. "You'll get used to it son," he said. And, of course, he was right. It just took a little steaming time in and out of Norfolk before I became very comfortable handling the huge *Colonial*.

Ballasting down and dewatering was another major learning lesson. Never having seen or even heard of such a capability before, I wanted to see how it worked. What I didn't know was that there were only two sailors aboard who had any experience with the system. It may sound routine to turn on the huge pumps, fill the well deck with water and observe how long it takes for her to

6. THE BERLIN CRISIS

sink lower in the water, but it was far from routine!

It started out problem-free. That is, the water was pumped into the well deck in large volumes. The after part of the ship started to sink, as designed. But... it didn't go down straight. She took on a severe port list (she leaned far to the left). We finally got the after end of the ship down ten feet but never could get it straight and level that first time. The next day I took the ship out in the bay and anchored. Then I ordered them to keep repeating the ballasting and deballasting until it worked smoothly. They didn't like the extra work but I think they were all proud of themselves when it got to be a routine process.

What I didn't realize at the time was that ballasting and deballasting alongside the pier resulted in sand at the bottom of the tanks. Fortunately we only did it once and there wasn't too much sand in the tanks. In any event, we didn't bother to remove it and it never affected operations.

A few days after reporting ready for training, we started the ORI, and even though we had received additional sailors, they were inexperienced. Most were nineteen years old and this was their first ship. But thankfully we did receive some petty officers who had been on other ships and had sea-going experience.

The authorized complement of the *Colonial* was 218 enlisted men. We had about 180 aboard when we started the training.

Normally, inexperienced people are reluctant to step up and take on challenging tasks that involve operating complicated equipment at sea. But there's another side to it. Almost all of them rise to higher levels of performance and make fewer mistakes when there is a good leader among them and they each have a clearly responsible task. Luckily, I had really good chief petty officer leaders so that the newcomers maintained their interest, were motivated, assumed responsibility and became so reliably trustworthy I couldn't believe it.

For example, ballasting-and-deballasting is actually a major operation that worried the hell out of me at first. But as mentioned above, the operation became so routine that I could start thinking of new ways to use the LSD's unique capabilities. Also, in the engineering plant a hesitant group of men quickly became skilled and ran the plant like they had been doing it for months.

Another example occurred the first time I anchored the *Colonial* – which was the first time in eight months the anchor had been dropped. I tried to back the ship to put some tension on the chain to make sure the anchor was holding. Surprisingly, there was no response to "back one-third or back two-thirds bells" (these are engine room telegraphic orders). We just sat there for a minute or so. Then, suddenly, the two-thirds bell was answered with what felt like a "back full" response. We picked up enough stern way to test the anchor and even drag it before the engineers responded to an "all stop" order.

Of course I picked up the phone and asked the chief engineer what had happened. He didn't alibi. Some of his new men had become flustered and didn't respond properly and that was it. Later I talked to him and we agreed that we should repeat that exercise and also run through a number of maneuvering drills so that all his people could get checked out.

There were a number of other mistakes that occurred, but they only occurred once and never again in the two years I was on the ship.

Though we thought we were ready for the ORI, I found that this particular ORI was far different than the ones I had gone through on the destroyer escort *Willis* at Guantanamo and Bermuda.

Indeed, this one was far more difficult and riskier than the others because of the utter incompetence of the training command team that was supervising the three-week long ORI.

We were the first LSD they ran through their ORI. And it showed! They had planned a number of exercises which would "test" our readiness for war and other emergencies. But they had not altered any of their exercises to fit some of the unusual characteristics of the LSD, including the operational use of our ballasting and deballasting to embark and debark landing forces.

The incompetence of the training group was demonstrated

6. THE BERLIN CRISIS

on the very first day of the ORI. About 35 evaluators with clipboards and pencils had stationed themselves throughout the ship to observe our response to different exercises. Most exercises were not announced ahead of time. We just had to be ready for any one of them,

We were at anchor at the start of the ORI, on the first day. The chief observer told me to get the ship underway (it was one of the exercises).

I gave the order to take in the anchor and we soon heard the heavy anchor chain being winched aboard. Just as the anchor was lifted clear of the water, I ordered "All engines ahead one third." That's when we saw smoke coming out of the forward part of the ship and received a report, "Fire in the paint locker."

"All engines stop," I ordered. "Prepare to drop the anchor." I knew the paint locker was right next to the anchor chain storage locker and thought it would be easier to fight the fire while at anchor rather than underway.

"Don't let go the anchor," Raab warned me. "We have two men in the chain locker."

"My God," I thought to myself. If I had dropped the anchor they would have been crushed to death by the heavy chains barrelleling up out of the locker.

"Stop off the anchor. Hold it where it is. Get those men out of the chain locker," I ordered. Raab had disappeared. He was on the way to the foc'stle where thick smoke was still coming out of the paint locker.

About 5 minutes later we saw a scuffle on the foc'stle. Then we saw Raab dragging the chief evaluator, a lieutenant, toward the gangway which was still down. "Bring a boat alongside for this guy before I throw him in the water," he shouted to the boatswain of the watch. In a few minutes a boat was alongside and the scruffed lieutenant was in the boat heading for shore.

In a few minutes Raab was back on the bridge. "That stupid son-of-a-bitch ordered a smoke pot placed near the chain locker for a fire drill. He didn't know we had men in the chain locker and he almost suffocated the two men in there." Raab was out of breath and his face was red with anger. I didn't say anything. I didn't need to. Everyone on the bridge knew Raab had done the right thing.

I sent for the next senior evaluator, also a lieutenant. "Your boss made a serious mistake," I told him. "You just don't set a smoke pot going next to the chain locker where people are stowing the incoming anchor chain when we are getting underway – and that's what he did. We were lucky he didn't hurt the men in there."

The lieutenant didn't say anything, but I knew he would pass my message on to the admiral.

"Let's get on with the training. Can you handle what we have to do?"

"Yes, sir, I can," he answered.

"O.K.," I said, "but let's not start it until I get the anchor secured for sea. Agreed?"

"Yes, sir," he answered quietly.

We spent the rest of the day running all types of exercises. An evaluator would hide one of the sailors. Then he would hand another sailor on deck a slip of paper that read, "Man overboard – starboard side." At the same time he would throw a dummy over the side. The sailor was expected to immediately throw over a life preserver with a whistle attached, and shout, "Man overboard, man overboard, starboard side" and report it by phone or by running toward the bridge, whichever was faster.

Once the Officer of the deck (OOD) got that information, he was expected to stop the starboard engine, order hard right rudder, have the word passed on the ship's loudspeaker system, inform the captain and turn the ship around so that it came to the same spot where the life preserver was floating. A muster of all hands would then be required to see if the missing (hidden) sailor was identified. Several actions were evaluated in this particular exercise including the responsiveness of all the ship's company, the performance of the OOD, as well as the time it took to recover the dummy.

6. The Berlin Crisis

The evaluators would then assign a grade to each participant in the exercise as well as an overall ship grade.

Similarly an evaluator would tell a lookout, "You see an aircraft approaching the ship. It is about 15 miles away bearing 020." And again, the lookout would be expected to immediately report that to the bridge. The OOD was expected to sound general quarters, notify the captain and train the guns in the direction of the target. Many exercises were performed over a period of three weeks, some of them more than once. The engineering department would be forced to operate on one engine, recover from complete power losses, and fight fires in the engine room.

The damage control parties were required to control simulated damage and even provide assistance to other ships. The Captain was also deemed a casualty in one simulated engagement and Lt. Raab had to step up and perform the duties of commanding officer.

Ballasting and deballasting exercises were also conducted, some with the well deck full of landing craft, along with execution of night landings on an unfamiliar beach. This latter exercise I added myself because the evaluators didn't know enough about the ship's capabilities to launch landing craft.

These exercises, including the firing of our guns at targets towed by aircraft and surface ships, were conducted at sea, day and night, over a three week period. All the time the evaluators took copious notes, identified what they thought were deficiencies and in general prepared themselves to assign an overall readiness-for-war grade to the *Colonial*.

I was not only proud of the way my crew performed but genuinely impressed with the way they responded to all the challenges.

The most serious and dangerous exercise for me personally was the towing task. A collision at sea is life threatening and unforgivable – as I was soon to learn.

Flagship Captain

✪ ✪ ✪ ✪ ✪ ✪ ✪ ✪ ✪ ✪ ✪ ✪ ✪

Figure 92: **LSD amphibious operations.** [Top] Although it appears that USS *Whetstone* (LSD-27) is sinking in this 1952 photo, she has instead flooded her well deck and ballasted down, enabling vessels to sail right into or out of her well deck. [Middle] Wet: Classic amphibious operations in modern amphibious ships. [Bottom] Dry: Air-cushion landing craft, pioneered in the 1960s, can drive into a dry well deck. Trucks can drive in from a boat, feet-dry.

Chapter 7

Learn by Doing

The huge 7000 ton attack cargo ship (AKA) (I forget its name) was stopped on a heading of 270 degrees as I made my approach in the *Colonial* to take him in tow. About the same size as my ship, the flat sea and slight breeze on my starboard (right) side were treating us the same. It was a nice sunny day as, on parallel course from behind and about 50 yards to his right, I very slowly overtook the stopped AKA.

When he was still slightly ahead of me, I ordered left ten degrees rudder and steadied up on a course that pointed my bow to a spot about 50 yards dead ahead of the AKA. My intention was to slide in front of him, come to a full stop, pass the tow lines, hook up, and start the tow. (See Figure 95.)

A towing-at-sea exercise, as this was, between two large ships is not a simple routine. It is only done during an operational readiness inspection (ORI), as we were undergoing, with a team of inspectors aboard watching and evaluating our every move.

Except for the special towing team of sailors in the engine room and on the bridge, and the deck hands ready with the tow line on the stern, most of the rest of the crew had lined the port side to watch.

While I had memories of being towed when I was aboard the USS *Gary*, this was quite different. The *Colonial* was about 60

7. LEARN BY DOING

Figure 94: **The almost-collision.** This is the USS *Rankin*, an amphibious cargo ship (AKA). Her 459-foot length was nearly that of the *Colonial's*. As the *Colonial* prepared to tow a ship of this class, a collision was barely avoided.

---

times the size of the tugboat that towed the *Gary* and her maneuvering ability was far less than any tug boat's. Most importantly though, I had never done this particular maneuver as the captain of such a large ship.

The weather was nice and clear. The sea was almost flat, with that slight breeze on my starboard (right) side. I was nervous at the start of the maneuver, but things were going so well as I made the approach that I began to enjoy the challenge.

When my bow was about even with the AKA's stern, I ordered "Stop all engines," expecting to coast slowly ahead of him to the spot I had selected.

I was doing nicely. Or so I thought, as I looked across the water at the hulking cargo ship.

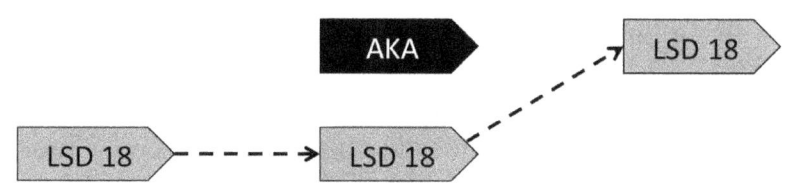

Figure 95: **Maneuver diagram.** This schematic illustrates my intended maneuver to pass the AKA slowly (at about 4 knots) on her starboard side, then slide into a towing position ahead of her.

Suddenly I saw that my ship was moving leftwards faster than it was moving forward. We were rapidly bearing down on the AKA and heading for a broadside collision!

Almost instantly I realized that my ship's huge superstructure had cut off the wind that had been affecting both ships and was now affecting me only. It was blowing me right down on the AKA.

Frantically I ordered, "Right full rudder steer course two seven zero, all engines ahead full."

"Ask the AKA to back down," I shouted excitedly to the officer of the deck (OOD). And heard him just as excitedly transmit the message.

"Coming right to two seven zero," responded the helmsman.

"Engine room answers all engines ahead full," shouted the quartermaster.

Slowly. Ever so slowly. The bow started to move to the right away from the AKA. At the same time we started to pick up some forward speed as we paralleled the AKA. But the wind had pushed us much closer to him. He was probably about thirty yards away. I heard a chief petty officer order my sailors to clear the port side and for an instant I thought we were going to have a broadside collision.

We were so close I felt I could reach out and touch the AKA's superstructure. With great relief I saw that my bow had crept ahead of the AKA's bow. Even so, I could see that, unless I did

7. Learn by Doing

something, the wind would push the after part of my ship into the AKA.

"Left full rudder," I ordered.

"Rudder is left full," came the almost instantaneous reply.

We started to move left – even closer to the AKA. However, at the same time, we were slowly picking up speed. And even though we were turning toward him our forward momentum from the turn pushed my bow ahead and just clear of him and my stern was swinging right – away from the AKA.

Thank God! I could see the danger of a collision was gone.

The left rudder had moved my stern and most of the after part of the ship away from the AKA. I was sliding forward and ahead of him literally wrapping my ship around his bow.

I waited until my stern was well clear of the AKA and our heading was about perpendicular to his so that we would cross well clear in front of him.

"Reverse your rudder. All engines stop."

"Rudder is right full. Engine room answers all engines stopped," came the word from the wheelhouse.

The bow's swing to the left slowed, stopped and then, as we moved ahead, started swinging in the opposite direction as the right rudder took hold.

I let the bow swing right for a while then ordered, "Steady as she goes."

"Steady as she goes. New course two four five," responded the helmsman.

We were still moving ahead slowly but the wind was no longer a problem We were still quite close but safely ahead.

Trying to get in position for the tow I ordered, "All back full" to stop our forward motion and not get too far ahead of him.

"Engine room answers all engines back full sir," came the response from the wheel house.

I wanted to swing the stern in closer to the AKA to make passing the tow line easier. So I ordered, "Right full rudder." I waited for a few minutes as the stern started to swing in under the AKA's bow. "Steer two seven zero. All engines stop."

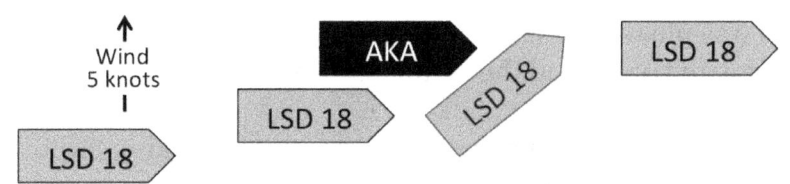

Figure 97: **Maneuver diagram – what actually transpired.** When the *Colonial* blocked the wind that had been affecting both ships, the effect was to push the *Colonial* toward the AKA. Only the *Colonial*'s emergency maneuvers avoided a collision.

"Steady two seven zero, engine room reports all engines stop," came the reply from the wheelhouse as the ship shuddered to a full stop – just a few feet ahead and on the same heading as the AKA.

I was amazed at my own ship-handling skills. We had slid in and stopped dead in the water just a few feet in front of the AKA. We had missed her by about 15 feet.

This all happened in the space of just a few minutes. After we cleared the AKA I saw his propellors create a small wake. It was his late response to my urgent back down request. The wake quickly disappeared as he realized the danger had passed.

Looking aft, I could see we were so close to the AKA that my sailors just handed the end of the towing cable up to the men on the AKA foc'stle above them. The latter quickly pulled it through the bull nose and placed the eye of the cable over a bollard. And in what seemed just minutes, reported the tow line secured.

Lieutenant (Lt.) Raab, who was in charge of the towing detail on the stern, reported the tow line secure, ready to start the tow.

"Tell him Wilco," (will comply) I said as I ordered, "Starboard engine ahead one third. Keep her steady on your present course."

"Engine room reports starboard engine ahead one third, steady on course 270, sir," came the acknowledgement from the wheel house.

7. Learn by Doing

I was pleased to see my phone talker, without being told, repeating my order and the responses from the wheel house to Lt. Raab's group back aft.

I was out on the port wing of the bridge looking aft for the tow wire Lt. Raab's group was paying out as we moved slowly away from the AKA. The danger here, I knew, was that if we had too much slack in the tow wire it might get pulled into our propellers and really mess us up.

"Mr. Raab says that the wire is well clear of the propellers," reported my talker.

As the distance between us increased I could see the wire slowly come out of the water. It had a reasonably long catenary (a long dip in the line) and didn't show much strain.

"Mr. Raab recommends stopping all engines so we can secure the tow wire."

We stopped until they secured our end of the tow line.

"Mr. Raab recommends one third ahead on one engine."

"Ahead one-third on the starboard engine," I ordered. We saw the tow wire take a heavier strain, then slack a little.

"Mr. Raab reports the tow is underway. He recommends all engines ahead one third." Because it is difficult to see from the bridge how the tow is riding, it is essential to have an experienced, reliable officer in charge back on the stern. And for me, that was Lt. Raab.

"Good old Raab," I said to myself as I ordered all engines ahead one third.

After about ten minutes, the strain on the tow wire increased until it rose out of the water then slacked as the AKA gained towing speed behind us. I remained at one third speed for about fifteen minutes and was starting to increase to two thirds when the senior evaluator announced, "Towing exercise completed, please secure from the towing exercise."

After we had retrieved our towing cable, I sent a message thanking the skipper of the AKA for his help and we headed for port. I got on the ship's loudspeaker system and complimented my entire crew, especially the engine room and those on the fantail (the stern) for a very successful towing exercise between two very large ships.

But deep down in my heart, I knew I was damn lucky to have averted a serious and very dangerous collision that could have injured a number of people and put both ships out of commission for a month or so. I really learned a ship-handling lesson. Never again would I forget to consider the large sail area of my LSD or any other ship.

It is remarkable how forgiving a crew can be. There was no way they could have missed the desperation in my voice when I asked the AKA to back down or my frantic stream of orders to miss the AKA and start the tow.

But they never seemed to have seen that part. All they saw and experienced was an outstanding maneuver that placed the huge *Colonial* just feet ahead of the massive AKA and reduced a complex two hour exercise to just minutes.

I can't explain it but for some strange reason their compliments to me on my ship handling ability, especially from Lt. Raab (who had not been on the bridge) gave me a great deal of confidence. At the same time, I gained a confidence in the professionalism of my crew. They really performed all their tasks in a top notch way with no supervision from me. This mutual confidence, in many ways, turned out to be a hidden blessing. In the days to come, when I had to issue many unwelcome orders before and during violent, dangerous storms, and when carrying unusual cargo in our exposed well deck. Not once did they question these orders, even when in hindsight some may have been seen as unnecessary.

No question, one way to crawl into the psyche of your crew is to share and succeed well in a challenging and dangerous experience.

The remainder of the ORI was all down hill. We managed to complete all the scheduled events, some by the skin of our teeth, and some like real professionals.

7. Learn by Doing

Surprisingly, at the final critique of all the ORI exercises, the admiral commanding the training group stated, in front of his evaluation team and in front of all my officers and Chiefs, that we had not completed all the required training.

"Therefore," he said, "I am assigning an unsatisfactory evaluation for the ORI." He tried to be gentle with us, noting that the *Colonial* had not been operationally active for eight months prior to the ORI, that it was only at seventy percent of its authorized personnel ceiling, and that it had temporary commanding and executive officers with limited or no LSD experience. Also, that because of these shortcomings, he had initially recommended against an ORI for the *Colonial*. However. the Commander Amphibious Force had ordered them to do their best to get it operational "And that goal was accomplished," said the admiral.

All this occurred in a gymnasium with the *Colonial* officers and chief petty officers in one set of stands and all the ORI evaluators and the admiral's staff sitting opposite us in another set of stands. I knew the admiral intended his talk as a compliment, but I could not restrain my anger.

With all the ORI evaluators and all of my officers and chiefs looking on, I raised my hand and stated that I was the commanding officer of the *Colonial* and would like to speak about the ORI and the unsatisfactory evaluation.

"Please do," he said expecting, I guess, that I would express my thanks for their endeavors in improving our readiness.

"Admiral," I said, "with all due respect for your command's efforts in our behalf, I can not agree in any way with your assessment of our performance in the ORI. We satisfactorily completed every exercise. None of the initial evaluations we received for a single one of those exercises was unsatisfactory. I am sure a careful review of all the evaluations will show that we completed them all successfully. We worked very hard night and day during this ORI and I don't think we are being treated fairly."

I could see that he was stunned by what I said. He turned to his chief of staff and we heard him ask, "Is that right? Did they complete all the exercises?"

The Chief of Staff, a captain, turned to the senior evaluator who was sitting a few rows behind him. We couldn't hear what they said but it was obvious that the senior evaluator, a lieutenant, was reluctantly agreeing with what I had just said.

After about ten minutes of discussion among themselves and the handing back and forth of some papers the admiral said, "Apparently you are right. You did complete all the exercises that were required. We will review the final evaluation and make a written report to the Commander Amphibious Forces and yourself. This meeting is over."

He didn't apologize or say anything else. They just got up and left as my group sat there and watched. As we left our seats to return to the ship, several of the Chiefs and Lt. Raab thanked me for speaking up. They all agreed that it was the inexperience with an LSD type ship that confused the evaluators and I agreed with them. It was the most incompetent training group that I had ever worked with.

Four days later we received a letter that informed us and Commander Amphibious Forces that we had completed the ORI satisfactorily. And that was it!

Actually, with our personnel shortages and no operational experience I thought we should have been commended for completing it. I passed on to my crew the fact that we had received a passing grade and commended my entire crew.

By this time (April 9, 1948), the newspapers were reporting the Soviet blockade and the growing Berlin airlift, so we all knew why the *Colonial*'s readiness was important.

The Soviets had completely blockaded the incoming surface transportation that carried supplies. However, air transport was a different story. There was a twenty mile wide air corridor over which the Soviets had no control. And, miraculously, it was through this corridor that the Allies started making aviation transport history.

At first, the air supply problem for West Berlin appeared unsolvable. For example, a single C-47 cargo plane could carry only

7. Learn by Doing

3.5 tons. Using them alone would require over 2,500 flights a day.

From that depressing, almost insurmountable beginning, however, the Allies persevered and surprised the world. One way or the other, they literally filled that air corridor with transport aircraft bringing supplies that sustained West Berlin.

The blockade lasted 13 months, until May 12, 1949, when the Soviets relented. But to play it safe the Allies continued the airlift until September 1949.

During a fifteen month period, using that 20 mile wide air corridor, a total of 277,804 flights were completed by the U.S. and Great Britain.[1]

It was a tremendous accomplishment and a stunning Cold War setback for the Soviet Union.

The *Colonial* was not needed for the Berlin crisis. We were instead assigned to an operational amphibious group that included the only other operational LSD in the Navy, the USS *Catamount* (LSD 17). We participated in landing force exercises from Puerto Rico to Newfoundland.

One experience scared the hell out of me when our task force of about 20 various ships was anchored off Virginia Beach. We received a storm warning predicting winds up to 60 knots. That is a lot of wind!

It was obviously very dangerous for all those ships to be anchored that close (about a mile) from the famous resort of Virginia Beach.

All ships were ordered to leave the anchorage and operate independently at sea to ride out the storm.

The weather prediction was right and the wind really started to blow, One by one all the ships got underway and left the anchorage – until I was the only ship remaining. I was reluctant to leave because I knew my anchor was holding well. I had about 80 fathoms (480 feet) of anchor chain out and we were steaming ahead into the furious wind at one third speed (about 6 knots). But we were not moving. We had the engines ahead at one third

---

[1] Royal Air Force Museum. https://bit.ly/2qnrHpR

to ease the strain on our anchor chain. This kept us riding and holding well.

Out of the mist I saw a large merchant ship that was dragging its anchor rapidly approaching us. At first I thought he would hit us and I ordered the anchor detail to start taking in the anchor chain, while preparing to move us out of the anchorage. But the wind was so strong that our anchor winch would only bring in one or two links every three or four minutes no matter how much steam we applied to the winch. I even went ahead two thirds on both engines (10 knots) to see if that would ease the strain on the chain and help the winch bring the chain in. It really didn't help much. Luckily, by that time the merchant ship had passed well ahead of us, still dragging its anchor.

We weren't the only ones being tested that day. Over the inter-ship radio, I could hear the ships that were underway at sea. They were having a terrible time with poor visibility and the strong winds. Several of them bumped together and caused significant damage that later kept them in port well after the storm.

I decided that I was going to stay there – no matter my orders. And stay there we did, steaming one third and sometimes two thirds ahead at anchor riding out the storm. Late that night, when the storm abated, other ships came back in and anchored nearby. They had all had harrowing experiences at sea while I really had it safe and secure with the anchorage all to myself.

Figure 104: **Well deck from above.** Top is the USS *Oak Hill* (LSD-7). Slightly older than the *Colonial*, the risk from boarding sea coming in from the beam (side) during heavy weather, described on page 71, is apparent. The many vehicles in its well deck, while impressive, do not fully illustrate LSD capabilities. The *Colonial* put an "LSM" ship, shown in the bottom figure, in her well deck. The LSM, having a deck of its own, can deliver five medium tanks and 200 marines to the beach.

Chapter 8

Land the Landing Force

The problems in Germany, that had initially prompted my quick elevation to command of the *Colonial*, grew worse. The Soviet Union was still fuming from the failure of its West Berlin blockade and the Cold War was getting hotter.

The outlook for avoiding World War III was grim.

With the media full of the problems between the Soviets and the U.S., it was easy to see why the Navy was increasing its readiness.

Shortly after our contentious ORI, while I was still in command of the *Colonial*, our personnel increased to 250 enlisted men and 10 officers. We became a fully operational unit of the Atlantic Fleet Amphibious Forces.

That increased readiness meant a lot of underway training, including an interesting "opposed" war game, where we were required to put a "large landing force," on the island of Ponce in Puerto Rico.

As I recall, there were seven of us who departed from the naval operating base at Norfolk, Virginia: six large amphibious force ships (troop transports and heavy cargo ships) plus my ship.

This amphibious task force was different from most of its predecessors. My ship was that difference.

8. Land the Landing Force

Before departure, we had ballasted down outside of the harbor to allow a large LSM (landing ship medium – Figure 104) to drive slowly into my well deck. We pumped the water out of our tanks and the snugly fitting LSM was high and dry on our well deck. The *Colonial* was ready to go.

The LSM carried five medium tanks and could beach itself. So the five tanks and the 200 Marines we had aboard could quickly go ashore without getting their feet wet. Even better, the resulting time and exposure to enemy fire during those activities were about one tenth of what the large, old-fashioned cargo ships experienced.

The night before we were to arrive at the landing area on Ponce, I received orders from the task force commander to leave the formation and proceed independently to a new landing area on the opposite side of the island from the planned original site. He gave me the specific time and location where I was to debark the LSM with its five tanks and Marines.

I was really happy to get those orders. I realized there was some one else who understood the flexibility and value of the LSD to make surprise landings almost anywhere.

Unlike the other ships, I didn't have to anchor to unload my landing force. I could ballast down, flood the well deck on the way to the spot where I was to discharge them, stop, and, without anchoring, open my stern gate and let the LSM drive out carefully under its own power. Then off she would go to the beach where the tanks and Marines she carried could all debark.

It was a "no brainer" for the Marine major in charge of the *Colonial* landing force. It was to be a surprise landing behind the defenders.

At 6 am the next day, that's exactly what we did. The surprising appearance of that group of Marines and their tanks, coming up behind the defenders, was the key to a very successful landing that earned the task group commander some well deserved praise.

I think it was an exercise that awakened the Navy to the tremendous potential of the LSD.

Of course we got a "well done" from the task force commander and the satisfaction of knowing that we were a key part of a more vigorous and innovative amphibious force.

After a very busy six months, I received the disappointing message that I would be relieved as commanding officer. I was just starting to understand and enjoy operating this unique LSD. I had known that I had been assigned as a temporary commanding officer, but I also hoped that I might remain in the job for a full tour (a year or more). But the Navy finally found a higher ranking officer whose career progression required command experience of a large ship.

On June 1, 1949, I was relieved as commanding officer. My new skipper was a Commander Phil Smith USN, and I, in turn, took over the job of executive officer. This moved Lt. Raab back to his old position as First Lieutenant.

Raab and I had been through a lot together and there's no denying we both felt bad.

While we didn't say much about it to each other, and the Navy didn't give us an official pat on the back, we both knew, that in the past six months, the *Colonial* had been transformed from a useless liability into a new, cutting edge, valuable, war-ready ship. A ship, which fourteen months later, on September 15, 1950, during the Korean war, participated in a very dangerous behind-the-lines surprise landing of U.S. Marines at the strategic port of Inchon, on the west coast of Korea. That landing changed the course of the war and earned the *Colonial*'s captain a combat decoration.

For me, however, on that June 1, 1949 day, going from being the number one cheese in the morning to number two in the afternoon was an abrupt change. For some time, the sailors inadvertently kept calling me "Captain."

My living accommodations went from three spacious rooms with my own steward to one medium room and no steward. But that wasn't the biggest adjustment.

Even though, officially, the scope of my responsibilities had changed, I had trouble shifting my full time concerns away from

8. Land the Landing Force

those of a commanding officer. To a degree, Lt. Raab, had the same problem, but only for a short while, as first lieutenant responsibilities demanded his full attention.

Strangely, my new captain kept pushing me back into my old concerns. He was a nice guy and treated me well. The *Colonial* was his first command and he wasn't the type to dig down and learn his ship. Instead he depended completely on me. Whenever there was a problem of any type or a decision to be made his first words were always, "Does Mr. Sotos know about this?" Or, "Ask Mr. Sotos."

For every maneuver, no matter how trivial, he insisted I be on the bridge. At first I didn't mind too much. But his near-universal insistence that I be on the bridge when he was cut down the amount of time I could spend on important duties with respect to the administration and operation of the ship, duties that naturally fall to the executive officer.

Worse yet, for every course and speed change, or every sighting of another ship, the standard routine on all Navy ships is that the captain must be informed. Well, my new captain instructed his officers of the deck (OODs) to include me in all those reports. That routine, which normally should not include the exec, continued day and night when we were underway. It was beginning to get me down.

Not long after the Ponce landing we were ordered to load some landing craft, plus two railroad cars full of aviation gas, a small tug boat, and some other cargo. We were to be part of what I believe was one of the Navy's first large amphibious operations in an arctic region – Newfoundland.

It was a big operation that included another LSD, the USS *Catamount*, plus a fleet oiler and a large number of other massive amphibious force ships loaded with troops and equipment for a cold weather landing.

I was standing on the crosswalk above the well deck watching our crew pack the cargo into our well deck. Normally we would ballast down and our cargo of landing craft would just drive into the well.

But this time it was different. We were alongside a pier and a huge crane was placing the cargo at different locations in the well deck. We were eminently suited for outsize and hard-to-stow cargo and that's what was coming aboard. I watched as the railroad cars full of aviation gasoline were secured against the side of the well deck with a small tugboat immediately behind them. Almost all of the cargo was secured with heavy chains connected to large pad-eyes welded to the top of the well deck.

When we left for Newfoundland I thought we were ready for any kind of weather. However, I soon learned that on an LSD readiness for sea means something quite different than it does on a destroyer escort.

About three days out of Norfolk the entire task force ran into some terrible weather. Our cargo took a beating from the incoming waves and the rolling and pitching of the ship. Two of the boats and some of the wooden cargo broke loose and before long the huge well deck drainage system was partially plugged up with all sorts of trash.

Requesting a course change from the task group commander to prevent the sea from boarding us and filling the well deck was out of the question. We were in a large formation and I thought the course we were on was probably as good as any to minimize water coming into the well deck.

In really heavy weather, course changes might help reduce the amount of water entering the well deck, but that wasn't a risk reduction solution. One huge wave could deposit massive amounts of water in the well deck and there is no course in heavy weather to prevent that. We could slow to almost a stop and that might help, but in the present formation there was no way the captain would have done that.

Lt. Raab and I stood on the catwalk that crossed the well deck and watched as our cargo shifted and banged together with each roll. I knew that once the cargo started to break up from that activity, it would just be a matter of time before splinters would plug the drains. And then the well would fill with enough water to break the chains holding the cargo.

8. Land the Landing Force

Sending men into the well deck to clear the drains was out of the question. The shifting cargo could crush a man in seconds. I could see that a chain holding the small freight car with aviation gasoline had parted. The freight car was now sliding back and forth and banging from side to side. In addition to the plugged drains, I was worried about aviation gasoline leaking into the well deck.

Frankly, failure to assure drainage of the water under heavy sea conditions was a major design problem. Notwithstanding the futuristic ideas that had been poured into the construction of this marvelous ship, it was clear that a wide open well deck with no protection from heavy seas was a big mistake.

That's when I recalled the advice I received from the *Colonial*'s first skipper, Captain Patterson, on the last day of Line School.

His words suddenly became very vivid in my mind. "After the well deck filled, it overflowed and entered the engine spaces below, causing the ship to lose power. We were reduced to using small portable gasoline pumps and bucket brigades in an effort to move water out of the well deck and save the ship. We were at the mercy of the heavy seas. I thought that the weight of the water in the well deck would break the back of the ship and cause it to sink."

With his words swirling around in my head, Lt. Raab, Captain Smith and I watched our sailors unsuccessfully try to lasso the freight car with some heavy lines so they could cut down its shifting.

In Patterson's experience the storm abated after they lost power and were left drifting helplessly, until rescue tugs arrived and towed them back into Norfolk.

Luckily for us the weather abated somewhat before we got into serious trouble and we were able to send men into the well deck.

It didn't take them long to clear the scuppers and secure all the cargo with heavy lines. But the most important action we took was what Captain Patterson had recommended in the first place and I had not followed up.

"Before leaving port," he had said, "remove the tops of the tanks on the floor of the well deck itself." There were about thirty two of these tops, each tightly bolted down with about fourteen heavy bolts. By removing the tank tops the water could then drain into the tanks where we could handle it with our pumps. But removing and then later replacing them when in port was a formidable job.

Nevertheless, whenever we went to sea, that's what we did. We didn't take off all the tank tops just about half of them in the after part of the well deck. Also, I required that the ballast pumps be manned and ready at all times if needed to pump the water out of those tanks.

All this meant a lot of extra work and extra watch standing that the sailors didn't take to kindly. No matter how many times I told them the story of Patterson's experience on this very ship they thought I was being too cautious.

Captain Smith didn't think so as he assented to everything I ordered. And you can bet we subsequently included removing half of the tank tops and replacing them with strong wire mesh in our standard readiness for going to sea.

For the remainder of the trip we manned the pumps and managed to keep the well deck dry enough to prevent any water build-up there. Raab's sailors also managed to insert some heavy planks between the loose railroad tank car and the adjacent boats, stopping further movement.

For now, our cargo was riding OK, but the ship was still rolling and pitching heavily.

Then early one morning we got a message from the task force commander. "All ships prepare to fuel from the tanker." He then provided the sequence of fueling for the different ships.

I thought it was a really stupid order and prepared a radio message to the task group commander, "Unless otherwise directed *Colonial* will not fuel. Current fuel above 90% level." I

8. Land the Landing Force

walked it over to the captain who was also on the bridge for release. But to my surprise he refused to send it.

"It wouldn't look good, George. This is a training cruise and that's what he is trying to do. Forget it, we will go ahead and take our turn."

Quietly, so only he heard, I tried to talk him out of it, "This weather is too bad for fueling. There's no way the helmsman can steer a course straight enough for us to go in close and get fuel. It is too dangerous."

"No, George," he replied, "he knows what he is doing. Get ready to fuel."

Inwardly I was furious that the task group commander and even my own captain would attempt to fuel in this kind of weather. But I shut up, said, "Aye, aye, sir" and told the OOD to pass the word to set the fueling detail, which he promptly did.

We were number two in the fueling sequence. The other LSD, the *Catamount* was number one.

"Mr. Sotos will take the conn for the refueling," the captain said much to my surprise.

The OOD turned to me, told me the base course and speed and that the fueling detail was manned and ready and said, "Do you relieve me, sir?"

Still inwardly boiling I answered, "I relieve you. I have the conn."

"The executive officer has the conn," shouted the quartermaster of the watch as the captain nodded.

Not only was I hot under the collar, I was worried. I could see that the helmsman was having a terrible time keeping the ship on a steady course. And I could see that even the oiler was wobbling left and right, having a tough time remaining on a steady course.

On most ships, having the exec take the conn for a replenishment maneuver would be considered good leadership on the captain's part. That's the way to train officers for higher responsibility. And that's the way it might have looked to the bridge personnel on the *Colonial* that morning.

But I knew better. Not only did I have much more ship handling experience than the captain, I had the feeling he was afraid to do it himself. I don't think that he had ever done it before.

We all watched as the *Catamount* started to pick up speed to overtake the oiler and move into fueling position. All three ships were plowing into a head sea a little on our starboard bow. In the process we could see the *Catamount* start to move right to approach fueling position about 50 feet to the left of the oiler.

There was no doubt that she was having a very difficult time. Her bow would swing right toward the oiler then it would move left as the helmsman corrected. They would steam parallel for about five minutes as the *Catamount* finally got in position with the oiler about sixty feet to its right. We saw the *Catamount* throw over the lines at about the same time a huge wave pushed her bow within twenty feet of the oiler's bow. Pitching and rolling badly the *Catamount* straightened out but she was damn close to the oiler.

Suddenly another huge wave picked up the *Catamount*'s bow and pushed it right into and above the oiler's bow. We saw that huge bow with its starboard anchor come down on the oiler's bow with a smash we couldn't hear, but could almost feel. In the next instant the *Catamount* was free of the oiler but her giant anchor was gone. We could see it sitting on the oiler's bow!

For two big ships like that to collide in a heavy sea without personnel casualties was extremely lucky. All that resulted was a lot of sparks, the loss of the *Catamount*'s starboard anchor, about twenty feet of stove-in side plates on the tanker's port bow, and some anchor chain dangling from the *Catamount*.

The captain of the oiler immediately signaled that there would be no more fueling this morning. And in a few minutes the task force commander cancelled the fueling altogether.

I was personally very relieved. I knew full well the same thing could have happened to us.

My captain didn't utter a word. I turned the conn back over to the OOD and left the bridge.

8. LAND THE LANDING FORCE

The remainder of the trip to Newfoundland, except for the continuing bad weather, was routine. However, when we made landfall on the channel leading into the bay where the landing site was located, we ran into a snow blizzard and visibility went to zero. It was so bad the task group commander ordered all ships to proceed independently.

That's what we did, but I think I aged a few years in the process.

That order was a smart one. That's because the channel had a tragic history for the Navy. On February 25th, 1942, the supply ship USS *Pollux* and two of her escorting destroyers, the *Wilkes* and *Truxton*, ran aground trying to navigate this same channel in a similar, vicious, blinding snow blizzard. It cost the lives of 203 men.

Yes, we had a full time navigator, a young lieutenant who had been an aviator just a year earlier. He had transferred to the surface Navy when he could no longer pass the flight physical. He was a sharp officer but, like the captain, he had no experience in low-visibility navigation.

Prudent navigation in zero visibility usually dictates anchoring somewhere until visibility improves. But we didn't even consider that as an option in this treachorus area. While we and the other ships had radar, it was an early version not intended for channel navigation in zero visibility.

I discussed with the captain what we should do. While I was the only officer on the ship who had been through this channel, what I remembered most were the details of the *Pollux* tragedy and not anything that would help our navigation. We agreed that I would go down into the combat information center (CIC) and navigate with the radar from there while he stayed on the bridge.

We were very fortunate in having a really good radarman second class named Simon who was very smart and had a lot of confidence in his own ability to read what little information the radar offered.

He had developed a particular skill in reading azimuth bearings that, along with ranges (distances), could be used for navigation. That is not an easy skill. When navigating close to land, the radar we had in those days was normally used to provide just the ranges to land. The ranges were not always useful because we were never sure if the radar was picking up the closest land or the first rise or hill on that land, which could be well beyond the shoreline.

The trick was to make sure that the islands and hills he was looking at were the same ones we were looking at on the navigation chart. He and I had practiced that a lot and developed a confidence in our communications.

We could perform two other cross-checks. First, we could check the plotted positions with the depth of the water shown on the chart. Second, when he got accurate ranges on well identified land marks, such as light houses or even channel buoys, this gave us a reliable check on our position. It required a lot of talking and coordination to make sure we were both on the same target.

Together Simon and I plotted the courses which I sent to the captain on the bridge. He followed our recommendations and after several hours we finally made it to the area in which we were to anchor. Visibility was still zero. The people on the bridge couldn't even see the ship's bow.

I picked out a spot in the lee of a small mountain that Simon recognized on the radar and I saw on the chart. Simply by providing tangents to the mountain, interspersed with ranges and information from our fathometer (depth reader), we gave courses and speeds and even stop, back down and let-go-the anchor recommendations from CIC.

The radar, of course, made it possible for the ships to follow and avoid each other. However, without the specialized skills of someone like Simon, navigating that channel would have been impossible. It was a job well done by all hands but especially Simon. He was doing things with that radar that I don't believe even its inventors anticipated.

The next morning when I went out on deck, it was nice and

8. Land the Landing Force

clear, but I couldn't believe my eyes. We were in the lee and very close to the shoreline of a fairly large round mountain. It looked many, many times bigger in real life than it did on that chart the night before. When I saw Simon, with a big smile on his face as he talked with a bunch of his shipmates, I complimented him effusively for bringing us to this beautifully protected anchorage.

Later we moved to an anchorage closer to the landing site where all the other ships had assembled to land the landing force.

We took our time unloading our cargo and soon our well deck was empty. Our primary role in this landing, besides carrying the outsize cargo, was to act as a repair ship for all the landing craft. By late evening we had a half dozen landing craft in the well deck undergoing repairs.

Two days into the landing, the task group commander issued the order for all ships to refuel from the oiler that was anchored way out where the swells were big.

Again I prepared a message for the captain to sign, telling the task group commander we did not need any fuel and, unless otherwise directed, would not fuel from the oiler. There was no way I thought we should try to go alongside the oiler without the assistance of tug boats – and there were none. Besides, we still had about 90% of our fuel, much more than enough on which to return home.

Again my captain refused to release the message.

We got underway and as we approached the oiler, the captain again ordered me to take the conn and bring the ship alongside the huge oiler.

I anticipated his order and had Lt. Raab put three of our large boats in the water to help push us into position as needed.

The weather was excellent with just a slight breeze that swung the oiler back and forth in a wide arc. There were swells but I didn't think they would bother us.

I was wrong!

I waited until the oiler was at one end of her arc and I went ahead slow, aiming for a spot about where her anchor was. My plan was to get in a position where we could close her and stop about the time she would swing slowly into us.

I instructed Raab to have lines to our boats so that if we closed together too rapidly they could pull us away from the oiler and minimize the impact when we came together. My plan worked beautifully. We stopped at about the right spot. The oiler swung broadside slowly into us. Our boats pulled mightily and the coming-together impact was just a small bump as our large pneumatic fenders, which both ships had hung over their sides, absorbed the impact as they were designed to do.

In no time at all we were taking on fuel and I was silently patting myself on the back. Bringing a large ship like the *Colonial* alongside a huge oiler without a pilot or tug boats is really something to be proud of.

But my self satisfying glow didn't last.

The slight swell affected the two huge ships differently. The oiler rolled a little toward us and we rolled a lot toward her. The rolls got bigger and our superstructures smashed together. As the two ships surged and rolled against each other, our superstructures kept touching and hitting. The noise scared the hell out of us. The big life rafts both ships had rigged outboard were smashed and torn loose, and the large pneumatic fenders we had both rigged between us were flattened.

"Stop all fueling! Take in all lines! Standby to get underway," I ordered without even asking the captain.

As soon as I heard, "All lines aboard, engine room ready to answer all bells," I ordered, "All back two thirds." We were lucky we didn't tear anything loose from the oiler as we backed away, because she was still trying to swing in our direction.

We returned quietly to our anchorage minus two large life rafts whose pieces were brought aboard by our boat crews.

Later that evening the captain released a message to the task force commander. "Fueling completed, ready for sea." He was right. We did receive 8,000 gallons of fuel.

A few days later the exercise was over and we all got ready to return to Norfolk. The weather was good on the return trip.

8. Land the Landing Force

Earlier, not too happy with my skipper, I had volunteered and been accepted as officer-in-charge of an air, naval gunfire, liason, intelligence team (ANGLICO) whose primary role in Korea was to spot our own naval gunfire. I was looking forward to the change – even though it was a risky, parachute behind-the-lines, combat job. But a week after we returned to Norfolk my orders were surprisingly cancelled and I remained on the *Colonial*. I had no way of being sure, but I always thought my captain interceded and had them canceled.

At the time I was pissed off with the cancellation, but in retrospect it probably saved my life. Not many of the people who went to those jobs in Korea returned alive.

While still in Norfolk, my captain was relieved by Commander Thomas Greene. He had been chief engineer of the battered carrier USS *Franklin*. Hit by a devastating Japanese air attack in WWII, she was expected to sink. However, her crew miraculously saved the ship and sailed the crippled carrier back to the U.S. for repairs. As chief engineer, Commander Greene was one of the senior officers still alive, and it was under their leadership that the ship was saved and sailed back home. He was awarded the Navy Cross.

I liked him right away and knew the ship was lucky to get him.

In January 1950, just before the *Colonial* was ordered to participate in the Korean war, my tour was up and I received orders to report to the Recruit Training Command at Great Lakes, Illinois.

I can truthfully say that I learned more in two years on that ship than in any other two years during my entire career.

It's worth repeating that, under its new captain, the *Colonial* did very well in the Korean war. Especially commendable was its participation in the Inchon landings, for which Commander Greene was decorated.

The Inchon landing took place on September 15, 1950 and included 261 naval vessels and 75,000 Marine and Army troops. It led to the recapture of the South Korean capital of Seoul just two weeks after it had been occupied by the North Korean army. The landing also cut off the North Korean army's supply line and completely reversed its string of victories.

Initially, the Navy was reluctant to undertake the Inchon landing because of serious navigational hazards. However, under General Douglas MacArthur's prodding, at a time when the North Koreans thought they had a major victory in their grasp, the Inchon landing placed a formidable force of Marines and soldiers behind enemy lines and changed the war.

The *Colonial* went on to win seven battle stars in the Korean war. And I had the satisfaction of knowing that all my hard work to get the ship ready for war paid off.

Figure 120: **Welcome aboard.** During their first week of training recruits at Bainbridge attended a "welcome aboard" talk presented by the commanding officer or executive officer. Here, I am delivering the talk.

Chapter 9

Boot Camp

It was 2 am when my bedside phone rang. The voice at the other end was unrecognizable.

"Commander Sotos?"

"Yes," I answered sleepily.

"This is Chief Morris of base security. You better get over here. The fire fighting unit is on fire."

"What! What did you say?" I shouted – now fully awake.

"There's a big fire at the recruit fire fighting unit. We have all the base firetrucks here and some are coming in from Port Deposit (the small town near our Bainbridge, Maryland base) to help us."

"I'm on my way," I said as I hung up, quickly drew a pair of pants over my pajamas, grabbed a shirt, slid into some shoes and was downstairs and out the door of the bachelor officer's quarters in a couple of minutes.

That's when the frigid air hit me and really woke me up.

When I got to the fire fighting unit, just a ten minute drive from my quarters, I found the roads around the fire fighting compound clogged with fire trucks and base police cars amid a sea of flashing red and white lights. I also saw huge flames leaping into the night air. As I ran to the scene I couldn't believe what I saw.

9. Boot Camp

Our fire fighting compound seemed to be on fire. That's where we taught the recruits realistic shipboard damage control and how to fight fires. It consisted of a large building, plus two smaller ones, all in the center of a wide concrete apron that sloped into a large pond that was about 300 feet in diameter. One side of the compound was packed with trees that separated the compound from the base hospital about 400 feet away.

I ran as close as I could to the fire which, much to my surprise, was mostly confined to the pond. Believe it or not, the surface of the entire pond was on fire.

It was an immense fire with flames leaping twenty to thirty feet into the air. The wind threatened to spread the flames to the trees and perhaps to the nearby hospital.

I could see that almost all the efforts were aimed at keeping the fire confined to the pond and away from the trees.

Even though I was the senior officer on the scene I was completely ignored. I didn't feel bad about that because I knew there was nothing I could contribute to the process of fighting the fire. So I just stood there, in the freezing night, near the edge of the burning pond getting soaked by the water spray from the hoses.

After about a half hour I realized my boss wasn't there. I went to a phone, woke him up with the bad news and returned to my freezing spectator spot – convinced that I should make myself visible there.

Captain Fred Wolsieffer, my boss, showed up in about ten minutes and we stood there together in the freezing night air watching the fire fighters do their job. He was smart enough to have dressed for the foul weather. But foolish me, I stood there in no more than a light sweater, soaking wet and shivering.

After a couple hours the fire was extinguished and the danger of it spreading was gone. We went inside the building for some coffee and made arrangements for investigating the cause.

About five days after the fire, after I started to cough up blood, I was admitted to the hospital with pneumonitis (very like pneumonia).

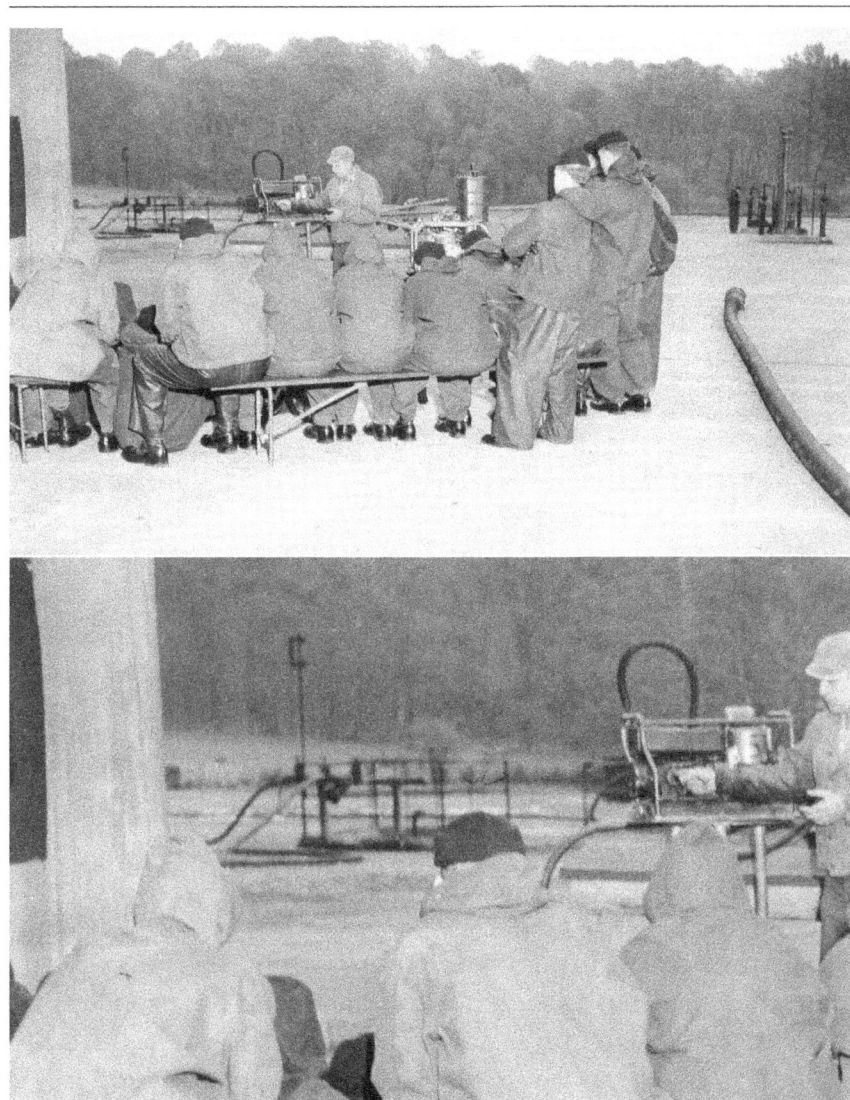

Figure 123: **Recruit fire training.** A recruit at Bainbridge spent considerable time learning how to fight fires, a life-saving skill at sea. The top photo shows an instructor, R.M. Winton BMGC, demonstrating to some chilly recruits a P-60 "handy billy" pump which can be used to bring in water from over the side. The bottom image shows the firefighting pond that caught fire, visible above the dark-hatted recruit's head.

9. Boot Camp

Figure 124: **Realistic fire training.** To simulate typical shipboard fires, we put oil in a tank of water, ignited it, and then – with supervision – let the recruits extinguish it. This was the source of the oil in the pond that caught fire.

It was my first experience as a patient in a hospital since I had my tonsils out as a child. It wasn't a bad experience since I knew most of the nurses and the doctors. However, the treatment I received was unexpected. That's because my room was kept dark and I wasn't permitted to read anything. As a result the days were very long and boring as I just lay there in a dark room for most of the day.

This gave me a lot of time to think mostly about about my early days training recruits. One experience involved the start of my involvement with recruit training, a year earlier, during my first visit to the recruit input center at Great Lakes, Illinois....

* * *

"Hold down the noise," shouted a boatswains mate first class (BM1/C), who was standing on a raised platform at the side of a vast room, addressing the new recruits. "This is the Receiving Unit. This is the place where we get you ready to form in a company and start your training. See those white squares on the deck. Each one of you pick out one of those squares and stand in it until I tell you what to do."

With very little conversation each of the sixty young men was soon standing in one of the white squares that had been painted neatly on the deck. Sharing the square with each man, was an open, medium size cardboard box. It was empty, except for a magic marker, a roll of scotch tape and a large white towel that was draped over one of the sides.

These were all brand new Navy recruits. They had just arrived at the Great Lakes Naval Training Center early that morning or the day before. They were dressed in civilian clothes. And they were all apprehensively waiting for something to happen.

"O.K. Give me your attention and listen carefully so we all do this right." The boatswain mate's voice was not too loud but everyone heard him.

"You are to remove all your clothes." He paused for an instant as he saw some facial reactions. "Yes, remove and put your clothes in the box. Fold your clothes neatly, so they fit, and that includes your shoes, socks, shorts – everything. You will not be using them for at least the next four years. So you have to get rid of them, You get just that one box. You will keep only your wallet, toothbrush and any small personal items."

He paused again, saw that they were all listening and continued, "When you are all buck ass naked you will take a shower, and come back to your square – so remember where it is.

"After the shower you will seal up your boxes, write your home address and your return address on the boxes and leave them right in the square. Your return address is – Seaman Recruit whatever-your-name-is, Recruit Training Command, Great Lakes, Illinois – just as it is on this blackboard." He uncovered a large blackboard that had been sharing the platform with him.

9. Boot Camp

"The tape and magic markers for this are in the box. We will pick up and ship the boxes." He paused and looked around noticing that several recruits had their hands in the air.

"OK? If you have any questions about shipping your personal gear home ask one of my assistants." The hands went down as six young sailors already in training, appeared and walked up and down the rows of white squares answering questions and helping where needed.

The boatswain mate knew from past experiences that one, two and sometimes even three recruits would state that they have no home to which they can send their personal gear. In those cases the boys usually wound up giving their gear to the base Navy Relief Chapter.

He waited and watched as the 60 recruits removed their clothes and stored them in the boxes. Some who had finished and were standing there with towels draped around them were holding their wallet and toothbrushes.

"You can leave your wallet and valuables in the box until you return from the shower," he said. "Don't worry about them. We will make sure they are safe.

"OK let's get it done. We'll go to the showers in groups of twenty starting from the front. Remember the square your box is in."

As the first group was returning from the showers the second group was rounded up and that's the way it continued until all 60 men had showered.

Then in groups of twenty, clad only in the towels and holding their wallets, they were marched to a line of medical people for their vaccinations. The medical staff was all business. Any recruit who resisted was pulled from the line, talked to quietly, and in almost every case inserted back in the line. There was an occasional fainting incident, but for the most part all were vaccinated without delays. Rarely did any recruit refuse.

Still in groups, they were marched to a room where a complete uniform including shoes, stockings and hats were issued.

Inconspicuously watching the whole scene was a spotlessly uniformed Chief Petty Officer named Sam Chapman.

Sam, a slender, dark haired Chief Machinist Mate (CMM) with 12 years service, most of it in the bowels of destroyer engineering plants, was on his first tour of shore duty. It was not the job he had envisioned, but now, as the experienced commander of a company of recently graduated recruits, he had adjusted to the very rigorous routine and was actually beginning to enjoy the job.

Unknown to the young men he was watching, Sam had been assigned as their company commander. That meant he would be with them from the time they awakened in the morning until they went to sleep every day for the next ten weeks.

He knew he could learn a lot about these young men by observing their behavior during input processing. He would need some of the recruits to help him do his job. For example, early in the training he would appoint a "recruit company commander" to assist him and be his alter ego. And that particular recruit had to be a special type. There also were a half dozen other similar appointments he would be making. A good recruit staff could make his job a lot easier and the overall training better for all.

So, as he watched, he was making mental notes about the behavior of all the young men.

It was just after noon when the 60 recruits carrying the uniform articles they had not put on were taken outside, assembled in formation and turned over to Sam.

"My name is Chief Machinist Mate Sam Chapman and I am your company commander," he told them. "I will be with you night and day for the next ten weeks. From now on unless I tell you differently, you take all your orders from me."

Sam assigned two young sailors to help form up the company and march it from the receiving unit to the recruit training barracks. After about fifty yards he brought them to a halt.

"Yes, you are all brand new recruits," he told them, "but we will be marching on a public road where people who see you don't know that you are new. So I don't want you looking like a

9. Boot Camp

bunch of drunks. Try to stay in step and keep the ranks straight." Then with one of his assistants shouting cadence they marched to the recruit camp about a mile away.

Sam was right. Civilians in passing cars observed and sometimes hailed the young recruits usually with friendly remarks. After about a fifteen minute march Sam's company entered the main gate of the recruit camp.

My office was in one of the first buildings inside the recruit camp, from where I would often watch as the new companies marched in. Then a few days later I would greet the weekly input of recruits in a "welcome aboard" talk (Figure 120).

Once Sam and his company arrived at their barracks they were greeted by other petty officers who helped the men get squared away.

The Receiving Unit was just one of the first steps in the life of a new recruit. But it was a quiet, serious, life-altering step that none of the recruits ever forgot. Nor did I.

You can imagine the complexity and the demands of Sam's job: sixty vigorous, eager, healthy, curious, energetic young men on his hands literally 24 hours a day.

It was Sam's responsibility to turn these young recruits into U.S. Navy Sailors. For each one of his 60 recruits, he is their role model, judge, jury, confidence builder, career advisor, character builder, disciplinarian, big brother, and proud "father."

The first week is the roughest for both the recruits and their company commander. Almost all the recruits get homesick and depressed. And the company commander's problems are at their highest level during that week. Starting with the second week, things begin to get better and all of a sudden the company becomes a cohesive and friendly home where everyone seems to know what is expected of him. The company becomes like a large team as it competes with other companies for military appearance, training awards and other accomplishments. Winning flags for their achievements and proudly carrying those flags as they march to their classrooms, they make an impressive sight.

I was quite surprised and very apprehensive on January 15, 1950, when I received orders to Great Lakes. There was another training center in San Diego, but Great Lakes was the top one.

My official assignment was as the military training officer of the Recruit Training Command (RTC). I didn't know what that meant, but the implication was that I would be responsible for converting civilian kids into young sailors. If there was a subject in the Navy that I knew nothing about, that was surely it! But I didn't let myself worry about it. I had asked for an assignment to Great Lakes which was near my home, and I got it.

Of course my family was sure I was going to be an admiral in just a few years and they thought the Great Lakes job was just another step in that direction.

My new boss was a man named Captain Nutting. He welcomed me and spent a few minutes discussing the criticality of my new job.

There were about 10,000 recruits in training and I was to be the third in command. Moreover, my office was right in the boot camp itself, as opposed to where the Captain was located.

Captain Nutting, a tall good looking man and quite pleasant, was obviously very serious about his job. And there was no light banter. He spent considerable time emphasizing that I was the senior officer who would be closest to the recruits and the one they would see the most.

He let me know that I would be completely responsible for the military training of all those recruits. Finally he stopped and asked, "Do you have any questions?"

"No sir," I answered shaking my head slightly.

"O.K., then let's get you started," he said, as he took me by the arm, headed for the office next door and left after introducing me to Commander Hansen, the executive officer.

After a few pleasantries, Hansen got right down to business. "The officer you are replacing has done an outstanding job and it will be hard to match him. You will shadow him for a week to learn the details of your job and the responsibilities that go with it. When he leaves it will all be in your lap. If you have any ques-

9. Boot Camp

tions or doubts you come right to me and we will work them out." He paused for a minute, then said, "Perhaps the most important thing for you to know is that, in many ways, because of the distance between us, the job you have is almost like a separate command, one which you run mostly by yourself without too much input from the captain or myself, The captain and I can always be reached quickly by phone. But after you have been here a while you probably won't have to call us."

We were interrupted by a knock on the door. A tall, slim, crewcut lieutenant commander walked in. His uniform was impeccable. He held out his hand before we could be introduced. "I guess you're my relief. Welcome aboard. I'm happy to see you."

"George this is Stan," said the exec, "You'll be sticking close to him for the next week, so it's important that you two get to know one another."

As I shadowed Stan for the next week, I grew to like him and was grateful for the way he broke me in. He didn't miss a detail. Nothing was too small for his attention. In fact I got the impression that he was worrying too much about details that should be the concern of his subordinates.

One of the first things we did was to tour the entire boot camp, which consisted of about 20 buildings such as classrooms, barracks, mess-halls and giant drill fields. Everywhere we walked there were "boots," that is, recruits with the leggings that covered their legs from knee to shoe. It was probably the reason they were called "boots."

I was never saluted so much in my life. For the recruits, who didn't see many officers, the salute was important. For many, it was still quite new. Stan spent some time telling me that while it might be burdensome returning so many salutes as we walked around the camp, every single one was important and should be responded to in smart military fashion. I could see his point.

I was surprised at the number of subordinates that were responsive to my position. There were four regimental commanders, each with multiple battalion commanders, classroom instructors, company commanders and many, many others all responsible for some facet of recruit training. And, of course, there were the recruits. As I walked around I could see it was their home and their camp. Some were in formations under the leadership of a company commander. Others would be walking alone on some errand. They were everywhere, marching to and from classrooms, or as sentries outside the barracks, large groups in recreation areas, varied numbers hanging or retrieving clothing from designated drying areas and, in general, a very busy scene.

As I accompanied Stan the first few days. I wondered if I had the experience to handle the job. Besides constantly being involved in some aspect of a recruit company's problems, Stan's office was responsible for scheduling of classroom training and many other activities.

You might ask how one officer can be responsible for the discipline of 10,000 recruits, who were converting from teen age school kids to U.S. Navy sailors?

The answer, of course, is the chain of command. A recruit company consisted of 60 sailors whose immediate superior was the company commander. The latter, specially selected men like Sam Chapman, were either first class or chief petty officers. As mentioned earlier, they probably had the toughest and most important job in the Navy.

Among the recruits, like any large group, there is always one percent who seem to have various persistent problems that adversely impact their performance. Sometimes they carried the problems with them from home, or they just were unable to adjust to their new routine.

There was considerable pressure on all the recruits to avoid demerits. Besides hurting the company's performance record and its chances to carry a merit flag, the demerits could result in extra instruction, extra drill and other distasteful chores. The demerit system is a good method for establishing discipline without spoiling a young recruit's official service record. It is a priceless teaching aid.

9. Boot Camp

In the Navy, the only officer authorized to award formal punishment for infraction of good military discipline is the commanding officer. And when he does so the incident is formally entered in the sailor's service record. From the beginning everyone is cautioned over and over again to "keep your service record clean!" A blemished service record is a guaranteed bar to promotions and the type of duty one likes.

One of my jobs was to review all the infractions that couldn't be handled by the demerit system. I saw and talked to those recruits whose offenses were too serious to be handled through the demerit system. These recruits were recommended by their regimental commander for Captain's Mast. This was a formal appearance before the captain who would hear all the evidence and adjudicate the offense. If found guilty, punishment could range from brig time to separation from the Navy with a formal notation in the man's service record.

I would review each case in a formal atmosphere. In almost all such cases I did my best to extract from these youngsters a promise to straighten out, hoping to avoid sending them to Captain's Mast. In about 95% of the cases I was successful. However, we had our share of serious infractions that required official action by the Captain. It was the part of my job that I disliked the most.

In any population of 10,000 young men who come from all walks of life it is almost impossible to avoid really serious problems. However, during my 14 months at Great Lakes it wasn't the mast cases that got me down. It was the suicides.

The first one was a quiet 19 year old kid from a rural town in New York state. He went AWOL (absent without leave) from the recruit camp, then made his way on foot to the closest village (Lake Bluff), about ten miles south of Great Lakes. He broke into a home, found a gun, wrote a note, and shot himself.

We were all shaken when the police notified us. "My God," I thought, "is our training that hard that a kid would leave the camp and kill himself?"

The captain appointed me as the command's official investigator and I looked into all the details of the young man's history. We knew very little about him. He was a well behaved young man who seemed to be getting along ok, according to his company commander and fellow recruits.

The young man's father arrived and I went with him to the morgue so he could identify the body. It was a chore that I have never forgotten. When the morgue attendant pulled open the large drawer containing the nude body of this good looking well built young man, both his father and I saw immediately the little round black hole in his forehead. His father stared at his son for a few seconds and then turned away.

The morgue attendant quietly closed the drawer. We went into another room and a member of the local police department asked the father if he would sign some papers confirming the identify.

The father did so quietly and he and I left. I had driven the father there, and once back in the car, I asked him if he read the note his son had left. I had seen it earlier. It didn't say much except that he was very sorry for the disgrace that he had brought upon his family.

He said "Yes."

"Do you know why he did this?" I asked.

Again he said, "Yes," as he shook his head and continued. "He got into some trouble at home and that's why he joined the Navy – to get away from all the trouble."

I didn't say anything while he paused. "It happened last winter. He and his little sister were in school when everyone was sent home because of a coming snow storm. He went to his little sister's class room to get her. I had told him to never leave school without her. Anyway he went to her class room but her teacher would not let her go. She was being punished for something she did and her teacher was making her remain after school.

"My son got into an argument with the teacher and he wound up picking the teacher up and dropping her on the floor, hurting her. He then took his sister and they got on the bus and came home."

9. Boot Camp

He was speaking quietly and I had trouble hearing him, but I did not interrupt him.

"The teacher wasn't hurt badly but they suspended him from school and the whole thing was spread out in our local newspaper. Everyone thought he had disgraced our family. He never went back to school and that's why he joined the Navy. I knew it bothered him, but I never knew it bothered him that much."

The Navy Department accepted my official report closing the case for us. However, they did tell my captain that I should never have been assigned as the investigating officer since, in my position as training officer, I might have been a party to the investigation.

We had a second suicide before my tour was over. One of our recruits cut his own throat – not an easy thing to do. After a formal investigation by the Navy Department it was determined that the principal reason for the suicide was a mental problem.

Despite the suicides and the six a.m. to nine p.m. hours, I grew very fond of my job. It was almost impossible to share such an environment without getting caught up in the really wonderful, progressive, developmental changes that I saw in the fine young men all around me. To a man, I had the feeling that the graduating recruits were champing at the bit to get aboard a ship, or go on to an advanced school with eager confidence. It was very satisfying to be part of an immense process that did so much good for individuals and for the Navy at the same time.

Naturally, there were exceptions. Almost all of them related to persistent problems on the home front: problems that resulted in sailors being absent without leave and sometimes other more serious offenses. But, considering the size of the recruit population, the number of these problems was very small, less than one percent.

In my previous jobs I never had to think much about discipline. But this was different. The sheer number of recruits forced me to think more about discipline.

For some young men, military discipline is a no brainer. They adapt to it like ducks to water. The key, I learned, is communication. Yes, communication! The tough drill sergeant you see in the movies raising hell with his troops is using a form of communication. And like it or not, for most of the troops, it is effective communication. Our company commanders weren't permitted to use that type of communication, which made their job tougher. And it probably lengthened the training time for our company commanders because it meant more explaining, especially for slow learners.

A great deal of time was invested convincing the recruits that buying into military discipline was really in their self interest.

Beyond a doubt, almost all of the recruits start out wanting to do the right thing. That number includes even young potential criminals for whom a kind, sympathetic judge withheld jail time if the culprit agreed to join the Navy. It included those kids who had a rotten home life. It included many, many young men who simply could not adjust to the rigor and demand of school programs and who wondered if there was some place they could fit in. It included young men who had problems with their sexual orientation and were desperate to be seen as "normal" as the next guy. It included well off, successful, hardened young criminals who had never been apprehended by the police but were smart enough to know that what they were doing was wrong and wanted to stop. It included young men with mental illness who, with their families, hid their problems in an effort to find a normal life. After all, the opportunity to serve in the Navy was available to all young men. And, if there was no official record with information that would prevent enlistment, physical qualification and a couple years of high school were all that was needed.

There were no statistics on the number of young men who fell into the different categories I describe above. But make no mistake, after three years in recruit training – one at Great Lakes and later two at Bainbridge, Maryland, where, as you'll read, I was executive officer of the RTC and chairman of the neuropsychiatric review board during the Korean war – I personally witnessed or interacted with young men in each of those categories. It was no fun.

9. Boot Camp

Lest the reader get the impression that these categories applied to all our recruits, it is very important that I make the record clear. By far the greatest percentage of the recruit population came from wonderful, loving, perfectly normal homes where, as in my own family, the kids entered the Navy because of patriotism and all the wonderful attributes that military service can impart to a youngster growing into manhood. For the most part the desire among almost all recruits to do what the Navy wants of them is very strong.

So, from my extensive experience, 99% of all the recruits, no matter their background want to do the right thing. Invariably, when they didn't, I learned it was a matter of communication. They either didn't get the word or they simply did not believe what we were trying to teach them.

I thought discipline would be a big problem for me, but it wasn't. Almost all the infractions were the result of poor communication among the recruits themselves or between the recruits and their company commanders, classroom instructors and sometimes with my office.

I rarely saw repeat offenders. When I did I knew I had a problem. Legally I had no authority to punish any recruit. Only the captain had that authority. And every Monday morning we would have a Captain's Mast where the captain himself would review the cases I sent to him and determine appropriate punishment,

Our goal was not to render punishment as punishment, but to have it in the context of encouraging corrective behavior on the part of the recruit. In 99% of the cases that's what actually happened. But, just as aboard ship, there were alway exceptions. Aboard ship that would apply to about two percent of the disciplinary cases. Here at boot camp, it was about one percent. And sometimes in that one percent we would have really tough cases.

We did have young men who were convinced that Navy life, for many reasons, was not for them. And despite our efforts to avoid punishments, administrative and, sometimes, bad conduct discharges, we did have them.

There is a danger here that I am over-simplifying the word communication. Especially among large groups of young men from all walks of life, it is by no means, a simple process. When communication is defined as a vehicle for altering behavior as I have here, it is far more than just exchanging words. Trust and confidence between the speaker and listener is essential if communication is to be effective.

This is where some company commanders excelled while, unfortunately, others did not. Recruits lucky enough to have a company commander who could instill trust and confidence among his men invariably produced companies with high performance scores and, in my opinion, better men.

The company commander, then, is really the most important person in a boot camp. At Great Lakes we were fortunate in having a high proportion of excellent company commanders. And both the recruits and I learned a lot from them.

So, just who are these sailors who become company commanders? In the peace-time Navy they are carefully selected and well trained. In almost all cases they have considerable sea going experiences, are already Chief Petty Officers or First Class Petty Officers on their way up.

Is the prospect of being a company commander in a boot camp something to which these men look forward to?

The answer to that question is both yes and no. An important point is that it is shore duty, most desirable for sailors with extensive sea going time. Those who would answer "no" are well aware of the exceptionally long hours that must be devoted to the job. For married men it is not that attractive.

"Yes" answers would come from unmarried aggressive men who like a challenge and for whom leadership skills come naturally. Thankfully the Navy has a very large reservoir of these men.

Each week we would graduate about ten companies – about 600 men total. And it was at these graduation reviews that I, and I'm sure most of the 500 staff we had, saw and appreciated the results of our efforts. Along with hundreds of proud parents and

9. Boot Camp

other guests at the graduation ceremonies, these recruits somehow managed to show us all the wonderful things about boot camp.

The reader might find it hard to believe that when I first reported for duty at the Great Lakes RTC I had little in common with the new recruits. I never had any basic military training, except for the 90 day indoctrination course as a midshipman (early 1941) in a converted Chicago office building (Tower Hall at 9th and Michigan Blvd). Our group did march back and forth to classroom buildings, but that was primarily to facilitate getting there on the crowded Chicago streets. We had no company commander. No one was in charge. Cadence was shouted by anyone who felt he was in good voice. But most of the time we sang marching songs as we walked along.

I had never seen a recruit training center nor had I ever even heard of a recruit curriculum. It was just as new and strange to me as it was to any incoming recruit.

Even though I had been through the entire war at sea and had command of a destroyer escort and landing ship dock I was as nervous and apprehensive about my role at Great Lakes as were the incoming kids about theirs.

But I learned very quickly that the knowledge and experience I had acquired was exactly what the Navy was trying to teach the recruits. Once I realized that, my role and duties became clear and I dove into my job with enthusiasm,

I had been there about a year when I suddenly received orders to be executive officer of a new recruit training center at Bainbridge, Maryland. It was big step up for me and for a brief moment I thought I was following in the footsteps of the famous Fleet Admiral Chester Nimitz, whose portrait hung behind my chair and who had my job there at Great Lakes when he was a commander.[1]

The impetus for my orders was the Korean war. In order to

---

[1] As told in my other book, *Living with the Torpedo*, I had earlier followed in Nimitz's footsteps by running my ship aground while an ensign.

avoid going into the Army, a great flood of draft eligible young men was enlisting in the expanding Navy. An additional training center was urgently needed. And the run-down, abandoned WWII training center at Bainbridge was still on the Navy's property list. Also, I had done a decent job at Great Lakes and knew the system well.

That was my boot camp experience before I got to Bainbridge. And as I lay there in my hospital bed I knew I was damn lucky to have had that experience. Without it, I would never have become the executive officer at Bainbridge. Worse yet I would never have known what coming into the Navy was like for the enlisted men.

That hospital dark room treatment lasted about four or five days and I rapidly became better. In about eight days I was well enough to go back to work.

Figure 140: **Esprit de corps.** To simplify administration, control, and discipline, each incoming recruit class was divided into companies of 60 men – or even 120 men during times of large input, such as the Korean War. To help create esprit de corps, the companies competed for flags that would recognize outstanding performance in values we wished to foster, such as teamwork, loyalty, pride in the organization, group productivity, group morale, and a sense of belonging. The large number of flags displayed by the company here marks it as a top company.

Chapter 10

More Boots – The Korean War

I thought the Navy's readiness for war could never get as poor as it was at the start of WWII.

But I was wrong.

Readiness for the Korean War, which started June 25, 1950, was worse. I got my first indication of this when the person selected to be the commanding officer at Bainbridge RTC backed out of that job. Informally I heard that he was dissatisfied with the level of readiness at Bainbridge.

And was he right!

When I arrived at Bainbridge as the acting commanding officer in January 1951, the place was a beehive of activity. Much larger than the Great Lakes Naval Training Center, the 800 acre site was to be home to an RTC, a group of advanced training schools called the "Service School Command," an Administrative Command, a prep school for the naval academy and several other ancillary organizations.

The RTC was by far the largest command, both in numbers of people and physical requirements. We had four regiments with a total capacity of 40,000 recruits who would live in 224 barracks. And there were many other buildings, including staff living quarters, classrooms, offices, mess halls and four huge hanger-sized indoor regimental command drill buildings. There were also four large "grinders" (outdoor paved drill areas) that

10. MORE BOOTS – THE KOREAN WAR

could hold a regiment of recruits.

To my disgust and surprise, I found that almost all of the above mentioned structures were still being worked on. I use the words "worked on" because most of the buildings were not new. Bainbridge had been a training center during WWII, but had been closed and abandoned when that war ended. People surrounding the center, and some from further away, stripped all the buildings of anything that could be used or sold, including all the toilets in all the barracks.

When I reported in, I was directed to an officer who was the acting RTC captain. His desk, and that of his yeoman (secretary), was a large wooden box. There simply was not enough furniture to staff the offices.

All of the recruit barracks had been scavenged. There was not an intact window in any of them. Almost almost all the piping had been stripped, as had all the electrical wiring. It was a disgrace and a terrible reflection on the Navy's custodial practices.

All of a sudden I found myself as the acting commanding officer of a sprawling training center that was still being put together. That didn't bother me too much until I was notified by the Navy Department that the recruits would start arriving in April 1951 – just three months away!

At the same time I discovered that I was the only officer there who had any recruit training experience. But my biggest surprise came when I ordered a muster of all the RTC staff. Expecting to see a large military formation of about 900 people, I saw a disorganized motley looking formation of about 900 men who looked as though they just walked in from the streets. There was every combination of Navy uniforms and civilian clothes one could imagine. Even when I had them called to attention it was impossible to visualize what I saw as a military formation. I soon learned that all of them were sailors recalled to active duty from the Fleet Reserve and other Naval Reserve units. And at least seventy-five percent of them were not happy to be there. Fortunately for my morale, there was a substantial number dressed in regulation uniforms who appeared happy to be back on active duty.

I issued orders for all of them to acquire the proper uniforms and that we would muster every day until I saw all of them in uniform and a proper military formation.

That same day I talked with all of my officers and assigned them to specific jobs. I was lucky. Whoever ordered these officers to Bainbridge knew what he was doing. While none of them had recruit training experience, almost all of them were educators or worked in academic environments. For example, one officer I appointed as a regimental commander had been an athletic director at Gallaudet University in Washington, DC.

Each of our four regiments was, to a large degree, an independent command with its own barracks that could house 10,000 recruits. Each had its own drill hall, mess hall, classrooms, and so on. They were Camps Rogers, Perry, James and Barney.

Captain Fred Wolseiffer reported aboard and relieved me as acting commanding officer a few weeks before the recruits started arriving. I was lucky to have him. He was an enthusiastic, hard working, fine naval officer. As I got to know him, I thought he was an ideal skipper for a recruit training command.

He told me to keep doing what I was doing and that's the way we worked. I still ran everything by him, but he pretty much told me to run the organization.

I gave detailed orders to the regimental commanders that they would be responsible for the readiness of all the buildings and barracks in their regimental area. This responsibility was later extended down to requiring personal inspections of the heads (bathrooms) and an inventory of working toilets in every barrack.

The latter was necessary because, for some strange reason, completion of the bathrooms and getting all the toilets to work remained a constant problem.

Before my boss arrived, I called Captain Nutting at Great Lakes. I asked if we could send our military training officer, reg-

10. More Boots – The Korean War

imental commanders, some company commanders and other key personnel to Great Lakes to shadow their counterparts for two to three weeks. He very graciously said yes and that he would help in any way. We immediately started sending those men to Great Lakes for instruction.

Before they left I made it clear that they would be completely responsible for setting up an operation in Bainbridge identical to the one they were going to at Great Lakes. They also would be expected to set up and operate training programs for the rest of the staff at Bainbridge. And that's exactly the way we got started.

I also contacted the administrative command at Bainbridge and inquired about the status of having uniforms and other supplies ready when the new recruits arrived. That drew a complete blank. They were unaware of those detailed requirements. In fact they had no idea about the detailed contents of the new recruit seabag (a complete uniform outfit for new sailors).

Again I called Captain Nutting and he promptly instructed the Great Lakes Administrative Command to send me all that information, which I passed to our Administrative Command.

Actually there was no dragging of heels at Bainbridge. Once people knew what had to be done they moved quickly. One of my key roles was to put people in touch with the right people at Great Lakes. Thankfully that was easy because people at both ends were anxious to help Bainbridge get started.

Contractors were everywhere trying to get the buildings in shape. Things were so chaotic that I repeatedly emphasized to the regimental commanders the importance of having a place for the recruits and incoming staff to live.

I focused on working with and talking to the incoming staff, officers and the enlisted groups. Aside from being disgruntled at having been called to active duty, the officers didn't complain too much. They all very quickly saw the magnitude of the job ahead and were eager to get started. However, except for the one officer who had been acting commanding officer until I relieved him, none had any idea about the operation of a Boot Camp.

Almost all the officers were mature and responsible men

who learned quickly. All I had to do was point them in the right direction. That direction, of course, was to send almost all of them to Great Lakes for indoctrination. That was one of my smartest moves, since after their return they knew exactly what to do and they did it.

It was a little tougher with the enlisted men who had been recalled to active duty. I don't think any of them had been instructors or company commanders in a boot camp. Most remembered dimly their boot camp training. At first they were reluctant to take on the responsibility of being company commanders, mainly because they were not in good enough physical shape to keep up with the young recruits. However after working with them for a while I realized that they were really good men with a great deal of war time experience.

For example one of them, a very modest man, Chief Machinist Mate William Badders, was the recipient of the Congressional Medal of Honor. He earned it on the 23rd of May 1939 for assisting in the rescue of 33 out of a crew of 62 men from the damaged, bottomed submarine USS *Squalus* (SS 192). In the first and, to this day, only such rescue in world history, he operated inside a large wire-guided rescue bell that travelled repeatedly from a surface ship to the submarine which was sitting on the bottom in 240 feet of water. The unprecedented rescue effort, which overcame serious problems, took place off the northeast coast of the United States.

There were many more decorated men among the recalled fleet reservists and they turned out be excellent role models for the recruits.

As mentioned, we sent a number of staff to Great Lakes to learn its complete curriculum for company commanders. When they returned and set up the company commander training course, I couldn't have been more pleased with the results. There were two main parts to recruit training. One was the outdoor training which included all aspects of military drill and other outdoor activities. The second was classroom instruction. We had to develop an expertise in both those areas as well as

10. MORE BOOTS – THE KOREAN WAR

the related administrative functions. The company commanders, of course, had to become proficient in all of these areas. For many of them, getting back in physical shape was difficult, as was catching up with all the subject matter that had changed since they were on active duty. The training challenges were formidable. Very quickly, as a result of the draft, we found that the educational range of our recruits, even in a single company, ranged from college degrees to illiteracy.

I can't over-emphasize the challenge we all had. It may be hard to believe that the U.S. Navy could be so unprepared, but it was! I was the acting commanding officer from the start and then the executive officer for the next two years.

What the Navy did right, however, was selecting the people it assigned to Bainbridge. About 100 officers and 1000 enlisted men from the naval reserve and fleet reserve were recalled to active duty at Bainbridge RTC. Almost all of them had WWII experience and required very little guidance. We just had to tell them what had to be done and show them how it was done at Great Lakes RTC.

But it wasn't all roses. It was tough for many of the first class and chief petty officers assigned as company commanders, because there was a good deal of marching required. It wasn't unusual to see a company (120 recruits) marching well in front of their struggling-to-keep-up company commander.

Very quickly the company commanders learned to use the command "To the rear march!" as a way of staying with their recruits. As a result we would see the recruit companies going back and forth to match their company commander's pace.

Initially we started with 500 recruits per week, but the rate soon doubled. We graduated the first 500 recruits on June 23, 1951.

A recruit graduation review is a big deal, not only for the recruits, but for their parents, friends and everyone on the base who had a hand in their training. We always had an invited celebrity, like a flag officer or the Secretary of the Navy, who who would make a short talk, award achievement medals to outstanding recruits and stand at attention as the graduating recruits passed in review.

From the marching band to all the orders controlling the hour long review, the ceremony was run entirely by the graduating recruits. Not only was it always an inspiring sight, it was a reflection on the quality of the recruits, the RTC staff and especially their proud company commanders.

Invariably a very strong bond developed between a recruit company and their company commander. So strong was this bond that we had to caution the grateful recruits against presenting farewell gifts to their company commanders.

By far the most numerous of the attendees at the reviews were the recruit family members. Many came long distances and it was a good feeling to see the pride in their eyes as they saw their young son or daughter turned into a U.S. Navy sailor. In many ways it helped us see and feel the value of our hard work.

It wasn't long before all four regiments were in operation.

One of the subjects we taught was "ship board damage control and fire-fighting." Built into our fire fighting school was an 80 foot long partial ship. If the recruits didn't do the damage control properly, the ship would sink. We also replicated actual serious shipboard fires where the recruits could get burned if they got careless.

This training was very realistic. I went through it myself and it really taught me how to fight fires. We used fuel oil to start and run the fires and, after each day, any remaining oil would be washed into a pond about 100 feet from the building.

That's where the fire of the previous chapter occurred.

How did that fire start?

For a while we entertained suggestions of sabotage. However, after looking into that possibility, the captain and I both rejected it. The speculation we accepted was that the pond, which had received great amounts of oil and gasoline residue when used for training during World War II, had never been cleaned. And, with the additional residue from our training, the pond had become saturated with oil and gasoline and was just waiting for

147

10. More Boots – The Korean War

an adequate spark! Whether true or not, with that theory we closed the book on the incident.

The fire was a very serious embarrassment for our command and the fire fighting school. Fortunately there was no damage or injuries and no interruption of training.

Another problem that bothered me all during my tour at Bainbridge was discipline. Like the Great Lakes RTC we had an excellent demerit system which was used to correct infractions without requiring the recruit to go before the commanding officer and spoil the recruit's service record. However, the sheer number of recruits that came into Bainbridge assured that the number of serious cases requiring the captain's attention was still large.

As mentioned earlier, I was the officer who determined which offenses went before the captain. So, for example, as the center population increased, I would hold hearings on about 15 to 20 recruits every Monday morning. Each of these cases had been screened by a company commander, a battalion commander and the regimental commander before being sent to the captain, for whom I was screening.

Almost all the cases were complex and required careful investigation.

One of the most forceful actions I could take, without sending a recruit to Captain's mast, was to remove a recruit from his company and assign him to one much earlier in the training phase. In addition to delaying his graduation, it meant loss of all his friends.

For almost all the recruits this was the worst possible punishment. They would rather go to the brig than be transferred to another company.

I took this action only when I thought the recruit would benefit from a change in scenery and a change in company commanders.

While most of the infractions weren't serious, we had some that we could not straighten out. For example, we had thieves who stole from their shipmates. And we had bullies who wouldn't change. There also were a few recruits who picked on homosexuals.

According to Navy rules of that era, once a recruit admitted to being a homosexual he was usually sent home with a less than an honorable discharge. One day an officer from the Navy Department visited and gave us some surprising information. The Secretary of the Navy, he said, was concerned about the large number of young men being discharged for homosexuality and being burdened for life with such a discharge.

He wanted the recruit training commands to consider setting up a program that would inform all the recruits about homosexuality.

I don't recall the detailed contents of the proposed program. However, I do recall a key issue was that innocent, inexperienced, young Navy men were being apprehended and discharged after unknowingly becoming involved in homosexual activity.

One objective of the proposed program was to fill this knowledge void. I initially resisted the idea, as did my boss and most of our staff and all the company commanders. It wasn't the content of the instruction that we objected to, but our apprehension about how the media would twist it and seriously damage the Navy's image.

Nevertheless, we were asked and so we agreed to give it a try before we made up our minds. The group responsible for implementing the instruction proposed that it be taught by a team consisting of a line officer, a company commander, a Red Cross worker and a chaplain.

After a large number of recruit companies had received the instruction, their company commanders called them together to obtain feedback.

We were all surprised at the reaction of the recruits. A large number of them did not know what homosexuality was and had never heard of it. They actually appreciated the information. Their reactions convinced the company commanders to recommend that it be taught. We followed their recommendation and

10. More Boots – The Korean War

included the instructions in the recruit curriculum using the same four person teaching team.

This incident occurred in 1948 and I believe all the Navy boot camps subsequently instituted the same program. It took more than 60 years for the military to lift fully its restrictions on homosexuality.

Another major change to the recruit curriculum was initiated by some of our chief petty officers and one of our staff officers, Lieutenant (Lt.) Larry Sharpe, USNR.

About six months after the recruits started to arrive and our population had increased, Lt. Sharp came to me with a proposed solution to a problem we were all aware of, but had been unable to solve.

Significant numbers of our young recruits were doing very poorly in their classification tests and were failing the academic subjects. Though bad from a morale perspective, removing the recruit from his company and friends, and making him repeat the training in a different company, was the only action we could take (short of discharging the recruit). That still didn't solve our problem, since the basic reason for these failures was often the recruit's inability to read or write!

All of us saw this unpleasant experience happen to recruits who had perfectly fine military aptitude and we thought would make good shipmates.

But the personal impact on these fine young men was very disturbing. We dreaded doing it and even established a tutor program in every company. While that helped some of the handicapped recruits, it was just a temporary fix. We knew they would have a tough time competing with their peers in the fleet.

I don't recall the actual number that tested below the third grade level, but it was too great to ignore.

In his research, Lt. Sharp determined that almost all of those recruits that had this problem had, for one reason or another, dropped out of school before learning to read or write. Many of them had joined the Navy to avoid being drafted into the Army.

Lt. Sharp proposed that we test all incoming recruits upon arrival, and that we assign those who could not read or write at the third grade level to special pre-training companies. The academic focus in these companies would be on reading and writing.

I thought it was a wonderful idea, as did my boss. We appointed a small group to figure out a way to get it done without adversely impacting the morale of those to be pre-trained.

It was given the title "Recruit Preparatory Training" (RPT) and folded right into our over-all operation.

This was not a simple matter. For example, we had to let those recruits know that they were being treated differently and that it would double the amount of time they spent in recruit training.

I was somewhat surprised at the reactions. All of them wanted to learn to read and write, so that part was not really an issue. The most sensitive issue was they wanted be considered "boots" just like all the other recruits and that they receive the training that the other "boots" did. And we assured them that would be the case.

A lot of these youngsters were tough, independent kids from the rough parts of New Jersey, New York City, and Philadelphia who could easily have accepted administrative discharges and gone home. But I was happily surprised to see that they recognized the opportunity the Navy was giving them – and though we had many hundreds in the program, we never had a morale problem.

We made sure the program was not publicized in a way that other recruits would know about these special companies. Being treated differently in a boot camp makes one very conspicuous so we made sure that didn't happen.

The program worked and was soon copied by other Navy recruit training centers and, I believe, by the Army recruit training commands, as well. It worked so well at Bainbridge that we soon considered it part of our regular training program.

10. MORE BOOTS – THE KOREAN WAR

Does that mean all the preparatory graduates did as well as the other recruits in the academic portions of the training program? Probably not. But almost all of them did well enough to complete the training program and graduate. We did have some exceptions, but by and large it was a solid success.

We were doing so many new things at Bainbridge and were so busy training the recruits that we didn't take time to pat ourselves on the back when we accomplished something really outstanding. We should have given Larry a medal for his idea and efforts, but, regretfully, we didn't. However, we let him know, and he could see, that he changed the lives of many many young men who entered the service unable to read or write.

Another incident which we were proud of, was the discovery of a strain of the Streptococcus bacterium (type 19) by a medical research team that was seeking ways to prevent rheumatic fever and the kidney disease caused by Strep throat. This discovery would not have been possible without the voluntary cooperation of many recruits.[1]

In 1952, the training of women accepted for voluntary emergency service (Waves) was shifted from Great Lakes to Bainbridge. I knew most of the Wave training officers from my tour at Great Lakes. They were all exceptionally competent and it wasn't long before their training program was functioning as well as, if not better than, at Great Lakes.

The senior Wave officer insisted that the women stand inspections by the commanding officer just as the men did. However, the captain was usually busy and I conducted the personnel inspections on Saturday mornings.

I had to be briefed by the wave officers on what to look for in the inspections. Nevertheless, I was uncomfortable making those inspections. At the time I was 33 years old, and still single.

---

[1] Dr. Charles Rammelkamp headed this team. In 1954 his team won a Lasker Prize, second in prestige only to the Nobel Prize. As late as 1977, the Bainbridge type 19 bacterial strain was still being used in medical research [Cunningham], and the type 19 bacterium continues to be discussed in the medical literature.

After my third inspection, the captain sensed my discomfort and took over the job.

Every day at Bainbridge was interesting, exciting, often quite unusual, but always inspiring in one way or another. There were so many wonderful things the recruits did with unbounded verve and pride that it was very hard not to get caught up in their enthusiasm. This was especially true at the weekly graduation reviews where the recruits ran the whole show.

With their proud company commanders, parents and invited celebrities looking on, a thousand or more recruits assured everyone that the Navy was in good hands.

Ask almost any veteran and I'm sure 95% will agree when I say the officers and staffs of their training commands shared that wonderfully satisfying feeling of accomplishment that is the essence of a boot camp.

Yes, there are exceptions, and one occurred on a hot summer day when the noisy unmilitary behavior of multiple recruit companies came to my attention. It was not an unusual incident, one often corrected by the assignment of additional marching and drilling. On this particular very warm evening, a number of recruits fainted during the extra drill.

The incident happened to be observed by a senior naval officer. It also was brought to the attention of a chaplain who became upset at what he labelled "inhumane treatment." Words of that type in a boot camp can create a firestorm, and that is what happened.

Fortunately I learned of the incident and visited the barracks of the recruits who were involved.

I talked to all the recruits until late in the evening. It was not unusual for me to be in the barracks talking to them since I had made a habit of doing so, asking them questions about their training. In any event I acquired enough information to satisfy myself that while mistakes were made, the treatment was by no means inhumane and did not warrant the charges that were being drawn up.

10. More Boots – The Korean War

The next morning a formal inquiry was initiated and my captain, as well as the regimental commander and other officers including myself, were required to respond to accusations of inhumane treatment of the recruits during that incident.

It was a lengthy hearing, but it wasn't until I requested the opportunity to address the details of the charges that the investigation was resolved. I went through all the information I had acquired the night before from the recruits involved. It became very clear that everyone in the company, with the exception of two recruits, considered it routine corrective drilling and by no means excessive or "inhumane" treatment.

After I finished presenting my information the convening officer – a senior Navy captain who was also the center commander – declared the investigation over and the charges were dropped. He then asked everyone to leave except for me. After the room had emptied he walked over to me quietly, put his arm around my shoulder and much to my surprise said, "George, don't let them make a Sunday School out of this place." He then thanked me and left.

That evening his aide delivered a package to my room. It contained the record of the hearing that we had attended that morning. "The boss wants you to have this record. It is the only copy and it is yours." Of course I was both gratified and surprised. I still have it.

After two years at Bainbridge, during which we trained well over 100,000 recruits, I was confident, interested, and still gaining experience on how to train recruits. That's the way it was when I received orders to assume command of a destroyer, the *Harlan R. Dickson*. Lucky for me, I was happy in my current job and still happier to be a destroyer skipper.

Figure 156: **USS *Tolovana* giving fuel.** USS *Shelton* (the destroyer, on left) and USS *Antietam* (the carrier, on right) simultaneously take on fuel from *Tolovana* during the Korean War. This is a straightforward maneuver in good weather. In bad weather it ranges from challenging to impossible, and tricky to catastrophic. Figure 61 shows the refueling hoses in their stowed condition.

Chapter 11

Collision

"What do you think, George?" asked Admiral William G. Cooper as each of us held onto an overhead beam to steady ourselves.

We were in the enclosed bridge of the destroyer *Dickson*, standing behind the helmsman as he tried to maintain a steady course.

Steaming parallel to our refueling tanker, which was about two hundred yards to our right, both of us on a base course of 135 degrees at 12 knots, we were having a rough ride. A 30 knot headwind slightly on the tanker's starboard bow had kicked up the seas and our rolling and pitching destroyer was bouncing heavily up and down, moving from left to right and then back again in response to the helmsman's efforts.

Even the giant tanker, ten times our size, was having a tough time steering a straight course. Heavily laden with fuel, and low in the water, her bow would dig down deep into the oncoming waves which shaved a half knot from her forward movement. Then the bow would slowly come up as masses of water cascaded rapidly down her deck. Down again would go her bow exposing much of her stern to the air sometimes even the spinning propellors. But while her pitching was violent, she didn't wobble left to right and right to left as much as we did. Even so, she was far from maintaining a steady course.

The tanker's steering wasn't my problem. I was focused on

11. Collision

my helmsman, Steve Clark, Quartermaster Second Class. He had his hands full, working hard to maintain the base course. In particular I watched how far to the right or left the waves pushed us and how quickly he could recover to bring the ship back on base course and hold it there. Sometimes, the waves would push our bow as much as 10 to 15 degrees to the right or left of the base course, forcing Clark to swiftly apply full rudder in the opposite direction to stop the swing.

With the big tanker on my right, it was not a pleasant feeling to see my ship's rudder at a full right angle as Clark tried to stop a wave-induced swing to the left, a type of swing that would easily tear fuel lines apart. On the other hand, if full right rudder was applied for just an instant too long after stopping the swing, this guaranteed a sharp turn to the right and a collision!

Rear Admiral Cooper was the flotilla commander of our group of twelve destroyers. We were about four days out of Newport, Rhode Island, on our trip across the Atlantic to relieve a similar number of destroyers in the Mediterranean operating with the Sixth Fleet.

A decorated WWII destroyer captain, Cooper was no rookie when it came to operating destroyers. His staff had directed the other eleven destroyers with us to stand by as we determined the possibility of refueling in this heavy weather. All 12 of the destroyers were of WW II vintage and notorious fuel eaters. We were down to about 30% of our fuel capacity and every ship now needed what that tanker was carrying.

We both stood there behind Clark and watched for about ten minutes. "I think I'll take her in closer and see how it rides," I said.

"Good idea. How does this course look?" responded Cooper.

"Looks OK sir, we'll give it a try."

"Tell the tanker we are going to make a dry run now and won't be sending any lines over," said Cooper.

"Aye aye, sir," responded our signalman who promptly sent the message by flashing light.

In seconds he reported, "Tanker acknowledges receipt of your message, sir."

I nodded to Lieutenant Vern Ware, my officer of the deck. "I have the conn."

"Yes, sir," he responded.

The quartermaster of the watch standing nearby shouted, "The Captain has the Conn."

I walked out to the edge of the starboard wing of the bridge and stood there with the wind and salt water blowing into my face. We had a gyrocompass and rudder-position-indicator repeater at that position, so I could see what course we were on.

"Come right to 140," I ordered.

"Right to new course 140, sir," repeated Clark.

I watched the gyro repeater as our distance from the tanker started to decrease.

"Steady on new course 140," shouted Clark.

"Roger," I answered.

We both knew there was no way he could steer a steady course. We knew from working together that when he said "Steady on new course," he meant only that the ship's heading would spend more time on 140 than any other course.

I waited as we rolled and pitched, but slowly closed the distance to the tanker.

When we were about 150 feet away I ordered, "Left to new course 137." The idea was to come a little closer to the tanker but still remain close to the base course of 135.

"Left to new course 137," repeated Clark who knew full well what I was doing.

Then, "Steady on new course 137," shouted Clark

Watching the gyrocompass, I could see the ship's heading swing left and right, but slightly more to the left as she responded slowly to the rudder.

When we were about 100 feet from the tanker I ordered "Come left to new course 135" (the base course).

"Come left to new course 135," shouted Clark even as he spun the helm to the left.

11. Collision

In a few minutes he shouted, "Steady on new course 135, sir."

"Roger." I responded and kept my eyes on the gyro compass even as I gauged our new closeness to the tanker.

By now we were about 80 feet from the tanker and, believe me, she looked huge.

In order to fuel effectively, such that the lines would all reach without too much stretch, we had to move in to about 50 feet from the tanker.

For some reason, I just didn't feel like going in closer.

We watched as Clark moved the steering wheel. It was constantly in motion – right to left and left to right – trying to spend more time on the base course of 135 than adjacent headings. And he was doing it. But every once in a while a large wave would pick us up and move us much closer to the tanker – even dangerously close.

Using full hard left rudder (meaning the steering wheel was spun left as far as it would go), Clark would stop the swing to the right and pull us away from the tanker. Then, almost immediately, to prevent an excessive swing to the left of 135 he had to reverse his rudder. And that's the way it continued without even a minute of steady steaming.

It is not a comfortable feeling to be pitching and rolling alongside a tanker that is also doing her own brand of big-ship pitching and rolling,

While stopping one particular surge to the left Clark didn't take off the full right rudder soon enough and we were suddenly within about 30 feet of the tanker before he could straighten it out.

It didn't take me long to conclude that it would be too dangerous to fuel on this course.

The admiral saw the same thing I did. Over the next couple hours we had the tanker change to several new base courses, but none of them seemed any better. He even had the tanker reverse course so we could try a downwind fueling. While the latter was much less windy and gave us a quieter bridge the following sea made steering control even harder.

I didn't have to make a recommendation to the admiral.

He cancelled the fueling and said we would try again the next day.

While the weather seemed to be just as bad the next morning, for some reason the ship behaved better and we could see that Clark had an easier time controlling her.

I was the first to fuel. While it was no picnic and almost all the sailors on deck got soaked by the boarding seas, we managed to quickly top off our fuel without any serious problems.

Not many people outside a ship appreciate the role of the helmsman. It is a routine job when the weather is good. But when going alongside another ship to fuel in bad weather, the helmsman becomes the most important man on the ship. And between the conning officer and the helmsman, there has to be a strong bond of mutual trust in the other's judgement and skill. For example, if I didn't have complete confidence in Clark's ability to sense when to use extreme rudder movement, I would be a nervous wreck as the ship was shoved back and forth across the base course.

Imagine for just a second how you would feel. The massive, heaving tanker, ten times your ship's size, is 50 feet to your right and you see right full rudder – yes, right full rudder, maximally turning you into the tanker – displayed on the remote monitor in front of you. There are times when that's exactly what I would see when the helmsman brings the ship back from a strong surge to the left. But that right full rudder is only there for a few seconds before he reverses the rudder to steady the ship and stay closer to the base course.

An inexperienced helmsman can easily leave the right rudder on just an instant too long and the ships can collide. Or he can leave left rudder on a little too long and the ships will separate, snapping the refueling lines and causing fuel oil to splatter over both ships.

If this type of back and forth ship steering occurred only once during a refueling operation in heavy weather, it wouldn't be so

11. Collision

bad. But this happens over and over again as you literally fight to keep the ship in position.

In a heavy weather fueling operation, the helmsman is the hardest working sailor on the ship.

Both the admiral and I could tell by Clark's timing and how hard he was working whether it was safe to fuel.

For his part Clark had to have confidence that the orders I gave him were orders he could carry out. But more than that, Clark knew that I trusted him implicitly, and would not second guess him, especially when he had to use heart stopping hard right or left rudder to maintain control.

Admiral Cooper and I both complimented Clark. We also complimented the rest of the fueling detail throughout the ship. One of the riskiest places to be was the wet slippery main deck where the men had to handle the heavy fuel lines in the face of boarding seas and heavy spray.

But what about the tanker? For that bulky, cumbersome Goliath, is fueling in heavy weather also a risky operation?

You bet it is! Later in my career, I would learn first-hand the risks involved. To finish this chapter, I'll jump ahead in time and share those risks with you now.

Seven years after I left the Destroyer *H. R. Dickson*, I was the commanding officer of the USS *Tolovana* (AO 64[1]). Over the course of a year in the southwest Pacific and East China Sea, I participated in probably over 100 refueling operations with every size ship in the Seventh Fleet, as well as a number of Japanese destroyers. For the most part, weather in the Pacific is much better than in the Atlantic. Nevertheless, we had our share of fueling experiences in extremely bad weather.

My biggest worry as skipper of the tanker was the safety of my men. Tankers have a very low freeboard, especially when heavily loaded (i.e., there is a short distance from the main deck to the water). With the ship moving at twelve to fourteen knots into them, parts of the waves sweep over the main deck.

---

[1] "AO" is the designation for a fleet oiler.

Once in a while, the sailors on deck would get knocked down or get pushed into a steel upright, leaving bruises. And sometimes they would be caught and sent five or ten feet down the slippery deck. For that reason, in heavy weather, we rigged safety netting that would catch them.

You would think that with the generally good weather in the Pacific refueling would be less of a harrowing experience, but no!

One day in beautiful weather, with a near flat sea and no wind, the destroyer *Henderson* collided with my tanker.

He approached my port side at too sharp an angle and when he was still fifty feet away I knew he was going to hit me.

"Clear the port side," I ordered.

The dangerous part of a collision with any tanker is the very volatile fumes that are unavoidably part of its environment. The smallest spark can ignite those fumes and cause an explosion. It was that danger that worried me as the *Henderson* slid toward me because there would certainly be sparks where our metal hulls collided.

In the few seconds between the moment I knew he would hit me and the moment when it actually occurred, time played out in slow motion.

Everything was exceptionally quiet. I was the only one on the port side of my ship. And as I looked down from the bridge across the steadily diminishing distance between us, I knew, and the captain of the *Henderson* knew, that he could not straighten out his ship in time to avoid a collision.

I didn't hear any orders on the *Henderson* to clear the starboard side, but the only one on the starboard side that I saw was the captain.

What I did hear was, "Aw shit!" followed by some quick orders from the captain to back the port engine.

He was rapidly decreasing the angle of the collision as he slid into me.

Because he had slowed considerably, his starboard bow hit the after (back) half of my ship and the impact caused him to rub against me in a parallel direction. Then while we were locked to-

11. Collision

gether, his ship slid back and under my counter (the high part of the stern), As he did so, my ship crushed two vertical steel uprights on his starboard side (boat davits) and smashed the boat it held. And then he was free and astern of me.

Thank God I saw no sparks!

However, the bruised *Henderson*, while still operational, left without refueling.

Sometime later the Task Group Commander sent his chief of staff (an old friend of mine) over to me by high line (breeches buoy transfer) to investigate the collision. He asked for my recommendation.

While I couldn't understand the *Henderson* captain's slip in judgement, I strongly recommended they forget about it. I had fueled the *Henderson* many times during that tour, some in especially bad weather and he had done an outstanding job.

All I had was a long scratch on my port side.

They followed my recommendation and there was no disciplinary action.

...

In 1954, getting command of a destroyer was the answer to every surface officer's prayer. Much like the fighter pilots of naval aviation in WWII, the skipper of a destroyer was the hottest surface line officer in the Navy.

Anyway, that's the way I felt when I got command of the *Dickson*.

Figure 166: **USS *Harlan R. Dickson* underway.** Photo is circa 1966.

Chapter 12

Destroyer Command

I took command of the *Dickson* on April 15, 1954. However, before I relieved Commander Edwin Finney, I spent several days on the *Dickson* getting acquainted and inspecting the ship.[1]

Getting command of a fast (about 39 miles an hour) destroyer is a major milestone in any naval officer's career. There is something quite special about them. In addition to their high speed, they carry three accurate 5"/38 gun turrets, a healthy stock of depth charges, a deadly torpedo battery, far ranging accurate general and fire control radars, and underwater sonar detection equipment. It all makes for a formidable stand-alone fighting ship.

Feared in combat by large and small combat ships, as well as aircraft and submarines, it is still small enough so that no one in the 335-man crew feels like a stranger. Everyone knows everyone else and everyone has a job that merits respect. Destroyer sailors possess the type of "can do" attitude where each crew is

---

[1] Lt. Commander Harlan R. Dickson of Washington, D.C, a graduate of the Naval Academy, was a carrier torpedo plane pilot. He flew off the carrier *Yorktown* and participated in aerial combat at Tulagi, Midway, and elsewhere in the early days of World War II. He was twice decorated with the Navy Cross for heroism and outstanding performance as a torpedo plane pilot, exhibiting exceptional courage and skill. He was killed in a crash in California in 1944.

12. DESTROYER COMMAND

convinced they have the best ship in the fleet.

At my first meal in the wardroom just after I met the officers, I was surprised by the lively, spirited and, I thought, disrespectful conversation among the senior officers, especially the chief engineer.

I thought it was for my benefit, but later Finney told me that was the way they always talked.

The chief engineer, a lieutenant, and veteran of WWII, had been recalled to active duty as a result of the Korean war. He was a competent chief engineer but he had grown to hate the Navy for recalling him. Apparently it had caused him to lose an accounting business that he had worked very hard to establish after being discharged at the end of WWII. At that time he liked the Navy well enough to remain in the naval reserve and collect pay for reserve duty. That, of course, was his mistake.

Another key officer, also a lieutenant, was just as vociferous as the chief engineer in his condemnation of the Navy's recall policies. All except one or two of the junior officers shared the attitudes of the two senior Lieutenants. I had not talked much with the enlisted crew, but I sensed that many of them (also recalled reservists) followed the lead of the unhappy lieutenants.

I was surprised at the executive officer's tolerance of the demoralizing conduct that I was witnessing.

I didn't say much during the first four days that I had command, hoping the lieutenants would just get tired and shut up.

But they didn't.

I called in the chief engineer and told him to either stop his tirade against the Navy or to request transfer from the ship.

"No, Captain, I won't stop expressing how I feel," he said, "Captain Finney told me the same thing. So I requested a transfer. But in his endorsement he stated that a qualified relief was required. That endorsement ruined my chances of getting off the ship since no qualified relief was available."

I interrupted him. "I won't endorse it that way. My endorsement will say that you are a competent engineer but that because of your attitude, your presence on the ship is detrimental to good order and discipline and that I want you off the ship – no qualified relief required. If you can live with that type of endorsement, submit your request for transfer right away."

He didn't back down. "Thank you, Captain," he said. "You will have my letter later today."

I then called in three more officers and told them the same thing. Two of them apologized and said they would stop cussing out the Navy. The third one, head of the deck department, also did not back down and, along with the chief engineer, they were both off the ship within about ten days.

I knew I was taking some risk in going to sea without an experienced chief engineer and deck department head. However, from my WWII experiences in seeing young officers rise to the challenge, I had no doubt at all that the same thing would happen in both those departments. I was right.

The departure of those two officers changed the wardroom immediately, and I'm sure the new uplifting attitude emanating from the wardroom spread throughout the ship.

My relationship with the exec, however, didn't improve until after an incident that occurred as we were entering Boston. That's when I had a good chance to see all my topside crew at their special sea detail stations. I didn't like what I saw. Their uniforms were unkempt and most of them were wearing their hats on the back of their heads. I thought we made a very sloppy appearance. I called the exec to the bridge and quietly (and privately) told him I was disappointed and pointed out specific reasons for my disappointment.

All he said was, "Yes sir," and left. That evening after we had tied up and were planning the next day's activities, I was informed that 32 sailors had been placed on report for being out of uniform and would be at captain's mast the next morning.

I was pissed off at the exec's irresponsibility. Taking a sailor to captain's mast is a serious action and can ruin a sailor's career.

I called the exec and told him to get those 32 men together and I would talk to them that evening. At that session I told the men that I was taking them off report and that they would not

12. Destroyer Command

go to mast the next day. I told them that they all knew better and we had other things to do besides having to make sure they are in the proper uniform. That was something I expected them to do on their own. That's all I said to them.

Then I called in the exec and told him that putting large numbers on report was not the way to get things done. I think he realized he acted too hastily because he didn't say much in response. After that we got along quite well and I found myself giving him less and less specific guidance.

While I did have some experienced chief and first class petty officers I couldn't say the same for my officers. It turned out that I had considerably more sea experience than any of them. Command experience is a special asset and I was lucky to have had a lot of that (as skipper of the destroyer escort *Willis* (DE 395) in 1945-1946[2] and the *Colonial*). By far the best teaching situations for anyone at sea are the mistakes that you make – especially the serious ones like failing portions of an operational readiness inspection, running aground, having a collision or near-collision, getting lost in a heavy storm, losing an anchor, trying to refuel in heavy weather and rescuing men who are in the water.

In varying degrees I had experienced all those "learning" mistakes and more. For example, on my LSD I had initially failed an important readiness inspection (page 100). On the *PC 476*, at the beginning of WW II, I was the navigator when we ran aground in the Miami Ship Channel. On the *Willis* I watched the navigator try to anchor us in water too deep for the reach of our anchor chain. Also on the *Willis* we rescued two aviators who had ditched their aircraft. After the war, when I was the captain of the *Willis*, I collided with another DE as we were going alongside because my engineers did not respond to a backing bell.

If your career progression withstands those mistakes without a court martial or censure, the experiences are like money in the bank. They give you a lot of confidence in your ability to handle such problems ... because going to sea means you are

---

[2] See *Living with the Torpedo*.

guaranteed to face challenges.

In any event, I had those experiences behind me and they, plus a lot more, gave me confidence in my ability to run the ship. One more incident that highlights the seriousness and value of those types of experiences is worth mentioning.

In our home port of Newport, Rhode Island I was surprised one day to get a call from the Chief of Staff for Atlantic Fleet Destroyers.

"Captain Sotos," he said, "Admiral Hartman (Commander Destroyers Atlantic Fleet) wants you to take him to Guantanamo Bay. Any reasons why you won't be ready in a few days?"

After I gulped a few times, I said, "We'll be ready sir." Two days later, Admiral Hartman came aboard, all by himself, no staff, no naval aide, just the top man himself.

We promptly displayed his two star flag at the top of our yardarm (crossbar at the top of the main mast used for flag hoists) – indicating my ship, the USS *Dickson*, was now the flagship for Commander Destroyers U.S. Atlantic Fleet – and got underway immediately.

A very friendly and outgoing guy, the admiral walked around the ship, introducing himself and talking to the sailors. Of course I already had announced that he would be coming aboard, so they all knew who he was.

The admiral used my cabin while I moved to the sea cabin, a very small room behind the bridge that was big enough to just hold a bed.

At meal time the admiral sat to my right. I had already explained to him that I had initiated a lunch time procedure where, on a rotating basis, each officer had to introduce a subject (no ship's business and no women) and then be prepared to answer questions about that subject. The admiral told me to continue our regular procedure and he joined in asking questions and even introducing a subject when it was his turn.

The one subject that proved very interesting was presented by our electronics officer, John Grant. A little nervous at having the admiral there when his turn came up, he talked about

12. DESTROYER COMMAND

his theory of space travel. This was 1954 and the Soviet Union's Sputnik satellite was still three years away, so John's subject was really a stretch for all of us. But the admiral joined in and we all got to know him better.

The weather was excellent and we had a good trip. The admiral spent a lot of time chatting with the officers and the sailors.

One day he nonchalantly asked me, "What do you think of the ORI (operational readiness inspection) and underway training at Guantanamo?" There was a large training group headquartered in Cuba's Guantanamo Bay which conducted operational readiness inspections, training and tests for most of the Atlantic Fleet combat ships.

Without much thought I answered, "Well you'll go nuts if you try to do everything they require of you."

"What do you mean?"

"On the day you arrive, about thirty or forty expert inspectors come aboard with clipboards. They spend half the day going around the ship making notes on what they call deficiencies. Then, late that evening, they hand you a twenty page document that lists the deficiencies they found. At the same time, they give you a detailed training schedule for the next three weeks."

I paused as I suddenly realized that I was criticizing the Guantanamo Training Command to a very powerful admiral.

"So, you get a list of deficiencies and your schedule. What's wrong with that?" he asked in a puzzled voice.

I knew I had my foot in it, But I also knew I knew I couldn't back down.

"The list is always unbelievably long and detailed. They even include the absence of compartment numbers and the labelling of the contents of every pipe on the ship in and out of the engine room."

He didn't say anything but I could sense his thoughts. "That's exactly what a ship needs for good damage control. Don't you agree?"

I stopped for a second. "I know that's important for damage control. But if you go from a Navy yard overhaul into an ORI, as most of us do, a lot of that stuff is painted over or modified. At the same time a large part of your crew has been changed and you have a lot of people who do not know the ship very well.

"There's no way you can correct those deficiencies and do all the training exercises in three weeks," I continued. "You have to work your entire crew every night to do it. And even then you can't get them all finished. It can drive you nuts trying."

"You seemed to have survived it," he said.

That's when I saw the light and understood why they had selected me to take him to Guantanamo. My ship had just finished the three week ORI with a passing but not career enhancing grade.

"Why didn't it bother you?" he continued.

"It did bother me, but I have been through three ORI's and I learned you have to work your people night and day to just come close to a high grade. I decided not to do that."

"I understand that you sent some people ashore every day to drink beer and play ball while you were going through the ORI."

I saw that he had been talking to the crew, "Yes sir, I figured they needed a break and it worked out well."

He nodded his head and that was the end of that conversation until the morning we entered Guantanamo bay.

The admiral was on the bridge as we headed in. We requested a berthing assignment and I was surprised at the response.

"Berthing assignment is Pier XY" (I can't recall the specific name).

"Christ!" I said, mostly to myself, as I went to the harbor chart to locate the pier. "I didn't know they had any piers here." But though he said nothing, I realized the admiral overheard me.

I took the conn from the officer of the deck and pointed the ship toward the pier which I could see through my binoculars. As we got closer a large tug boat stopped directly in front of us.

"He's lost power," reported the signalman who received a message from the tug.

12. DESTROYER COMMAND

Fortunately, we were not going to collide with him. The bay was flat. There was no wind and it was a beautiful day as we sat and waited for the tug to regain power and move out of our way. We were close enough to the pier to see and hear a large band at the head of the pier playing martial music.

"Admiral they are welcoming you." I said and added "Jesus, I didn't know they had a band here."

As we were sitting there waiting the admiral quietly asked, "George, I guess you are wondering why I have been asking these questions about the training here." He didn't wait for my responsse. "We've had some serious problems here. I've had one captain shoot himself, one run aground and another give up his command." Then he asked me, "Do you think that three weeks of ORI and training here is too long?"

I waited a few seconds before answering as I mulled it over. "Yes, sir, I think it is."

We were interrupted by a shout from the lookout, "The tug is moving."

The admiral didn't say anything else as I started in for the pier where we could see a large number of people waiting as the band played on.

I brought the ship in rather bumpily. That is, we slid forward rubbing alongside the pier into the correct berth. There were some rocks on the other side that I wanted to stay well clear of and that overcorrection affected the quality of my ship handling.

As a veteran destroyer skipper himself, the admiral understood why I hugged the pier. The skipper he had mentioned – the one that ran aground – had done it on those rocks that were on the starboard side.

A bunch of dignitaries came aboard and the admiral thanked us all as we rendered honors to him when he departed.

I never saw the admiral again until Hurricane Carol hit Newport, Rhode Island on August 31, 1954. However, I did learn later that the ORI training was reduced by one week, and every arriving destroyer was greeted by a Navy band and assigned a pier its first few days.

Figure 176: **Dickson on the cover.** This photo of the *Dickson* was unique enough to become the cover of the official information bulletin of the Commander of the Navy's destroyer fleet in the Atlantic ("COMDESLANT"). It was taken from a helicopter launched by the flag cruiser carrying the Sixth Fleet commander. The cruiser's commander gave us only 10 minutes' notice to get everyone dressed and in position. I am on the port side of the bridge, barely discernible.

Chapter 13

This One's Greek

On February 12, 1955, 12 fully loaded destroyers left Newport Rhode Island. Ours was one of them. Our destination was to join the Sixth Fleet operating in the Mediterranean Sea, for a six month deployment.

My ship, the USS *Dickson*, was selected to be the flagship for all the destroyers attached to the Sixth Fleet.

It meant that I didn't just have command of the *Dickson*. It was much more than that. I was no longer the captain of just another DD that had to conform to someone else's tactical orders. Instead, as the flotilla flagship carrying the flotilla commander, Admiral William G. Cooper, my ship was looked to for leadership around the clock. It gave me a heady and satisfying feeling.

It's no secret that, if he has the option, a flotilla commander will pick the best qualified ship to be his flagship. So, it is a nice pat on the back to be selected for that job. As I told my crew, it is good solid evidence that you have made the *Dickson* the best destroyer in the Atlantic fleet.

It took a few days before the 12 destroyers acted like an effective operating unit. During that time Admiral Cooper and his staff ran all of us through a series of maneuvers including some gunnery practice. I quickly learned that there is more to being a flagship then providing the admiral and his staff with a seagoing berth.

13. THIS ONE'S GREEK

Crowded as a destroyer normally is, we also had to handle the extra staff that came with the Admiral. Once again I had to give up my cabin, spending the next four months in my sea cabin (about seven by four feet). It contained a small bed built into the superstructure, a small toilet and wash-basin, a small chair and a chest of three drawers built under the bed.

I spent very little time in the sea cabin except to sleep or lie down when the weather was bad. There were some benefits to the sea cabin because the bridge people knew I could hear almost everything going on. As a result they became more professional.

The remainder of the admiral's staff of three officers and nine enlisted men were assigned bunks in different parts of the ship. It wasn't long before this arrangement folded them nicely into the crew. This was important because the entire ship's company became like a right arm for the Admiral and his staff.

The job of the staff was to help the admiral command the operation of the 12 DDs. But they could not really do that without help from the *Dickson* crew, especially the sailors in our combat information center and radio shack.

I had prepared my crew for their flagship duties through several briefings, so all in all it went well. My crew knew it was an honor to be selected as a flagship and they wanted to be the best.

The fourth day into our eastward crossing of the Atlantic, the weather started to get really bad and, to make matters worse, the storm was going in the same direction.

Despite the heavy weather, we refueled as I described in the previous chapter, and were scheduled to do so again when we joined the Sixth Fleet in the Mediterranean. In fleet operations, destroyers are kept busy screening the carrier and other large ships, and by performing any number of special missions. Much of their time is spent guzzling fuel at high speed (20-25 knots). As a result, fleet commanders like to keep them topped off (full load of fuel), so a destroyer can usually plan to refuel from a carrier or fleet oiler about every three days.

When we reached the Mediterranean and we rendezvoused with the massive Sixth Fleet, it was, as always, a stirring sight.

The Commander Sixth Fleet had scheduled a big replenishment operation where the entire fleet and the newly arriving destroyers would be refueled and restocked with food.

We and the fleet were on opposite courses heading toward each other. The Sixth Fleet ships were everywhere we looked: carriers, a battleship, cruisers, the 12 destroyers we were relieving, and countless huge supply ships.

We had all been assigned our respective replenishment ship and the task was to pick out that ship, go alongside quickly and smartly, receive our supplies and fuel, and relieve the outgoing DDs that were screening the fleet.

As flagship, it was my job to set the tone for all twelve DDs in our flotilla.

I was assigned to go alongside the carrier *Randolph* which was near the Sixth Fleet flagship. I was sure Vice Admiral Thomas Combs, the fleet commander, was watching.

As the lead DD in a fast moving (20 knot) column of 12 DDs about 500 yards apart, I headed right for the center of the fleet, all of whose ships were on an opposite course at 12 knots. We saw the *Randolph* on our port bow and I told the admiral I was ready to go alongside.

By flag-hoist he released all 12 DDs in our column from his tactical command and ordered them to their fueling stations. As he executed the flag hoist, without reducing speed, I ordered "Left full rudder," and headed for a spot just behind the *Randolph*, now steaming across my bow. I stayed at 20 knots until I completed another turn to the left that put us on a course parallel to the big carrier, about 50 yards behind and 75 feet to the right of her. Then I slowed and quickly slid left into our replenishment station about 40 feet abreast of the *Randolph*'s starboard beam.

It was a really great maneuver and from what I heard all the other DDs in our flotilla did just about the same thing. That's the

13. This One's Greek

way destroyers are expected to operate. And from what his staff told me later, the admiral was very proud of us.

The remainder of our tour with the Sixth Fleet had its ups and downs, but by far, more ups than downs.

We conducted training exercises with the fleet for about two weeks, then we broke up and headed for "liberty ports."

One of these ports was Malta, where Admiral Cooper had scheduled a reception for Vice Admiral James Fife, who was the U.S. Naval Commander in Chief, Mediterranean.

We had never hosted a reception on the *Dickson* and now we were on the hook to host one at a top level.

Neither Admiral Cooper nor any of his staff gave me or my staff any instructions other than the names of the attendees and their spouses. I was nervous as I knew arrangements for such an occasion were well out of my league. Fortunately, my chief steward knew exactly what to do. He prepared our small wardroom (about 26 by 20 feet) in a manner I had never seen before (Figure 181).

The reception was a huge success. My one contribution was to place, as a souvenir of the event, an attractive USS *H. R. Dickson* labelled silver cigarette lighter at the plate of each female guest. They loved it!

There is no doubt that the way my people handled the entire reception earned many brownie points for me in Admiral Cooper's book. In a way, my entire crew seemed to enjoy the pomp and ceremony that went along with this very formal, but intimate, destroyer event.

When it was over Admiral Cooper gave us all a hearty "Well done."

That type of event on any DD was rare. It was never repeated aboard any of my ships in my 32 years in the Navy.

We spent much of our time cruising in the Mediterranean with the Sixth Fleet. I always thought the Mediterranean was a very roomy sea. But the way we operated it sometimes seemed like a very confined space.

Figure 181: **Formal reception in the *Dickson* wardroom.** Held the day after we arrived in Malta on Feb. 8, 1955, the wardroom never looked so good. The officers are, from left to right, Vice Admiral James Fife, an unidentified Royal Navy admiral, Rear Admiral W. G. Cooper, me, and Admiral Guy Grantham of the Royal Navy. Grantham, a four-star equivalent, had two months earlier relieved Admiral Mountbatten as Commander-in-Chief, Allied Forces, Mediterranean. Fife commanded American naval forces in the Mediterranean.

One night, a large number of ships, including a battleship, two carriers, a couple of cruisers, and a large number of destroyers were formed by the fleet commander into a column to transit the Straits of Bonifacio, near Italy.

When the fleet commander takes charge like that, his subordinate commanders (like the DD flotilla commander on my ship) are out of the operational chain of command and are merely interested observers.

The straits are a narrow (6.8 mile wide about 40 miles long), crooked, and dangerous channel between the islands of Corsica

13. This One's Greek

and Sardinia. They are also home to many fishing boats that could care less about the powerful American fleet. They are so busy fishing they simply didn't seem to give a damn about the navigational rules of the road, leaving it to the other guy to take avoiding actions. All in all, even in daylight, it's no fun making that transit, and at night it is a real pain.

The transit requires frequent course and speed changes. Unfortunately, because of the fishing boats and the ineptness of the fleet staff running the transit, there were too many course and speed changes on this trip.

Multiple course and speed changes for different size ships, 500 yards behind one another, is not a comfortable way to operate – even in daylight in an open sea. Ships of different classes simply do not accelerate and decelerate at the same speeds. So, in a long column such changes can create an accordion-like effect, making it difficult for ships to keep their 500 yard spacing. In a crooked channel, at night, crowded with bright lighted fishing boats, it is plain foolhardy.

But that is exactly what we did that night.

After a third nerve-wracking incident where we closed to within a hundred yards of the cruiser ahead of us, I suddenly had enough. I told the OOD, "I have the conn."

"Aye, aye sir," he said and the quartermaster announced, "The Captain has the conn."

I promptly ordered "Left full rudder," to bring the ship out of the column.

It was dark and I had forgotten that the admiral was on the bridge.

"George, what are you doing?" shouted the admiral.

Fortunately we were not the formation guide for the destroyers and they were not required to follow us. But I suddenly realized what I did reflected on the admiral in his capacity as destroyer flotilla commander.

"They don't know what they are doing, sir. It's too dangerous in there," I answered as I gave orders to parallel the column.

Before Admiral Cooper could say another word we received a report of a collision near the end of the column. A destroyer had run into the stern of the cruiser ahead of him.

The fleet commander immediately ordered all ships to proceed independently (just as I had done) to clear the straits.

Admiral Cooper never said anything to me, but I realized I should have notified him before I did it.

The damage from the collision was not serious but the whole thing was troubling because we lost confidence in the skills of the fleet commander's staff.

Two months later Admiral Cooper and his staff left the *Dickson*. However, I still carried his flag and was treated as the DD flotilla flagship. That meant I was an escort for the fleet commander's flagship and accompanied him to the ports he visited. The first one turned out to be the Greek island of Rhodes.

When the Greeks on Rhodes learned that the skipper of the DD escorting the fleet commander was of Greek descent, you would have thought I was a returning hero. It was 1955, and the impact of WW II was still quite evident.

Rhodes, at that time, was a deathly poor island devoid of tourists and any income. The arrival of the two U S Navy ships with a couple thousand sailors eager to spend their pay was the answer to their prayers. We were the first U.S. Navy ships they had seen since the start of WWII.

The mayor of Rhodes, a practicing dentist, was a cheerful, gregarious, energetic man who kept talking about his island and its economic problems (Figure 184). I was a good listener and we became fast friends in just the three days we were there.

He not only told me told me how poor they were, he took me around to large shuttered hotels that hadn't seen tourists since before the war. In fact, the only open large hotel was the one they made ready for the Sixth Fleet Commander's visit.

In Greek he asked, "George what can I do to bring the U.S. Navy ships here to visit us?"

In my broken Greek and in all seriousness I tried to answer. "At the reception tomorrow night, tell Admiral Combs, the fleet

13. This One's Greek

Figure 184: **Our Greek hosts on the island of Rhodes.** We were the first U.S. Navy ships to visit Rhodes since before World War II, and they were really happy to see us. Left to right: a military guest, Mr. Boulas (Governor General of the Dodecanese Islands), the Mayor of Rhodes, and the author.

commander, personally, that you love the U.S. Navy and want their ships to make regular port visits here. Tell him that you will do whatever is necessary to make them feel at home and enjoy themselves. Then," I continued, "write a letter to the Commander-in-Chief U.S. Atlantic Fleet and the U.S. Navy Chief of Naval Operations. Tell them the same thing. Invite them to schedule regular port visits for all the ships of the Sixth Fleet." The mayor took careful notes as I kept emphasizing that he should not only contact those higher ups but to tell them that the people of Rhodes really welcome the U.S. Navy.

I'll never know if he wrote the letters I recommended, but four years later I received some surprising evidence that he probably had. I had been transferred to a job in Hawaii in 1958, and had just finished relating this experience to my new boss, Captain Fred Archer.

"Well, I'll be damned!" he said. "I think you not only helped that mayor but you also helped the Navy in a big way."

He went on, "I was the naval attaché in Greece not long after your visit to Rhodes. We had scheduled a major formal change of command ceremony for the Sixth Fleet commander in the big harbor at Thessaloniki. But the students there had organized a huge protest and were going to do all they could to disrupt the fleet ceremony and embarrass the Americans.

"We had a serious political and Navy problem and were not quite sure whether we should go ahead with the ceremony. It would have been a major embarrassment to cancel or postpone it. While this was going on, we received a phone call from the mayor of Rhodes. He wanted to talk to the naval attache. That was me.

"He knew about the student protests against the Sixth Fleet ceremony and told me to bring our ships to Rhodes. 'The Sixth Fleet is more than welcome,' he said. 'We have plenty of room (Rhodes does have a very spacious anchorage). We would love to have you.' He asked me to urge the ambassador to move the change of command ceremony to Rhodes."

Captain Archer told me they were elated at the mayor's timely invitation and that it got them out of a serious political hole.

"And that's how the Navy avoided a major international incident. The ceremony with all its ships and sailors was moved to Rhodes."

Overnight Rhodes became the top liberty port and favorite destination for the Sixth Fleet ships, even to the point that, in 1959, the Commander of the Sixth Fleet, Admiral Charles Brown, was featured in *Life* magazine when he attended a wedding ceremony of several Greek couples on Rhodes and provided dowries for the brides.

From my conversations with the mayor, I am convinced that he saw the U.S. Navy as the salvation for his struggling island.

13. This One's Greek

It was the U.S. Navy that turned around the economic disaster confronting Rhodes, and started it on the way to becoming a top tourist attraction.

Some weeks after our visit to Rhodes, Admiral Combs headed his flagship, the cruiser *Philadelphia*, for Izmir, Turkey, and I was ordered to go along as their DD escort. About a hundred miles from Izmir, we ran into some bad weather and the cruiser received a distress message.

Because the admiral had some appointments in Izmir that he didn't want to miss, I was ordered to go to the aid of the ship that sent the distress message while he took off.

After some searching, I found what I thought was the ship in distress. It turned out to be a tug boat that was steaming ahead slowly. He was rocking and rolling and we couldn't see him all the time because of the huge waves. I reversed course and paralleled him, trying to communicate, but they were afraid to come out on the bridge. I stayed with him for about twenty minutes until I was confident he was O.K.

Then I got the bright idea that he must have been towing something and that was the reason for the distress message.

I reversed course again and proceeded along his track in the opposite direction. After about 45 minutes I came across a very large barge that was adrift and at the mercy of the sea and wind. We saw three men on the barge who remained out of the weather. The barge had no propulsion capability, yet seemed to be in no immediate danger and there were no navigational hazards that threatened them. So I just stayed with them until it turned dark. The weather started to get better and I told my officer of the deck to keep a searchlight on the barge and circle it all night. Then we would try to help them in the morning.

I sent a message to Radio Athens reporting the barge was safe and giving our location. Had I been public relations savvy in those days I would have sent a catchier message, "Greek meets Greek," but I was quite proper and sent a formal one.

They replied that a large tug was on the way to tow the barge to the seaport of Pireaus, which is just south of Athens.

Figure 187: **Greek barge, adrift.** This fuzzy photo was taken from our ship, part of which shows in the lower left corner.

It turns out the smaller tug that I saw earlier had been towing the barge when the tow line parted. It was a big barge, about the same length as my ship but much wider. I could understand why the people on the tug had decided it was too dangerous for them to try and hook up again with it. The men on the barge were probably in less danger than the small tug.

The next morning was nice. The sea was rather smooth and the men on the barge came out and waved at us. I brought my destroyer within ten feet of the barge and my sailors passed them some coffee and sandwiches. I surprised them (and my crew) by speaking Greek and I could see they were quite happy to see and hear us. I also told them a large tug was on the way to get them.

Later that day the large tug showed up. I went back about three miles, turned, rang up 25 knots and headed for a spot close to the barge. As we passed them close aboard at 25 knots, our big flag streaming majestically in the wind, the three men came on deck and gave us a farewell and thank you salute.

We reported the situation to commander Sixth Fleet and Radio Athens and headed for Izmir.

Nothing exciting happened during our visit to Izmir. But, a later visit to Athens (through the port of Pireaus), was interest-

13. THIS ONE'S GREEK

ing. During this visit the Greek CNO hosted a reception for the Commander Sixth Fleet and all his captains. As I approached the Greek CNO at the head of the receiving line his aide introduce me in english.

"Admiral, this is Captain George Sotos of the destroyer *H. R. Dickson*."

The admiral, a tall dark good looking man, nodded, shook my hand and said "Welcome to Greece."

I replied in Greek, "Efkaristo para poly. Ei gonies mou ineh elineh." (Translation: Thank you very much. My parents are Greek.)

He was astounded! The receiving line stopped as he took the time to ask me (in Greek) where in Greece my parents were from. Still speaking in Greek I told him my parents were from Kalamata and that my dad was born in the village of Meligala. He continued chatting with me for several minutes then grabbed me by the arm and took me to Admiral Combs (a few feet away) and said in a rather loud, proud voice, "Admiral Combs, this one is Greek!"

I was surprised as he introduced me to my own equally surprised admiral, whom I had never met. Then, still holding me by the arm, he left the receiving line with me and called to one of his officers who hurried over. "This young captain is Greek, make sure he has a good time!" And yes, I had a memorable evening and met a lot of really nice people.

While in Pireaus I tried to send a seabag full of clothing to a remote village in Greece. It was destined for very poor relatives of some people in Boston who had asked me to deliver it. I didn't realize how bureaucratic and inflexible their customs officials were. As a result, a young clerk who tried to do it almost got fired before I talked his boss out of it. I never found out if the clothing was ever delivered.

A different kind of incident occurred when we were anchored near the town of Rapallo, a beautiful resort on the Italian coast. I had just come ashore with my operations officer when we were stopped by two very pretty American girls.

"I understand you are the captain of that destroyer sir," said one of the girls.

"Yes I am," I replied with my friendliest smile.

"One of your sailors told me I should talk to you and that you might be able to help me."

"Sure, what can I do for you?"

"Well, you see I am not feeling well and I think I need to see a doctor, but we are strangers here and don't know what to do. Can I see your doctor?"

I didn't hesitate. "Yes you can, but my doctor is not an MD, he is a pharmacist's mate."

She seemed a little dejected at that but I continued. "However, he is very competent. He takes care of all of us and if he can help you he will. Do you want to to go aboard and see him?"

Her companion urged her to go aboard. I felt a little sorry for her and suggested it might be a good idea to see him.

I instructed my boat crew to take her to the ship and inform the officer of the deck that I'd like our doctor to try to help her if possible. Then both girls got in the boat and headed out to the ship.

I learned later that "Doc" was able to help her.

A lighter incident occured off the coast of Cannes. We had anchored not too far from the town while the sailors went ashore on liberty. It was a rather windy day and we discovered that our anchor was not holding and we were dragging in toward the beach, so we had to move.

While searching through the local books and the navigation chart for a good anchorage, we discovered there was at least one island that was for nudists.

Since the anchorage near that island appeared to be OK, I said lets go there and take a look.

We found a good anchorage, but couldn't see anything on the beach. However, the sailors had a lot of fun trying.

One of the most interesting and worrisome parts of a captain's life is the behavior of his sailors when they go ashore.

13. THIS ONE'S GREEK

After a second visit to Malta, we were getting ready to rejoin the fleet, when a gondola-like boat with two people in it came close. One of the occupants was a very pretty girl who wanted to talk.

We had a few minutes to kill so I said OK and directed the boat to go to our midships main deck section, which is closer to the water. I sent a sailor down to see what they wanted.

The sailor talked to them for a few minutes then shouted up to me at the bridge, "Captain, the young lady wants to talk to Tom Jones."

Almost everyone topside heard this exchange, I instructed the bridge people to pass the word throughout the ship for Tom Jones to go to the quarterdeck to meet a visitor. With the whole crew topside watching Tom Jones ran to the quarterdeck. It was obvious he knew the girl and they started to have an animated conversation. We could see he was trying to break off the conversation but she quite obviously wasn't.

After about ten minutes, an embarrassed Jones talked her into leaving. As the boat pulled away he turned, looked up at us on the bridge, and waved a thank you. With a good laugh we got underway. I never did learn what they talked about.

On the down side was the behavior of four or five of our really reckless sailors. They simply could not handle their whiskey. Careful not to create incidents in foreign ports, I kept cautioning, reminding, and warning the crew that shore patrol incidents were serious and could get shore liberty for the whole crew cancelled.

Near the end of our six month cruise all the destroyers in our flotilla, except for mine, were restricted because of incidents ashore. Finally, in Monaco, it was our turn. There was a riot at a local dance hall where Marines, sailors, and some locals got into a huge fight. When the shore patrol brought back four of my men, drunk, disheveled and beaten up, we were placed on restriction. It was a disappointing ending to what had been a pretty good cruise.

Back in Newport, following a short maintenance period, we

began training with the other ships. Early one evening I was steaming number two in a column of three ships going upriver in Narragansett Bay.

"*Dickson*, you are trailing oil," messaged the ship behind us.

"Oh my God. Check it out!" I ordered.

The answer was swift and devastating. One of our valves was inadvertently turned to the open position and we were pumping oil overboard into pristine Narragansett Bay!

Quickly the valve was closed and I thought that was the end of it. But no! About 15 minutes later a local radio station broadcast an urgent message, "The USS *Harlan R. Dickson*, Destroyer 708, is pumping oil into Narragansett bay. The oil will affect the beaches."

The skipper of a nearby fishing boat had seen the same thing as the the DD behind me. However, instead of bringing it to my attention, he picked up his ship to shore phone and called the radio station. He got his one minute of fame but I got at least ten days of infamy.

Even before we tied up at the pier we were in deep trouble. That news broadcast was repeated over and over again by every radio station in the area. It seemed there was no other news in the Newport area except the progress of the *Harlan R. Dickson*'s oil spill, and what it would do to area beaches!

Even the New York *Times* weighed in the next day and printed a small report of the spill.

Of course I was upset. I looked into what happened and found out that one of my most reliable, responsible, and finest sailors, a petty officer first class, had mistakenly turned the valve the wrong way.

It affected him badly. Never having been in any kind of trouble, he was absent without leave the next day and for four or five days after that.

Commander Destroyers Atlantic Fleet, Admiral Hartman called me on the carpet and asked what happened. I told him about the mistake and the caliber of the sailor who did it. That

13. This One's Greek

was it. He did not discipline me, although the newspapers reported that he did.

For my part, when the sailor who did it returned I didn't even put him on report. He had punished himself. I told him to forget about it.

As a result of our incident a Navy-wide order was issued to all destroyers to chain that particular valve shut before entering port.

It was about two weeks before the radio stations stopped reporting on it. Fortunately the oil spill was contained and no beaches were contaminated.

I had another experience which I am convinced, but can't prove, affected the entire Navy.

Most of the men who fell overboard on destroyers and smaller ships were usually young mess cooks. These are the newer sailors who work in the mess halls. They help the cooks, but are not actually cooks.

One of their jobs is to dump the garbage over the side while cleaning up the galley. They would carry these heavy loads out on the main deck and walk aft (toward the back of the ship).

Being low in the water, destroyers always hit waves that keep their decks awash. Frequently these waves come aboard with enough force to knock an unsuspecting young man off his feet. If it is dark and the deck is wet, one of those waves can wash him overboard in just seconds.

Worse yet, being always in a hurry, young mess cooks often lean over the side or the stern to dump the garbage clear of the ship. In doing so they expose themselves to these boarding waves. No matter our warnings, we had many scares. And while I didn't have any men go overboard, other ships did.

In an effort to eliminate this particular man overboard risk, I wrote letters to three companies that manufactured garbage grinders.

If they would give me one of their large garbage grinders, I would install and test it on my ship. If it worked out as I thought it would, I would then make a recommendation to my force commander (Commander Destroyers Atlantic Fleet) that all destroyers have one installed. And perhaps his firm could be the supplier.

One company responded affirmatively and in a short while there was a large garbage grinder on the pier ready for my men to install.

The installation required that we cut a hole in the side of the ship out of which we could discharge the ground up garbage. And, if we were to do it, the hole had to be near the water line.

I told my engineers to go ahead and shift all our water and fuel over to the port side so the ship would lean over enough to cut the hole at the appropriate spot.

They completed shifting the liquids and with the ship leaning quite far over to port, they were getting ready to cut the hole for a discharge pipe. Just then a senior engineer from the admiral's staff walked by and asked what we were doing.

He ordered them to stop and came aboard to see me.

"Captain," he said, "there's no way you can do that. Only the Bureau of Ships can authorize cutting a hole in the side of your ship. You are asking for a lot of real trouble."

I told him why I was doing it and he sympathized with my problem. Nevertheless, he said I should not proceed without the Bureau's permission, even though that might take forever. I thanked him and reluctantly told my men to stop. I wasn't about to cross the Bureau of Ships, especially when a senior engineer on the admiral's staff had cautioned me.

We boxed up the grinder and returned it, with thanks, to the company.

I then sent a letter up through the chain of command recommending, that for safety reasons, the possibility of installing garbage grinders be investigated.

I was never told that my letter started the ball rolling, but the ball did start rolling and it wasn't long before every ship in the Navy had a garbage grinder.

Probably the worst experience for the *Dickson* occurred when I was in Chicago on leave. In fact, I was at the Oak Street

13. This One's Greek

beach on a date with Georgette (my future and current wife) when a newspaper blew near us. I picked it up and read that Hurricane Carol had hit Newport, Rhode Island, causing massive damage. I got to a phone as quickly as I could but all the lines were down. That ended my vacation and I returned to Newport as fast as I could.

I couldn't believe what I saw. The large parking lot in front of the pier where I had left my ship was a mass of jumbled cars, some turned over, some on top of each other, one laying on top of a lamp post it had struck.

I also saw that four destroyers were still nested alongside the large destroyer maintenance ship USS *Yellowstone*. Mine was the furthest out, just where I had left it. But I immediately noticed that both anchors were missing.

Everything was quiet as I made my way across the three inboard destroyers. I could tell that something had happened. Everything was just too quiet. When I got aboard the *Dickson* and was greeted by my quarterdeck watch, I asked the sailor. "How did things go?"

"Not so good, Captain."

Just then my exec, Lieutenant Commander John Lovell, who I had left in charge, came up to me. "Sure glad to see you Captain," he said as we walked to the wardroom. Once inside he opened up.

"Captain, it was terrible, really terrible. We got about four hours warning that the hurricane would hit here. We put out more lines and some extra wire lines forward and aft.

"At the time, as you know, our boilers were down and we had absolutely no power of our own. We were working like hell to get them back together when, all of a sudden, our lighting system went black. Our guys found themselves trying to put the boilers together with flashlights!

"In preparing for the hurricane the *Yellowstone* people had killed all the electrical power they were supplying to the destroyers. And we couldn't get them to keep it on for even a little while.

"When the wind hit we were still without power," Lovell continued. "They had sent a tug over to help us. And for a while he did. He put his bow on our outboard (starboard) side and kept pushing us and the whole nest toward the *Yellowstone*. All the lines including a two inch wire we put from the bow to the pier took a heavy strain. We were holding with a very heavy strain on all the lines when the tug captain told us he had to leave. Water was coming up over his stern and into his engine room. He had to leave or it would be flooded.

"Right after he left, all the lines took a really heavy strain and suddenly the extra bow wire we put on parted. And the bow swung out. Then as the wind got between us and the other ships all the lines, one by one, parted and we were blown out into the bay. All this with absolutely no power and the engineers down below working like hell with flashlights trying to get the engines going.

"One after the other, as we were being blown into the bay, I dropped both anchors but there was no way we could stop off the chains and both anchor chains ran all the way out and we lost them.

"The ship was drifting helplessly up the bay. We even passed a house with some people on the roof and a destroyer escort trying to get them off. The wind was still blowing like hell when a tug came alongside and managed to control us a little bit. Thank God the engineers finally got some power and I could use the main engines.

"We stayed in the bay with the tug until the wind abated and then came back to the nest. If the *Yellowstone* had not killed the electrical power when they did we could have gotten the engines together in time to have some power. And it might not have been so bad."

Lovell sounded close to hysterical as he explained all this. He ended by saying, "Captain I have to transfer out of this ocean. I simply can not stay on a ship in the Atlantic. I have to get to the Pacific."

John was a big guy, over six feet tall and a good 200 pounds,

13. This One's Greek

but with tears in his eyes he appeared to be a nervous wreck. I tried to placate him and finally told him I would see what I could do about getting him to the Pacific.

There is no doubt about it. Whether it was John's leadership, or just good luck, the *Dickson* avoided disaster.

Later, after the Admiral sent for me and got my side of the situation, he agreed that the *Yellowstone* people contributed to the *Dickson*'s problems and took no further action. Luckily, no part of the ship was damaged and none of my people were injured.

The next day I got underway and retrieved my anchors. Although the biggest losses were the damage to many of the cars belonging to my crew, I could tell from their demeanor they considered themselves fortunate. It could have been a lot worse for everyone.

As for Lovell, he got his transfer to a destroyer in the Pacific fleet. I had to agree with him on one point. The Atlantic is not the place for a fair weather sailor. The *Dickson* went through two more hurricanes before my tour was up and I was transferred to the Service Schools Command at Great Lakes, Illinois in June 1956. They were Hurricanes Edna on August 25, and Hazel on October 5, 1954. They were category 3 and category 4 hurricanes (winds in excess of 115 miles an hour). Luckily, both curved eastward before overtaking my ship. And while we experienced some really rough riding, it was never as bad as the fury of Lovell's Hurricane Carol.

I personally got nervous during the month of September (hurricane season) whenever I was attached to a ship in the Atlantic fleet. The primary source of that nervousness was our inability to predict the track of the hurricanes in sufficient time to avoid them. Most of the hurricanes form in the Caribbean and work their way toward the U.S. eastern seaboard, where they may or may not curve north or northeast. If your ship happens to be in the coastal area north of the hurricane, you simply can't be sure of an avoidance course.

John Lovell's transfer to the Pacific did not, by any means, guarantee him fair weather sailing.

For example, on December 17th, 1944, Admiral William Halsey's powerful Task Force 38, consisting of 7 carriers, 15 cruisers, 8 battleships, and about 50 destroyers was virtually put out of action by Typhoon Cobra. The force was 300 miles east of Luzon in the Philippines and starting to refuel when, as a result of bad weather forecasting, they collided with the 100-120 mile per hour winds and high seas of the typhoon. Three destroyers were sunk, ten other ships were damaged and 780 men were lost.

The Pacific does have a reputation as a fair weather ocean among most sailors, but it also has its share of heavy storms and deadly typhoons. While I did have substantial sea time in the Pacific I was fortunate enough to stay clear of its typhoons.

Figure 198: **Recruits at Great Lakes.** Great Lakes opened in 1911 just north of Chicago, training about 2000 recruits a year. During World War I, about the time this photograph was taken, it trained 125,000 sailors. This formation exceeds 10,000 recruits.

Chapter 14

Self Discipline – Navy Style

"Ready for preliminary mast, commander?" It was Jim Broffman, our legal officer, who had stuck his head in the door of my office.

"Yes, Jim," I answered. "How many are there?"

"One hundred and sixty men, sir."

"What! Are you kidding me?"

"No sir. That's the right number. They are all AWOLs (absent without leave)."

It was the first Monday morning after I had assumed the job as executive officer at the Service Schools Command, in Great Lakes, Illinois (near Chicago). We had about 5000 students in 8 different schools. Every weekend they would go on liberty with orders to be in class by 0800 the following Monday morning. If they didn't show up on time they were placed on report, which meant they would have to appear before captain's mast.

Considering that about two-thirds of our students take a train, some other transportation, or hitch hike into Chicago about 60 miles away, a reasonable view might be to forgive the three percent returning late. But the Navy, especially in the training segment, doesn't see it that way. Even one AWOL is bad news.

The officer I relieved had not briefed me on how he handled the discipline for such a large number. Taking 160 men (most of

14. SELF DISCIPLINE – NAVY STYLE

them petty officers – we were not training recruits) to captain's mast was something I did not want to do. It would be a very serious career damaging problem for each one and would probably consume the Captain's entire day.

I didn't have a lot of time to think through what I would do. Jim told me my predecessor would reduce the numbers to about 10 of the most serious offenses (over 8 hours or more late) and issue warnings to the remainder which did not go in their records.

I didn't like that way of handling it, but I also knew I was not taking that large a group before the captain.

I told Jim that we would not take them to captain's mast and that there would be no legal consequences for them. However, each one of the men who did not have a valid excuse would be required to attend a two day educational program on self discipline the following weekend.

I personally delivered this message to the group. I believe most of them realized that they were getting a break even though it meant attending the special course would cost them the next weekend liberty.

What I didn't appreciate was that even though my actions helped those men retain a clean record, some of them perceived my actions as punishment.

"You are risking criticism for taking actions that you have no authority to take," cautioned Broffman. I saw his point. While I believed that my job was to teach a level of self discipline, I listened to Jim.

"OK, what do I have to do to make these weekend classes on self discipline legal?"

He thought a while and said, "Develop a formal curriculum and get it approved by the training wheels in Washington." So that's what I did.

We had two experienced reserve officers on active duty with us who were juvenile court officials in their civilian careers at the state prison in Joliet, Illinois.

I called them in, explained my problem and proposed solution, and asked if they could develop a two day course on self discipline that would be forwarded to higher authorities for approval. They both agreed not only that they could do it, but they thought it was a good idea and would undertake the task with enthusiasm.

About two month later we forwarded the proposed course to Washington. And a month after that we had approval of both the course and its weekend scheduling.

The results were impressive.

Everyone who was AWOL, without an excusable reason, was required to attend the course and pass an examination on its contents. If they failed, they had to repeat the course the following weekend.

I am proud to admit that the results solved my problem. Our unexcused AWOLs dropped to almost zero.

Coincidently, the Navy had just introduced a chaplain-sponsored character guidance program for all training commands, including ours. It didn't bother me that they took credit for the drop in our AWOLs. I was just happy not to have 160 plus offenses every Monday.

Discipline in this job, however, was the least of my concerns. Our schools were all in the advanced category and the sailors we received were all rather high caliber.

We had one unusual educational challenge caused by the Navy's increasing use of technology. Specifically, we had about four hundred boatswain mates in one of our schools who, upon completing a 10 month course, would change their rate to electronic technician.

Converting to a technology-intensive rating such as electronic technician was not an easy task. I was amazed at the way most of them adapted to the new skills. But no matter their efforts, a sizable number of these dedicated, top notch, self-taught seamen just couldn't learn the intricacies of their new profession, and there were failures. It was tough to witness the dejection of these mature sailors who tried but failed to change.

The reader might ask, "If they were top notch sailors why couldn't they adapt?"

14. Self Discipline – Navy Style

That is a reasonable question, but an appreciation of the answer requires an understanding of the rugged life of a hard working boatswain mate. At sea on a destroyer or smaller-size ship, a captain depends on his boatswain mates to handle ship-wide security and non-engineering crises. And in small ships that go to sea, sooner or later there is always a crisis. It may be during a storm (perhaps a hurricane) or another life or death type of emergency that requires a combination of skill, courage, and leadership in the face of real danger. This is where the boatswain mate stands out. They were not only the undisputed enlisted leaders aboard ship, they helped immeasurably in establishing the character and morale of their ship.

I became involved in the provision of special tutoring and repeating of courses, which helped somewhat. But I thought it was the hard way to achieve the objective. I became convinced that the Navy needed to improve its long range planning to match personnel skills with ship-board requirements. As for the men who could not make the transition, we worked with them to provide assignments acceptable to them.

The ET (Electronic Technician) school was our largest, but by no means was it the most difficult. The courses in all schools were developed and maintained current by professional educators. The latter was no easy task since the Navy was constantly introducing new machinery of all types into the fleet. Graduates were expected to be qualified to handle all these capabilities.

I enjoyed this job a great deal. Our schools were probably the best vocational schools in the country and a great challenge. I often wished I could have attended several of the schools myself, especially the ET school. Our instructors were among the best qualified men in their field.

Another incident helped in the feel-good department.

My sister Virginia, who lived with her husband and four children in the Chicago suburb of Wilmette, introduced me to Georgette, a really pretty girl, when I was home on leave from my destroyer a few years earlier, in 1954.

I was lucky. Or perhaps Virginia really knew what she was

doing. She insisted, not in words but in deeds, that Georgette was the girl for me. Although she knew a lot of girls, she refused for three years to get me dates or introduce me to any other girls. In her eyes it was Georgette! And she was right! As I write this, Georgette and I have been married for more than 60 wonderfully happy years.

Georgette and I were married in Chicago on January 12, 1957. For those who have never witnessed a Greek marriage ceremony, it has a few interesting traditions that are worth mentioning.

Initially Georgette and I wanted to be married in the chapel at Great Lakes. However, Father Karras, one of the few Greek Orthodox chaplains in the Navy, who was stationed there, told us we had to be married in Georgette's parish, the Saint Andrew's Greek Church in the north side of Chicago.

That was OK with us but the big surprise was when we stood before the priest. He never asked us the traditional questions you see in the movies. I was never asked, "Do you take Georgette for your lawfully wedded wife?" And Georgette was never asked if she wanted me for a husband. I guess they assumed we did or we wouldn't be standing there. As the ceremony continued neither Georgette nor I knew when we were actually married. Father Karras was standing nearby and as Georgette and I, led by the priest, walked in a circle with small white ribbon connected crowns on our heads, I kept asking Father Karras, "Are we married yet?"

Only when he nodded and said, "Yes, George, you are married," did we know we were man and wife. There was no formal "You are now man and wife" announcement as seen in traditional marriages. I have to admit it was a really memorable and beautiful way to get married.

That June we left for Newport, Rhode Island and the Naval War College where I would be a student for one year.

W-128	SHEPARD,A.B.JR.,LCDR,USN		306	SWOPE,F.A.,LCOL,USA
W-260	SHEPPARD,C.W.,LCDR,USN		W-243	TAYLOR,L.S.,CDR,USN
E-114	SHINNEMAN,J.R.,CDR,USN		137	TAYLOR,L.T.,CAPT,USN
302	SIEGEL,P.J.,CDR,USN		164	THOMAS,J.M.,CDR,USN
E-227	SIMONS,J.T.,LT,USN		261	TITUS,J.C.,CAPT,USN
E-305	SIRIGAYA,A.,CAPT,THAILAND		125	TOLIVAISA,H.,CDR,USN
154	SKUZINSKI,C.F.,CDR,USN		142	TOUART,R.G.,CAPT,USN
W-254	SLASINSKI,F.M.,LCDR,USN		005	TRUM,H.J.,CDR,USN
001	SMALL,W.L.,CAPT,USN		104	TURNER,G.B.,PROF.
110	SMITH,C.E.,CDR,USN		W-241	TURNER,H.J.JR.,LCOL,USA
007	SMITH,C.H.,CDR,USN		259	TYSON,J.K.,PROF.
320	SMITH,W.C.,CDR,USN		323	VAIL,P.P.JR.,CDR,USN
004	SOTOS,G.P.,CDR,USN		137	VALIANTE,L.F.,LCOL,USA

Figure 204: **US Naval War College.** An exciting thing about the War College was the knowledge that it was a major crossroads for people who go on to do big things in the Navy. An excerpt from our class roster exemplifies this, with its inclusion of Alan Shepard, whom I didn't get to know. He would be selected as an astronaut the next year and become the first American in space three years later, in 1961.

Chapter 15

War College

It was at the Naval War College where I became immersed in subjects at the national and international level.

Before arriving at the college, my duties were primarily as the captain or executive officer of a ship. In those jobs I spent almost all of my time making sure the capabilities of each ship's departments were not only first rate, but were effectively integrated.

Most ships have an engineering, gunnery, deck, and operations department. In many ways each of these is independent. For example, the gunnery officer is responsible for all the ordnance, ammunition, ammunition storage spaces, and the upkeep and readiness of the guns. This a huge responsibility and his department has a dedicated number of trained officers and sailors whose primary duty is maintaining the readiness of their department.

The same is true of all the other departments. Each has specific responsibilities and dedicated personnel to carry out those responsibilities.

It is the captain's job to make sure all his departments are managed efficiently and ready as an integrated unit for combat at any time.

Running a ship leaves little or no time for study and acquiring knowledge about the larger national strategies which dictate how and when the ships are employed. It is institutions like

15. WAR COLLEGE

the Naval War College where up and coming senior officers are taught to think about the Navy's role in achieving national objectives.

To develop strategic and operational leaders, the U.S. Naval War College, since its inception in 1884, has produced more than 50,000 U.S. and allied foreign graduates. About 10% of the foreign alumni, from 137 different countries, have become chief of their country's navy. More than 300 of current U.S. flag officers and senior civil servants are alumni as well.

During the ten month course, among other tasks, we were required to do the research and write papers on national strategy and the achievement of national objectives. To help steer us toward our objectives, lectures and seminars that included national leaders, like the Secretary of State, were scheduled. An interesting and challenging aspect of most of those lectures was the opportunity to ask questions and receive candid answers from some of the nation's top leaders. Our papers, which were reviewed and evaluated by three faculty members, were the major challenges of our program.

One reviewer noted that my first paper had 234 erasures. But he begrudgingly admitted that I demonstrated knowledge of the subject.

What that reviewer didn't know was that my wife Georgette, who normally typed my papers, was pregnant with our first child and in no shape to do the burdensome typing. This was long before the introduction of computers. My hunt and peck typing did indeed provoke 234 erasures.

I did well enough on two of my papers to have them forwarded to the Navy Department in Washington for information and further review. Of course I was pleased with myself. But subsequent reviews poured cold water on my ideas.

Strangely enough, one of those ideas, directed toward improving the Navy's effectiveness in anti-submarine warfare (ASW), I think still has merit today. So, I am taking the liberty of repeating it briefly here.

In WW II, the greatest problem in the Atlantic Ocean was locating the enemy U-boats before they could do their dirty work. This "locate and destroy" problem would still be a major worry if war started tomorrow against a nation with many submarines – such as Russia or China. Even today this remains a serious concern.[1]

My 1957 suggestion was that eight LSDs (see chapters 4 and 5), each carrying six midget submarines be employed as hunter-killer groups in the Atlantic. Four of each LSD's midget submarines would be maintained in the water at all times, spaced to form an around-the-clock sonar barrier. The length of the barrier would be determined by sonar conditions and the listening-detection reach of each midget.

The four midgets in the water would establish a 90-to-100 mile or even greater passive (listening) barrier to detect and report transiting enemy submarines, whether submerged or surfaced.

Helicopters aboard the LSD would refuel, replenish food, and replace personnel aboard the midget subs, enabling them to remain on station for months at a time, returning to the LSD only for routine or emergency maintenance.

The LSD itself would have sonar equipment and underwater weapons and would be protected by five destroyer escorts as in the highly successful WWII hunter-killer groups.

In addition to its built-in listening equipment, each midget could tow a field of listening devices.[2] In lieu of the towed hydrophone fields, the midget could make good use of wireless sonobuoys. These are 2-foot portable underwater listen/transmission devices that can send what they hear to orbiting aircraft or nearby surface units, as was done in WWII. Also, with the LSD's transport capability, the bigger and heavier underwater listening devices used to protect the entrance to U.S. harbors could, with sea anchors, augment the midget's cover-

---

[1] Rear Admiral W.J. Holland Jr. "Submarines: Key to the Offset Strategy." *U.S. Naval Institute Proceedings.* June 2015.

[2] The range of such devices varies considerably, and depends on several environmental factors including water temperature and salinity.

15. WAR COLLEGE

age. For example, the entrance to Pearl Harbor was protected by huge buoys whose suspended listening devices provided a much greater range than the small sonobuoys dropped by aircraft.

Used as static or movable underwater barriers, the midgets along with the many other ASW tools, such as radio frequency detection, radar, sono-buoy fields, long range underwater listening systems, satellite coverage, and long range air patrols, the enemy submarine threat can be quickly controlled.

"The Navy does not have any operational midget submarines," was one of main comments when the idea was turned down. But today they are available. The Navy is also researching the development of midget submarine drones.[3] Even narcotic smugglers are using midget submarines.

An important reason for considering them today would be their contribution to minimizing the hiding places of enemy ballistic missile launching submarines. The latter is our most critical defense problem.

Another key part of my 10 month long course at the College was the realistic and very serious annual war game. The dirty business of killing the enemy had again thrust its head into my consciousness... but this time I was on the other side.

The war game pitted the Soviet Union (purple) against the United States (blue). As chief of staff for the purple long range transportation directorate, I was also a member of the council that made the major purple war decisions.

In the first phase of the war game, we (purple) gained a significant advantage over the blue forces. However, some members of our purple council were concerned that blue's retreat was a ruse to lead our forces into a trap. There was merit to their concern, since blue had not yet committed all their forces to the

---

[3]In late 2016 newspapers reported that the U.S. Navy is testing small, potent, drone submarine systems that can hunt enemy submarines and much more. I was about 59 years too early! [Christian Davenport. "The new frontier for drone warfare: under the oceans." Washington *Post.* Nov. 25, 2016, page A16.]

Figure 209: **War game in the electronic era.** A war game in progress at the Naval War College, 1958, in the newly installed Navy Electronic Warfare Simulator.

fighting. Also, our intelligence had reported ominous increases in activity within blue's nuclear forces.

As we discussed the available options, several council members expressed apprehensions about the artificial, self-imposed barrier against using nuclear weapons.

Blue losses were greater than ours and there was no immediate indications that the rate of those losses would change.

Putting ourselves in the shoes of the blue leaders, we concluded there was a probability they would reverse their losing position by immediate use of nuclear weapons. Their use of the atom bombs in WW II against Japan was clearly a precedent that would make such a decision easier.

15. War College

After much discussion, the council agreed unanimously that we had no choice but to pre-empt blue by immediately launching an all out attack with nuclear weapons.

And that is what we did! As far as I can recall blue did not launch any nuclear weapons. Our unexpected nuclear attack demolished them and the war game ended abruptly.

I'm not sure, but I had the impression that our class was the first to employ nuclear weapons in the school's war game. I believe that possibility had not been designed into the game. It was a shocking result because it implied that the use of nuclear weapons was inevitable in any armed conflict between the USSR and the U.S., even if the USSR was winning at that point.

We had been told the results would be communicated to senior officers in Washington, but, considering our unexpected actions, I wonder if that was done. I have also often wondered how subsequent classes and the college itself handled the use of nuclear weapons in the annual war game. There can be little argument that policies on the use of nuclear weapons are the most troubling and serious problems facing our military.

The war game, intense as it was, comprised just one part of our program.

To our surprise, the Soviets introduced a subject, not only for me and my fellow students, but for the whole world!

On October 4, 1957, the Soviet Union surprised the world by launching the first unmanned satellite into an easily viewable 96.2 minute orbit around earth. Our small group of War College students was very quiet as we stood and watched this small light move across the dark sky.

There was no cheerful "star-like" sparkle to this light, and there was no confusing it with the stars. A simple and steady light with a deliberate straight movement, it stood out in the dark night against a background of stars.

For us it was much more than that. We could feel the symbolism of military power projected by that light.

All in all, my War College experience was terrific. We were completely independent in almost all our studies. We were simply told what was to be done and we did it. I understand the college has changed considerably and is much more regimented today.

When school ended I received orders to be the U.S. Naval Attaché in London.

"Wow! What a wonderful job," I shouted to Georgette as I burst into our home.

But that glow disappeared quickly when a member of my class confessed that he had written the orders as a joke.

My friends all had a good laugh but I had the last laugh when my real orders came through. They were to Hawaii, where I would be the commander of nine destroyer escorts operating on the distant early warning barrier in the middle of the Pacific Ocean.

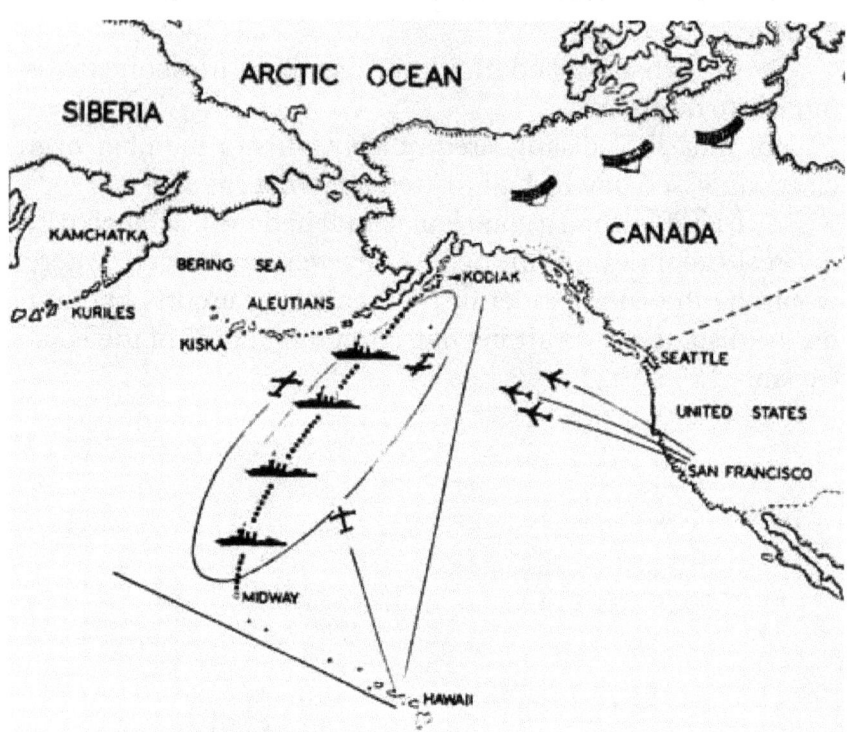

Figure 212: **Pacific Barrier segment of the DEW Line.** The Distant Early Warning (DEW) Line consisted of land, air, and sea radar stations that watched for missiles inbound from the Soviet Union. This chart shows the portion of the Pacific Barrier manned by my nine Destroyer Escort Radar (DER) ships, based out of Hawaii. Land-based radar stations in northern Canada and Alaska could detect missiles coming over the North Pole.

Chapter 16

The Pacific DEW Line

"Commodore, is that you?"

"Yes, I answered sleepily. Who is this?"

"Sir, this is Lieutenant Piccion, Squadron duty officer. I think you better come down here right away. There's been a death aboard the USS *Sturtevant* and the police are all over the place."

I looked at my watch. It was 2 a.m.

"I'll be there in a half hour," I said as I hung up and started dressing.

"Where you going?" asked Georgette sleepily.

"We've got a serious problem on one of my ships. I'll call you later."

This was the first time in the almost six months of my command of Escort Squadron Five that I was called during the night. I didn't have to be told it was serious. A death on a U.S. Naval ship is really bad news.

I arrived at the destroyer pier in Pearl Harbor at about 2:30 a.m. There were three police cars with their emergency lights, still flashing, parked on the pier alongside the *Sturtevant*.

Lt. Piccion met me and wasted no time filling me in.

"Three sailors in the black gang (engine room personnel) were drinking down in the engine room when they got sick. Apparently they thought they were drinking Coca-Cola and ethyl alcohol but it turned out to be methyl. Looks like it killed one

16. THE PACIFIC DEW LINE

man and two others are in bad shape. They've all been taken to the hospital."

I went aboard the ship and talked to the captain (Lieutenant Commander Roger Thelon USN). He had arrived about 15 minutes before I did and didn't really know any of the details. He was distraught as hell. He knew the men and spoke highly of them, saying he had no idea why they would be drinking aboard ship.

The naval investigative service (NIS) took over the case and for the next few days I didn't hear anything except that they were questioning a lot of people on the ship.

Three days after the incident I was visited by a Captain Harmon of the NIS. He didn't waste any time.

"Commodore I want you to order Captain Thelon to take a lie detector test."

"What?"

"We have administered lie detector tests to many of the people on his ship and now it is his turn."

I was both shocked and surprised. The captain of a naval ship in my eyes was beyond even being considered for a lie detector test. "Do you have good reasons to ask him to take the test?"

"I am not going to discuss any part of the case with you. He has refused to take the test and I am asking you as his immediate superior to order him to take it."

I wasn't used to being talked to like that, which made it easier for me to tell him, "Sorry I can't do that."

"Why not? You're his boss, and it is a legitimate order."

"No, I don't think so. I am not going to argue with you. I'm just telling you that I take anything he tells me as the truth and a lie detector order from me is out of the question."

"You realize this is a very serious case and your attitude is certainly not one of cooperation."

"Sorry sir, I am not about to order any of my captains to take a lie detector test."

"O.K. We'll see about that."

He got up and left.

Of course I wasn't as confident as I sounded. I just intuitively felt that it would be very wrong to order the captain of any naval ship to take a lie detector test. But I also knew that this might be different. It was my first time working with the NIS in this manner.

As soon as he left I got up and went to my flotilla commander's office. I explained what I had done and told him to expect a visit from the NIS. "George, you did the right thing. Thanks for letting me know. Why do you think he wants the captain to take a test?"

"I don't really know. But I have an idea that it might be connected to Captain Thelon's drinking habits. He likes his scotch and has a reputation for opening the medicinal locker for his crew after bad weather."

I paused, adding, "But he runs a fine ship and does his job."

"O.K., George, I'll handle it if he contacts me."

I didn't hear anything for a day or so. I knew the NIS was having a hard time figuring out what happened and I expected another visit from them.

Suddenly it was all over.

A young fireman told his chief that it was he, who, at the order of his senior petty officer, brought the drinks to the three men who were injured. He went to the alcohol locker, as he had done a number of times before, poured some of the alcohol into half filled cups of Coca-Cola and brought them to the three men. It wasn't the first time he had performed that service for his bosses. He wasn't on watch at the time and that's why no one connected him to the incident.

When the men became paralyzed and one died, he was too scared to tell anyone what had happened. But, as the investigation grew larger and larger, he got scared and decided to tell his chief.

While that explained part of the incident, there was still a mystery connected to it: who switched the alcohol from the drinkable ethyl to the poisonous methyl alcohol?

16. THE PACIFIC DEW LINE

Here again I thought the NIS was looking for a murderer. I was never privy to the final resolution of the investigation, but I believe that a similarity in the stock numbers contributed to the switch, and that eventually the case was closed without holding anyone responsible for what happened to the three sailors. A very unfortunate series of events, but one where the injured sailors were major contributors to their own injuries.

That incident was the worse experience I had in my job as commander of Escort Squadron Five.

There were nine ships in my squadron. Each one was a former WWII destroyer escort that had been converted to an advanced radar platform. The conversion was significant enough to warrant a change in the ships' official description from Destroyer Escort to Destroyer Escort Radar Picket (DER). Together with the Lockheed Super Constellation "Warning Stars" from the Navy's Airborne Warning Barrier Squadron, Pacific, the DER mission was to man the North Pacific portion of the Distant Early Warning (DEW) Line.

With DERs evenly spaced between the Aleutian Islands and Midway Island and the aircraft flying above the ships, we established a radar sea and air barrier which detected any Soviet activity. In addition, the DERs provided a limited anti-submarine coverage, navigational check points, and Search and Rescue assistance in the event an aircraft had to ditch.

We also performed a night ditching drill with the aircraft. The DER would release a long, narrow oil streak about the length of a runway. At intervals along the edge of the water runway, it would drop floating guide lights. Then the DER would post itself at the end of the runway and turn on its yardarm lights to give the pilot a horizon reference. The pilot would make an approach, coming in low much as he would during a normal landing at an airport. To see, hear, and help guide these huge aircraft down to just a few feet above the water and fly the length of the oil strip before climbing was a thrilling experience, especially at night. The DERs were also equipped to use this procedure with commercial aircraft that might be in trouble and require a water landing. I don't think the Navy or even commercial planes have this procedure in their emergency plans any more.

I commanded one squadron and Commander Dave King, a friend, the other. We were each required to keep 6 ships on station across the Pacific day and night. As best I can recall we did just that, never having a hole in our surface barrier.

One of our biggest problems was keeping the advanced air-search radars in peak operating condition. Even though we had priority access to spare parts, maintaining around-the-clock-operation was not easy. It was not unusual to swap parts between ships to keep those on the DEW line operational.

Each patrol was about a month long. During that month the ship would leave Pearl Harbor, and proceed in 3 to 5 days to its barrier station. Once there, to save fuel, it would just steam in a slow, 5 knot circle on one propellor. Except for the bridge and combat information center people searching for targets, it was very boring duty.

One captain proposed a test to determine sonar conditions along the mid Pacific barrier line. He wanted to see if adjacent ships in the barrier would hear depth charge explosions from his position about 300 miles away.

I thought it was a good idea. While we know pretty well how our sonar machines behave in the open ocean, there is a great deal we do not know about sound ducts. Sound ducts are certain regions of the ocean formed by temperature gradients, salinity, pressure, and other factors that permit sound to travel much further than we normally experience with our ships' sonar.

For example, even though we knew about such phenomena during WWII, we could not find and use such ducts to help us in our hunt for German U-boats.

An even more interesting example of such ducting is a wide sound channel at the bottom of the ocean. Once sound gets in this channel, it can travel clear across the ocean. Scientists, using hydrophones, have recorded a wide range of noise in this channel, including the sound of ship propellors and the singing of whales.

16. The Pacific DEW Line

I approved the captain's request to make the test, but it was stopped by higher authority. They were concerned that during the test we might inadvertently drop depth charges near a Soviet submarine and start something serious.

One day an unusual letter, addressed to the head of the bureau of supplies and accounts (responsible for provisioning our ships) came across my desk. Accompanied by a drawing, the captain of one of my ships was reporting the existence of a four headed chicken. Apparently his ship's cooks had analyzed the chicken parts sent to the ship and concluded that the number of chicken necks were far in excess of the number expected from normal chickens.

I forwarded his unique complaint with a routine endorsement that the phenomena was worth an examination.

We never received an official response. However, that ship never received another four headed chicken.

Given our type of operations, it was difficult to get the ships together for any squadron exercises or training. All of them took advantage of the time they had on the barrier to conduct operational exercises and encourage their people to study for advancement.

It was a real challenge for the captains to keep morale at a high level, and I did all I could to encourage them in that effort. Fortunately, except for that one fatal incident mentioned earlier, my captains did a fine job.

Operating out of Pearl Harbor was a lot different than out of an East coast port like Newport, Rhode Island, homeport of my destroyer in 1954. (Figure 220.) At Pearl Harbor we shared the harbor with huge carriers, cruisers, numerous destroyers, submarines, and supply ships. It was stimulating to be there and appreciate the size and power of the U.S. Navy.

But I was also reminded of the cost of failed leadership. Every day as I looked across the harbor I saw, protruding above the surface of the water, the skeletonized superstructure of the once powerful battleship USS *Arizona*. With her keel still sitting on the bottom of the harbor, I couldn't avoid thinking about the December 7, 1941 Japanese surprise attack on Pearl Harbor and the bombers that sank her. I often asked myself how eleven hundred and two sailors and Marines, still trapped inside the huge battleship, could be lost when a ship sinks in only 40 feet of water. The consensus today is that an explosion in the forward ammunition magazine trapped the men below decks and they couldn't get out as she settled to the bottom.

On the nearby battleship USS *West Virginia* a number of men trapped in the sunken hull survived for 16 days. During that time they tapped on the hull and people outside heard but could do nothing to extricate them. When the bodies were removed some months later a large calendar on which the men had marked the 16 days they survived was found with them[1] – a gruesome story and one which will probably be duplicated on the *Arizona* when the bodies are eventually removed.

The attack on Pearl Harbor was a complete surprise. So, why do I write that the casualties resulted from failed leadership?

The answer, one that I could never have written had I not experienced WWII, is simple and straightforward. No matter any extenuating circumstances, the readiness of his force is a leader's sole and absolute responsibility. It cannot be diluted. It cannot be explained away. Had the naval forces in Pearl Harbor been ready, the outcome would have been far different.

Being a DER squadron commander was an excellent job, primarily because all the captains that were sent to command my ships were outstanding officers. In fact two of them went on to become admirals. One, Lieutenant Commander Sam Gravely, captain of the USS *Falgout*, happened to be an African-American officer. I didn't know it at the time, but it was a historic event for the Navy. He was the first black officer to command a combat ship in the U S Navy. He did an excellent job and I was happy to see his steady progress in the Navy. He later became a vice admiral and an icon for both the Navy and the African-American community.

---

[1] See bibliography: Gregory.

Figure 220: **A corner of Pearl Harbor, 1959.** The two destroyers at right are DD-528 (Mullany) and DD-566 (Stoddard). The eight front ships at left are destroyers: *Epperson* (DDE-719), *Nicholas* DDE-449), *Renshaw* (DDE-499), *Philip* (DDE-498), *Taylor* (DDE-468), *O'Bannon* (DDE-450), *Jenkins* (DDE-447), and *Walker* (DDE-517). Behind them are seven radar-picket destroyer escorts, including *Newell* (DER-322), *Gary* (DER-326), and *Wilhoite* (DER-397). I had commanded *Gary* in 1946 (see chapter 2) and had operated with *Wilhoite* during World War II. If the US Navy were the same size in 1959 as it is today (just 286 ships), the 17 ships mentioned above would represent 6% of the entire Navy.

Note the empty Hawaiian landscape in the distance. The Boeing 707 jetliner, which entered commercial service about the time of this photograph, soon transformed Hawaii by making it easily accessible from the mainland.

Chapter 17

Carry Out Your Orders

"George," said Hank, "I've got some information for you. But I don't think you are going to like it."

"Can't be worse than this set of orders I have to Kunia," I answered.

It was April 1960, I was finishing my tour of duty as the commander of Escort Squadron Five operating out of Pearl Harbor.

As a senior commander with four sea commands and the War College behind me, I thought I knew my way around the U.S. Navy. But as my assignment to Kunia illustrates, I was dead wrong.

My wake up call appeared in the form of cryptic orders assigning me as the Officer in Charge of Kunia.

Certain that "Kunia" was a new, fast, large ammunition ship about to be commissioned, I was pleased with myself.

The happy glow didn't last very long. I quickly learned that Kunia was a large, underground building that would be the emergency command center for the Commander in Chief Pacific (CINCPAC).

Even though it was located in Hawaii on the island of Oahu, where I was, I could find no one who knew what a "command center" was, especially one for CINCPAC.

While I was trying to sort out the details, Commander Hank Easterling, Chief of Staff for Destroyer Flotilla Five and a good

17. Carry Out Your Orders

friend, came by to visit.

"It's about Kunia," he said.

Of course that caught my interest and I listened carefully,

"I've just returned from San Diego where I visited the chief of staff for all Pacific destroyers, Captain Heinz. We were shooting the breeze in his office when the phone rang. The call was from the captain detailer (the officer in the Pentagon who makes the duty assignments for Navy captains). I heard him mention your name. After he hung up I told him I was a friend of yours and asked if there was any information I could pass on to you.

"Heinz told me, 'Sure, you can tell George that he had been proposed as the chief of staff for our Destroyer Flotilla Two. That's our research and development flotilla here. The Admiral had accepted him and we expected him to receive orders to that effect. That phone call I just had withdrew his name for that job. The captain detailer said that Admiral Felt wanted George as the commander of his new underground command center at Kunia.'

"I told Heinz, 'Wow, that's too bad. I know George would have liked that destroyer job. Can I tell him about this?'

"Heinz said, 'Sure go ahead.'

"And that's it, George. I thought you'd like to know."

I was dumbfounded. Both Hank and I knew that the destroyer flotilla job was one of the best in the Navy and a top rung on the promotion ladder to admiral.

"I think you got screwed somewhere," said Hank, sensing my disappointment.

"Why would the detailer withdraw my name and substitute a two bit job as the commander of an underground building that no one knows anything about?"

"Damn if I know," said Hank. "He did say that Admiral Felt wanted you personally." Felt was probably the #2 admiral in the entire Navy, so that would be a big deal.

"Hell, I know that can't be true. Admiral Felt doesn't know I'm alive."

"Well that's what he told Captain Heinz."

Hank could see I was upset. "I don't blame you for being pissed," he said, "but I think you've had it. It's done with. I didn't think you knew anything about it."

"Thanks, Hank. I'm going to see if I can get to Admiral Felt and find out if he did ask for me personally."

"Good luck," he said as he left my office.

I didn't waste any time. I got in my car and drove directly to Admiral Felt's headquarters.

Instead of getting in to see him I was ushered into the office of his chief of staff for personnel.

I told him the entire story. He was an aviator but he understood the blow it was to my career.

"In answer to your question whether Admiral Felt asked for you by name – he did not. His request was for an officer who had a successful command tour as the skipper of a destroyer, and I guess that's how they got you. He put some pressure on them to get someone here in a hurry. I guess you were the closest candidate."

"Is it OK with you if I call the captain detailer and tell him that you don't especially need me by name – you just want a qualified ex-destroyer skipper?"

He didn't hesitate. "Go ahead and tell him you talked to me and I'll support you."

Feeling a little better I said goodbye and started planning what I would say to the detailer, who was a senior Navy captain named Baumberger. I had my thoughts in line when I called early the next morning.

The detailer didn't waste any time with me after I told him Admiral Felt just wanted an ex-destroyer skipper to run Kunia, and that it didn't have to be me. I also mentioned what Hank Easterling had told me and asked that I be assigned to the destroyer flotilla job. "The orders to Kunia mean an end to my career," I told him with some anger in my voice.

When he heard that he didn't even try to be civil. "Are you trying to tell me how to run my job?"

17. Carry Out Your Orders

"No, I'm not. I'm just trying to get myself out of this assignment and that's something I've never tried to do before."

In a hurried voice he tried to explain why it had to be me. The primary reason for withdrawing my name from the flotilla job was that the present incumbent of that job wanted to stay on for three more months until the end of the school year.

But I had a feeling he really hadn't tried to put me in that coveted job. There were any number of ways of permitting the incumbent to remain until the end of the school year. For example, I could have attended one of several schools before reporting to the flotilla. However, I never got a chance to offer any suggestions. The detailer was angry and I made him angrier by suggesting that I would ask Admiral Cooper to contact him and discuss it.

As noted earlier, I had been the Flag Captain for Admiral Cooper when, as a flotilla commander in the Atlantic, we had deployed with twelve destroyers to the Mediterranean's Sixth Fleet. I had done well as his flagship skipper and, when he left, he told me that if I ever needed him for anything to just ask.

"Are you threatening me?" was the detailer's angry response when I mentioned Admiral Cooper.

"No, I'm not. I just want to be treated fairly," I answered.

His final words were, "Carry out your orders." And he hung up.

I sat there for a while. I knew that if I called Admiral Cooper he would at least look into it and there was a good chance that he could turn it around. But for some reason I didn't call him. Perhaps it was the fact that we had just moved into a brand new, large house right on the edge of the ocean where we could see Diamond Head day and night. It was easily one of the nicest locations and best built homes the Navy had in Hawaii.

After thinking it over I admitted to myself that the captain detailer had a job to do and there was no intent to short change my career. I just happened to be in the wrong place at the wrong time. My proximity to Kunia, my qualification as an ex-destroyer captain, and the pressure to get the job filled probably left Baumburger with little or no room to be responsive to my desires. I concluded that there was nothing personal in the decision and that I should "shut up" and carry out my orders. After talking it over with Georgette, we decided to forget it and stick with the Kunia job, and that's what I did.

The key point here is that I wasn't selected for the Kunia job because I had experience or any specialized training in computers or communications, even though the job required those skills. Destroyer command experience was the priority.

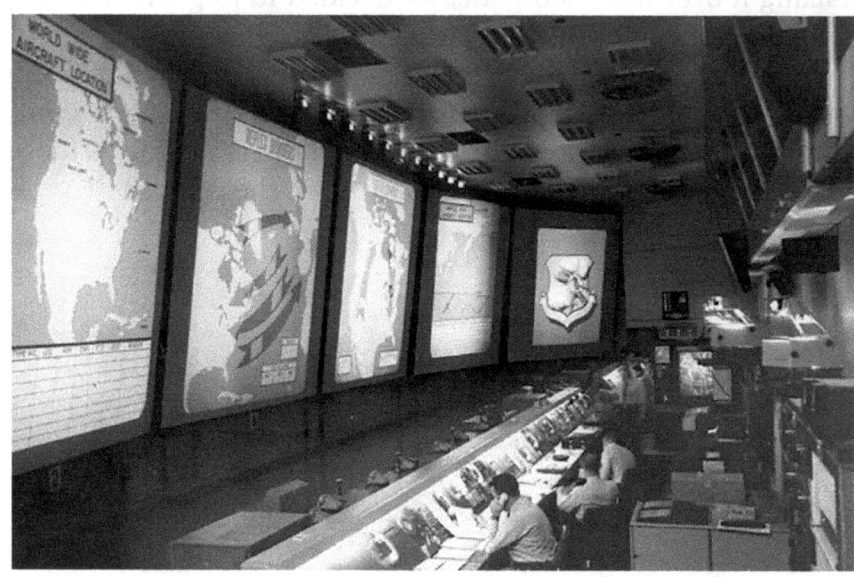

Figure 226: **Desks and displays in SAC war room.** This Strategic Air Command (SAC) war room is far different from the bare bones war rooms we started with at Kunia in 1959. In those pre-computer days, we were lucky to have a teletype, secure telephone, overhead projector, television screen, large chalk board, large presentation board, a few large desks, and an air tube message delivery system. There was no such thing as an on-line computer capability. However, with the help of contractors, the delivery of small and large computers, and an intelligent, curious, imaginative staff of operationally experienced people that quickly learned to program and use compeers for a variety of operational and administrative requirements, our nine war rooms were modernized and operationally productive by the end of 1961.

Chapter 18

Birth of a Command Center

With the decision to remain at Kunia, I set to work trying to understand what my new job really was. And, luckily for me, it turned out to be one of the most interesting and challenging jobs in my career to that point. I say "to that point" because it set me up for some subsequent exciting jobs that I never would otherwise have experienced.

Kunia was the beginning of nine years of work in applying computers and communications to command and control at the very highest levels of the nation.

I didn't realize it, but at that time in the Navy, there were not many planners, operators, or even administrators in the area of command and control of nuclear weapons. I was in at the start of something quite new.

Indeed, Kunia was designed to be the command and control center for all nuclear planning and operations in the Pacific.

The interesting part was the emphasis that Admiral Felt, an aviator, placed on destroyer command experience. There's little doubt that the Kunia commanding officer should have had a high level of technical expertise in communications and computers, none of which I had, nor, I suspect, did any ex-destroyer skipper. This was especially true when it came to knowledge of computers, which were then in their infancy.

Admiral Felt clearly knew what he was doing. He apparently

18. Birth of a Command Center

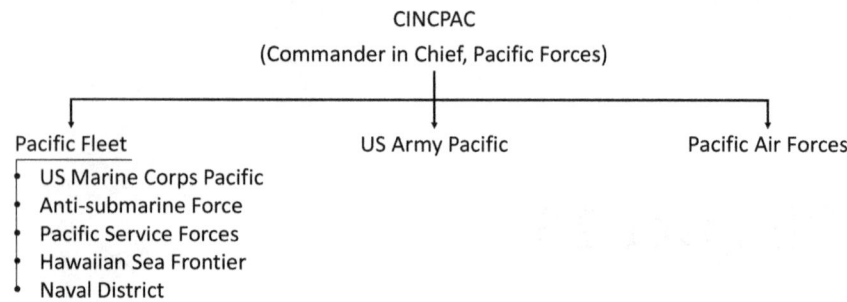

Figure 228: **Organization of Kunia (FOCCPAC) war rooms.** There also were offices representing the Strategic Air Command and a number of different intelligence units, but these did not rise to the level of being "war rooms." "Naval District" is the 14th Naval District.

---

valued the command experience well above technical expertise. It, therefore, should not have been a surprise to anyone why I ran Kunia like a ship.

It didn't take me long to understand what was expected of Kunia and to realize that we were pretty much on our own. To make sure our growing staff and the tenants in our building knew who we were and what we were doing, I spent some time preparing and publicizing to my staff the following mission statement (from page 20):

OUR MISSION IS TO:

1. PROVIDE AND MAINTAIN THE HARDENED KUNIA FACILITY.

2. PROVIDE CONTINUOUS SUPPORT AND ASSISTANCE TO THE WAR ROOMS OF CINCPAC AND TO MAJOR COMMANDERS ON THE ISLAND OF OAHU IN THE EXECUTION OF THEIR COMMAND AND CONTROL OPERATIONS DURING AN ATTACK ON THE U.S. *(The war rooms are listed in Figure 228.)*

3. MAINTAIN INSTANT READINESS OF THE COMPUTER BASED OPERATIONAL DATA SUPPORTING CINPAC'S NUCLEAR WEAPON MISSION IN THE PACIFIC.

4. Maintain and operate, around the clock, a major communications center and relay.

At the same time, I emphasized that we would be very responsive and sensitive to all the requirements of the flag officers and their staff who had war rooms in the Kunia building.

So, in the middle of the Cuban missile crisis in October 1962, when, on my own command authority, I ordered DEFCON 1 in Kunia, it was like going to general quarters on a ship.[1]

In DEFCON 1 everyone was required to remain in the "tunnel," which was our informal name for the underground Kunia facility. During war (DEFCON 1) drills, all war rooms would be manned around the clock. We provided berthing and messing.

But now there was no indication of how long we would all be staying in the tunnel. This, of course, generated a lot of questions, not just among my men, but also among the other services and the civilians who worked in the tunnel.

Why involve the civilians?

Because, as a result of several early fires in the tunnel, I began treating everyone in the tunnel as a member of my command.

The first fire occurred in an Air Force office on the third floor. The workers called the local civil fire department and the trucks roared up to the tunnel entrance. The bewildered Marine guards did not enforce security restrictions. They stood

---

[1] It is important to note that when I ordered DEFCON 1 that order excluded the personnel who were attached to and operated the war rooms in the headquarters of their respective commanders. All of the regular war rooms were located in buildings 5 to 15 miles from Kunia. In worldwide exercises the commanders would practice relocation of their staffs to Kunia. Such a relocation demanded error-free transfer of complex tasks and effective continuity of operations. Relocation of relevant operations was a major task in itself. My role in FOCCPAC was to assist in those efforts in any way that I could, including taking responsibility for significant data handing tasks essential for management and control of nuclear warfare. We spent a great deal of time practicing these tasks even when we were not going through formal drills. So, when I ordered DEFCON 1 in Kunia it affected primarily the entire FOCCPAC staff. But the war rooms were fully aware of our actions.

18. Birth of a Command Center

aside and waved the firefighters into the four-city-block-long entrance tunnel, which led to our top-secret areas.

It turned out to be a wastebasket fire which was extinguished by the time the firemen arrived.

Even before I could organizationally respond to the threat of fires we had another one in the middle of a workday.

Sailors in a highly-classified Navy intelligence space reported the fire. My first lieutenant and a group of men responded, but none of them was permitted inside – they didn't have the requisite clearances! Fortunately, those in the space managed to put out the fire. However, there was a lot of smoke which spread throughout the tunnel and made a lot of people uneasy.

I didn't need any more prodding, especially when I learned that both smoke and heat from an uncontrolled fire in a tunnel can, if not stopped quickly, spread rapidly and lethally. In our case, an unchecked fire could have have been catastrophic.

I raised hell with the intelligence officers for not permitting my people inside to fight the fire. The fire turned out to be in a large bank of batteries we didn't even know they had. The fumes could indeed have been a serious threat to the entire building had the fire not been extinguished quickly.

Without getting permission from anyone, and completely disregarding organizational chains of command, I issued orders that every organization in the tunnel help staff and support permanent fire parties. The fire parties would be scheduled for watches around-the-clock (0800-1600, 1600-2400, 0001-0800). The officer leading each section had the responsibilities to (a) muster his party at the start of each watch, (b) check all equipment, (c) report the readiness of his fire party to the command duty officer, (d) train and qualify each member of his fire party, and (e) schedule realistic drills that challenged his fire party. Each watch was capable of handling any emergency in the tunnel.

Despite some early murmurs of dissent, none of the tenants or other services objected.² I had included a vivid narrative about the dangers of fire in an enclosed tunnel so they all knew the reason for the fire parties. We never had another fire after that.

To make sure the fire parties would not be denied entrance to classified spaces, I requested the appropriate security clearance for myself and designated subordinates, but the response was negative.

I then notified the head of that organization that I was about to issue orders to the Marines to bar them from entering the facility. Very quickly we received the appropriate clearances to enter any space in the building.

No one really had any plans for the operation of this one-of-a-kind, highly secretive command center. The building design reflected a well thought out "joint" operational concept. But I never saw that concept in writing. I inherited a well-designed building and had to implement my own concept of how that building should be used. I had no supervisors watching everything we did. I would report status of completion of different operational areas that I defined. Very few, if any, questions were asked.

We made up our own rules as we went along. When you are doing this type of work for CINCPAC, no one really questions you. By running the center as a flagship for each of the commanders, I had almost unlimited flexibility. Not that we were freewheeling and without responsibilities or accountability. No, just the opposite.

After I made a call on each commander, as instructed by Admiral Felt (page 22), I found that it was easy to communicate and work with the staff of each of those commanders. The personal calls surprised most of them, and I had the feeling that it placed me in a good position for communicating with the top

---

²This does not mean that the 8-hours-on, 16-hours-off schedule was rigidly observed by every command in Kunia. All of them had enough people to cover their operational requirements pretty well on that basis, without excessive duty hours for their personnel.

18. BIRTH OF A COMMAND CENTER

members of each staff. The call I made on General Emmett E. "Rosie" O'Donnell Jr., the colorful and well-known commander of the Pacific Air Forces is worth reporting.

I entered his outer office one morning and explained to his surprised aide who I was and why I was there. Still not sure what to do, the aide went ahead and notified the general, who almost immediately asked me into his office. Of course I was quite nervous, but I was also curious. I had heard from some officers that General O'Donnell and Admiral Felt weren't really very friendly, even though Admiral Felt had been designated the senior officer in command in the Pacific.

The general received me very graciously, offered me a cup of coffee and with a wide grin on his face said, "You know young man, you are the first Naval officer who has ever paid a call on me." Then he went on to ask what he could do for me. I told him that I was essentially his flag captain at Kunia and that I was there to make sure that he knew I was personally responsible to provide any support he required at Kunia. I think he liked the idea of having a Navy flag captain but he didn't quite say so. I didn't even know if the flagship/flag captain concept was understood or used in the Air Force. I don't believe it was, because he asked me a few questions about it. I didn't have much to say except that I wanted to make sure that he knew I was available to him and his staff any time of the day or night for any support he might require at Kunia.

He thanked me and I was on my way. I knew the visit was a great success from the reaction of his aide. I saw the latter soaking in every word I said about being the general's subordinate and responsible for providing him with any support he required, day or night. I had the feeling he would pass those words on to all the Air Force people who used Kunia.

I'll never know if it was my visit to the general that was responsible for the wonderful relations I had with the Air Force at Kunia. There were at least a hundred of them working there, even before I became Kunia's commanding officer. By no means was I their boss. Actually I was their landlord whose job it was to help them in any way possible.

I made it a point to keep those relations at the most friendly and responsive level. It worked out beautifully. My staff worked directly with the staffs of all the commanders to prepare the support required for their war rooms.

Kunia did not house CINCPAC's main war room, nor the main war room of any of the flag officers we supported. Each had his principal war room at his regular above-ground headquarters building 5 to 15 miles from Kunia.

For all of them, including CINCPAC, Kunia housed an emergency command center (ECC) that included an alternate war room, as well as several offices and adequate berthing spaces. And all of the commanders who had war rooms – plus many others like SAC, the CIA, and various intelligence commands – had small full time operations staff in my building on a permanent basis.

For administrative purposes I reported to one of Admiral Felt's principal subordinates, the Pacific Fleet Commander, Admiral Herbert Hopwood. However, Admiral Hopwood seemed to have no real interest in Kunia. His Chief of Staff, with whom I dealt, had even less.

The only person, aside from Admiral Felt, who showed some concern was Commander Blair, the project officer for Kunia before I relieved him. Blair was on the logistics staff of Commander Service Forces Pacific. He was a very bright and imaginative officer who didn't seem to have a boss, since he made many important decisions on his own.

For example, he was responsible for supervising the implementation of the building design and procuring all the equipment that went into Kunia. He gave full and straightforward answers, including "I really don't know," to my many questions. He helped me set up a sound financial structure for our operations. In general, he did a remarkable behind-the-scenes job in an area where he had little or no experience. Almost all the problems I had in the early days stemmed from the complete absence of any written guide lines for organizing, not from anything he had

18. BIRTH OF A COMMAND CENTER

left undone.

Fortunately, Blair and the experts from the Navy Department had done an excellent job in drawing up the numbers of officers and enlisted men to be assigned to Kunia. I was lucky to find that my subordinates were excellent, responsible people who, once they understood our mission, didn't need a lot of detailed guidance.

One major problem for all of us was the extremely high security classification that was placed on everything related to Kunia. Essentially, I was the landlord of this immense facility, but both my staff and I were barred from entering many of our tenant spaces because we didn't have the requisite security clearances.

Our first "security related" problem involved the formal establishment of the command itself. I was instructed by Admiral Hopwood's chief of staff to have a formal commissioning ceremony and invite every one of the nine flag officers who had a presence in the building.

We issued formal invitations, planned a nice ceremony and made ready for the event. The day before the commissioning, I was told by Admiral Hopwood's chief of staff to cancel the whole thing. Then he sent me the reason for the cancellation. It was the invitation I had sent to Admiral Felt.

He had written "cancel" on it – just the one word. But I knew why he cancelled it. I had told the chief of staff that we should have a private ceremony and avoid any publicity. But the chief of staff had insisted otherwise.

Since the cancelled commissioning ceremony affected all of my staff, the other incumbents of Kunia, and all the invitees (including most top flag officers in Pear Harbor) everyone knew immediately who cancelled the ceremony and why. It was a loud and clear message from Admiral Felt to all of us: high security and absolutely no publicity for Kunia.

Shortly after the cancellation, my office (FOCCPAC) received an interview request from one of the local newspapers. Our answer was that FOCCPAC was a high security installation and

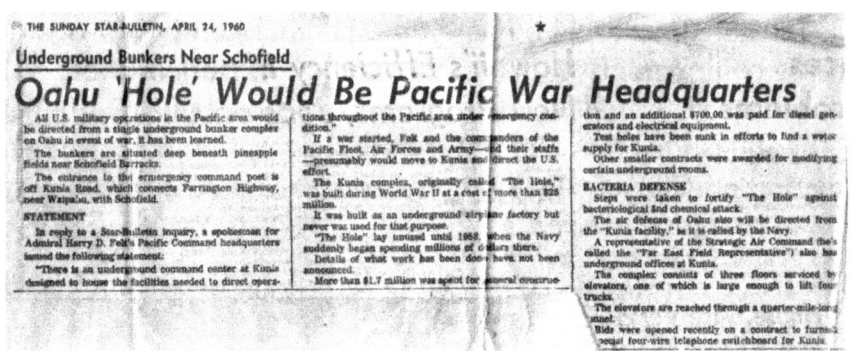

Figure 235: **If no news, send rumors.** This is the only newspaper clipping about Kunia that I saw in my three years there. It mentions a quarter-mile-long tunnel that leads to an elevator capable of lifting four trucks. It also mentions the upcoming installation of a "special four-wire telephone switchboard."

---

there would be no interviews or other publicity about the installation. Although the newspapers never contacted us again, we learned that reporters did visit the area around our installation (Figure 235). The abrupt and outright cancellation of the commissioning ceremony was an important security lesson for both Admiral Hopwood's staff and myself.

I was often asked why the security of Kunia was so strictly enforced. Very few people knew that we had multiple tenants that were highly classified intelligence units. And even those who knew about the intelligence tenants complained about the unusually high security safeguards. At times I even asked myself the same question. I really never got an answer.

But, while researching this book, I developed what might have been a reason for the unusual security level.

In 1961, none of us knew that the President had delegated to senior commanders the authority to use nuclear weapons if they could not reach the president and considered that circumstances warranted their use. Admiral Felt was probably the most senior commander in those days and although it has never been

18. BIRTH OF A COMMAND CENTER

so indicated, it would be hard to argue that he was not one of those commanders so delegated. Such a delegation would not only have answered the security level question, but a number of other questions that had developed in my mind as we worked hard to provide a really top notch computer assisted capability for use in a nuclear war.

FLAGSHIP CAPTAIN

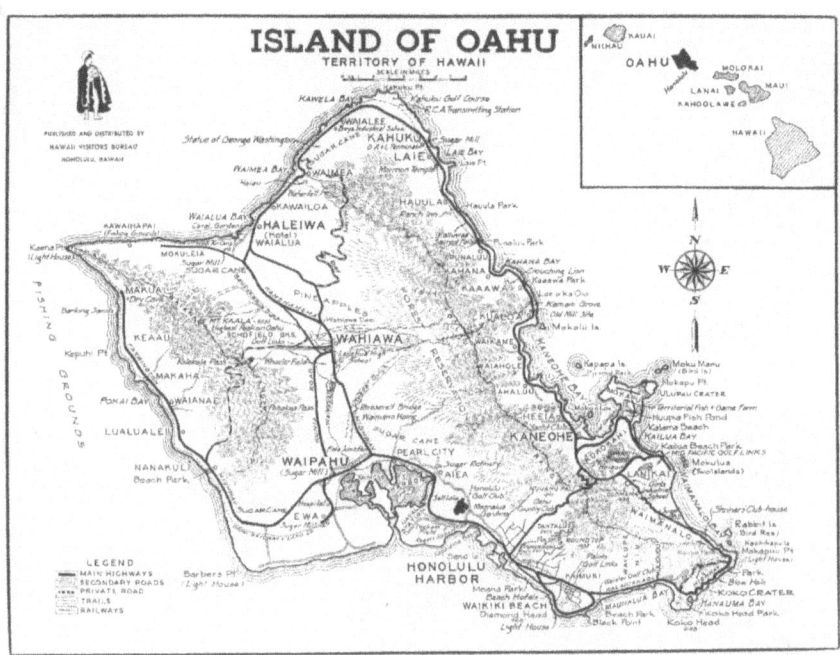

Figure 238: **Map of Oahu.** Oahu is the most populous of the Hawaiian Islands, and includes the city of Honolulu. The Kunia tunnel is located near the center of the island, just off Kunia Road, which is the dark line running vertically from Waipahu to Wahiawa. Pearl Harbor is at bottom center of the island. Notice that the map refers to the "Territory of Hawaii" – as it was in early 1959 – not the "State of Hawaii."

Chapter 19

Kunia II

I can truthfully say that on the day we commissioned the Fleet Operational Control Center Pacific (FOCCPAC), only one member of my staff of 250 (a graduate of the Naval Post-graduate School in Monterey, California) knew what a computer program was. And for some time, none of us knew the intended use of our computers.

I recall searching frantically in all the services and universities in Oahu for a course that would help us. When I did find one, which I attended, it was a voluntary course presented by an Army major, and it focused mainly on the technical basis for the operation of computers.

I had many previous experiences in the Navy where we had to start organizations from scratch, but there was always an organization to which we could turn for some assistance. That was not the case for Kunia. There was absolutely no organization in the Navy that was doing, or had done, what we were heading for.

Our situation changed dramatically one day when a team from the David Taylor Model Basin showed up. We learned that they had been working on a Navy computer project called the "Sea Surveillance System" (SSS). Almost immediately, another contractor team – this one from IBM, working on computer support for nuclear war operations – showed up.

The Sea Surveillance System had started in the office of the

19. Kunia II

Chief of Naval Operations. The highly classified work of these contractor teams had been followed for some time by an office on the CINCPAC staff (see footnote on page 40). For some unexplainable reason, partly due to its highly classified nature, we were not included in on the details of the planned project. At some point, someone in that office realized that these projects would result in something called software programs that were to be operated on the computers slated for Kunia – and that's when I got involved.

Our lack of knowledge about computers would have been far worse had we not been so friendly and close to the Air Force personnel in Kunia. They already had two small computers in operation, along with a great deal of experience. And they were eager to assist us.

It wasn't long before 15 or 20 of my officers and enlisted men, mostly self-taught and attendees in small specialized classes, became quite proficient in programming.

But that didn't solve all of my problems. One of the biggest was the operational implementation of the SSS, which would maintain information in the computer about every ship in the Pacific. In those days, the computer was considered somewhat of an assistant brain that could do things your own brain could not. Anyway, that's what most of us thought.

Partly because of questions I was raising about who was planning for the use of my computers, I was invited to a briefing on the SSS at the CINCPAC headquarters. Presented by a team from the Navy's David Taylor Model Basin, the briefers literally walked us into a computer-based future where critical operational information about all ships in the Pacific would be at our fingertips. It was very impressive!

Despite my controlled anger at not having being invited earlier into these classified briefings, I made it clear to the team and the contractors that I was the officer who was getting the computers and who had full responsibility for implementing all the wonderful things they were talking about.

They could see my obvious enthusiastic support for the

project. And when I told them that henceforth all briefings on the project would be presented to my staff at Kunia, no one objected.

In fact, while they didn't say so, I had the feeling they were a little worried about the implementation phase and were happy with what I said. From then on, the team spent its time at Kunia working with members of my staff.

The initial focus of my staff was on the input to, and and the output from, the SSS. These were issues that neither the team nor the contractors had any control over – but I did.

At the time, I knew that many of the technical details of the software were beyond the grasp of my staff. At first I didn't get too concerned because I had been assured that the team and the contractors would remain in Kunia as long as we needed them. But soon I had trouble visualizing just how the payoff would be achieved and I started to get nervous.

For example, I did not know to whom I would deliver the output reports that were being developed. It was clear those reports would be of value to all the directorates of the CINCPAC staff and other commands. However, not only had none of those offices been involved in the design of the outputs, they had existing systems and methods which they may or may not have wanted to change. Further, before I could even suggest that they consider using the planned outputs, I had to be in a position to guarantee their accuracy – a guarantee that I was in no position to make.

I quickly learned that these complex machines simply converted massive amounts of English words about ships and their locations into something called bits and bytes that were then stored and retrieved in response to questions that had similarly been converted to bits and bytes. Programming skills were required to communicate with the machine in order to manipulate these bits and bytes. I learned also that it was rare to find an individual with fleet operational experience who also had programming skills.

One of my first challenges was to extract the operational value from the SSS so that I could "sell" the output to the opera-

19. KUNIA II

tions staffs of the Kunia war rooms. In the process my relations with the project team became frayed.

My staff and I learned a great deal about computers in a very short time, due in a large part to the staffs of our Air Force tenants. They had been using a computer in Kunia well before my organization took over the building. One incentive for them to help us was my promise to allow them free access to the new Control Data computers, among the largest in the world, that were scheduled for installation.

With the help of the Air Force, some training courses, and the guidance of the project team, we managed to get key portions of the SSS operational. What proved to be most valuable was the ability to use elements of it for other capabilities.

For example, as mentioned earlier my supply officer, Lieutenant Quinn Morrison, taught himself programming. Working with the Service Force war room officer who was responsible for supplying the fuel for all Navy ships in the Pacific, he wrote programs that linked with a few of the SSS software segments to provide, at a moment's notice, the location, quantity, and ownership of all military and civilian cargo fuel in ships throughout the Pacific.

Also mentioned earlier, another such program – for contact correlation – would provide the identification of all ships within a specified radius of a particular location anywhere in the Pacific Ocean. We finally convinced the operations staff of the Hawaiian Sea Frontier Commander that it was more effective than his present system, based on handwritten 3x5 cards to identify nearby ships for rescues at sea. The officers from the Commander Anti-Submarine Warfare (ASW) staff saw its value immediately and became key users.

Another of our in-house teams was working with CINCPAC's operations staff to develop programs that could be used to support his command and control mission for nuclear war.

Working with our nuclear options team, the IBM contractors produced a number of computer programs that all the war rooms eagerly embraced.

One really new and very effective procedure was the way we used our television system to link all the war rooms with each other and with the large combined conference and briefing room. We arranged it so that CINCPAC and his subordinate commanders could ask for, and immediately see, a televised picture of the plots, and get a current briefing or answers to questions from any of the nine war rooms.

Once they got used to it, the war rooms would use the TV system to exchange information among themselves, probably making us the most cooperative "joint" operation in the military at that time – and it was done without any formal requests or instructions. It occurred simply because the capability was there, and it was helpful, and made good sense to use.

In this manner, any of the war rooms could be inserted into a briefing. It was a smooth operation since all nine of the war rooms listened to briefings during worldwide exercises or other conferences and knew when they could help. Often they volunteered information to my operations officer.

I was really proud of the way my people pulled that entire operation together. It made everyone look good, not only during the Cuban missile crisis, but especially during worldwide nuclear war exercises.

This sort of coordination and presentation of information is routine today. But in 1962 it was a first!

HEADQUARTERS OF THE COMMANDER IN CHIEF PACIFIC
FLEET POST OFFICE
SAN FRANCISCO, CALIFORNIA

CINCPAC
1611
Ser 2285
4 OCT 1962

From: Commander in Chief Pacific
To: Captain George P. Sotos, USN
Via: Commander in Chief U.S. Pacific Fleet

Subj: Letter of Commendation

1. Upon termination of your current assignment in the Pacific Command, I wish to compliment you on your superior performance of duty as the First Commanding Officer of the Fleet Operations Control Center, Pacific, during the period 4 January 1960 to 20 October 1962. During this period, you were responsible for the condition of facility readiness of an activity having major importance to the Commander in Chief, Pacific.

2. I have observed with great satisfaction the steady progress and improvement in the readiness condition of the facility under your command, as well as its increased capability to assume additional functions beyond those assigned. I note also that the cordial relationship existing between members of your command and my staff, an essential ingredient of effective teamwork, is attributable in large part to your personal leadership, enthusiastic cooperation, and thorough understanding of the command arrangements peculiar to a unified command.

3. I take great pleasure in commending you on a job well done. Your splendid performance of your duties reflects great credit upon yourself and your command, and is in the best traditions of the United States Navy.

H. D. FELT

Figure 244: **Writing about secret matters.** How does one write a public letter of commendation for someone who has been doing a secret job? This is Admiral Felt's answer. He offers no specifics about Kunia's function, referring to it only as a "facility [of] importance," its readiness, and cordial personal relations.

Chapter 20

Nuclear War Readiness

Early in my tour I learned that security at Kunia was a very serious issue.

Virtually unkown throughout the Navy, Kunia was probably the most mysterious military installation in all of Hawaii.

CINCPAC insisted that nothing at all be issued to the public. This only made the newspapers more aggressive to get information. For the most part they were not successful, and all they reported was that the "Tunnel" or "Hole" was a highly classified installation.

But this made many people curious, and the multiple acres of pineapple field that covered our installation was an object of intrigue for many people. We had the entire area fenced off and a guard tower manned by Marines. They became targets for the curious, and, regrettably, some of the local thugs would shoot at the Marines with BB guns from the pineapple field.

It is not a good idea to irritate Marines. Our Marines took their job very seriously, and I worried that they might lose their tolerance. So, with CINCPAC's approval we decided to do something about the security above my installation.

A well qualified consultant detective from Chicago came to Kunia and after two weeks' inspections, recommended a high electrified fence all around the area above our installation – at a cost well over several hundred thousand dollars. Initially I sup-

20. Nuclear War Readiness

ported the recommendation and subsequently we received several bids from local contractors to build the fence.

That's when I started to ask questions. For example, what happens if a large bird sits on the fence?

"Well it won't kill the bird but it will set off an alarm" was the answer. We had hundreds of these birds, meaning that we would have hundreds of alarms.

I killed the project.

But we still had a problem. I don't know where the idea originated, but I instructed the Marines to go to the Honolulu dog pound, pick out the two meanest dogs they could find, and turn them loose in our fenced-in pineapple field.

They found two dogs. Both had to be handled with well-padded gloves. I recall one was a huge brown boxer who really took to his Marine handlers. But they always wore gloves.

Surprisingly, the dogs solved our problem immediately. They had the run of the pineapple field and the number of curious onlookers and locals with BB guns went to zero.

Topside security was just one of our problems. Getting it solved so quickly was a relief. This allowed more time to focus on a major part of our mission that was completely new to me: readiness for nuclear war.

Like almost every officer in the Navy at that time, my knowledge of nuclear war was very limited, even though I was a graduate of the Naval War College. It was a highly classified, need-to-know subject, and until I got to Kunia I had no need to know.

I quickly learned that CINCPAC had an important second strike role in the execution of nuclear war in the Pacific area, and that Kunia's support for that role was critical. My job was to provide the facilities and the technological support that would help the planning and operations people discharge their Pacific-wide responsibilities in a timely and efficient manner.

But it was the scope of their support requirements that got my attention. CINCPAC's command responsibilities covered about one-half of planet earth. It doesn't take a genius to appreciate the vastness of the information required by his planning and operations staff for the targeting, command, and control of nuclear weapons.

With two of the nation's most advanced computers from Control Data Corporation, some ancillary computers, and what became the largest communication center in the Pacific, my staff and facilities gradually integrated our support capabilities into the plannning and operation of the CINCPAC war room.

But the learning process wasn't all roses. My personal experience in the development of our communications center was a particularly rocky road.

In the early days I focused on the installation, development, and operation of our vast computer system. At first I was not adequately aware of the criticality of assured communications and its importance to continuity of operations and governance. Kunia opened my eyes and my mind.

The largest and most critical part of our over-all operation at Kunia was the communication center. I knew even less about running a communication center than I did about computers. But thanks to my communications officer, Commander Gil Clark, I learned in a hurry. But my learning process was really hard on him.

I would hold command inspections every Saturday morning, just as we did aboard ship. I couldn't believe what I was seeing every week in our two story communications center. I knew what a ship looked like before it was placed in commission and started operating. And that never really bothered me. But I had never been near the startup, from scratch, of a large communications center, and what I was seeing bothered me.

The first floor was a sea of desks, a large number of teletype machines, several offices, and a large (about 10-by-6 foot) bank of hundreds of air tubes for in-house delivery of communication messages throughout the building. This big room always seemed to be a mess, filled with teletype machines and wires (Figure 30). Although bothered, I decided I could live with what I saw there.

On the second floor, it was a different story. In a huge room

247

20. Nuclear War Readiness

we were installing a giant relay center. It was a mass of teletype machines and wires strung all over the place. Instead of progressively becoming better organized and orderly, it was going in the opposite direction: even more teletype machines were squeezed into the room. Beside each machine were many strips of punched paper tape hanging on nails waiting their turn to be inserted into the correct teletype machine. Each week I saw more wires all over the floor.

There must have been three rows of forty machines each, side by side with wires connecting them to the war rooms, and to other offices in Kunia, and to an antenna site many miles from Kunia.

Gil obviously had a big, responsible job, but the tough part was, I didn't know how difficult it really was. For a long time I was pushing him to better organize the relay and, at least, make it somewhat presentable. He would say, "Aye aye sir," and fortunately continue doing his job the way he knew best. That meant ignoring my admonitions and continuing to string wires and moving communications traffic the best way he knew. I became increasingly upset at his disregard of my inspection reports to clean up what I saw as a mess, and it started to bother Gil.

Finally, one day he sat down and wrote a 12 page, single space, long hand, private letter to me. When I received it my first reaction was one of anger. However, I took it home and reread it carefully. He let out all the stops in his letter. He wrote that I was unknowingly interfering in the establishment of the communications center by prioritizing spit and polish over important operational requirements, and that it was starting to affect the morale in his department. He literally asked me to "lay off" and give him the time and support he needed to get the job done.

He was flat out telling me I had the wrong priorities.

I had never received a letter of that type from a subordinate, or even a senior. But, as much as it bothered me, I started to appreciate the courage it took for Gil to write such a letter. He was fully aware that it could ruin his career, but he still had the courage to tell me I was wrong. I remained angry that he felt he had to write to me, vs. come in and discuss it. But I also realized that the communication center was my communication center, and this guy was dedicated to making it work right at the risk of losing his job.

The more I thought about it, the more I realized that I had to change. It became clear that unless I changed and let him run his department as he saw fit, I would probably have a major problem on my hands. In other words, I had to admit to myself that he knew far more about that responsibility than I did, and that I should try to help instead of putting obstacles in his way.

I met with Gil the next morning and told him that I would lay off him, as he put it. I asked him to let me know what I could do to help him get the job done.

That was the end of the matter between us. I did alter the way I inspected his center. I focused more on what he was getting done operationally than what the place looked like. It wasn't long before he had a well organized, neat communications center that operated at top effectiveness.

Looking back, my decision to "lay off" was a good one. We soon had a first rate communications center that was the subject of many compliments, especially from the CINCPAC director of communications. And, believe it or not, I started to learn communications well enough to have it added to my formal qualifications as a sub-specialty.

We both forgot about his letter and our relations kept getting better. I gave him an excellent evaluation, which I'm certain helped him some months later be promoted to the rank of captain.

Spurred by the growth and effectiveness of our communications center, more tasks were assigned to us. For example, Kunia became one of two major recovery control centers for NASA's astronaut spaceflight program. When assigned our first recovery – Walter Schirra's *Sigma 7* spacecraft in October 1962[1] – many of

---

[1] This was the first manned American space mission to be recovered in

20. Nuclear War Readiness

the senior officers in the Hawaii area wanted to reserve seats in our building to witness the event. To accommodate them all I seated them in our large auditorium, which was right next door to the control room. We had a lot of jury-rigged wires for the first recovery and the men running it asked us to make sure only authorized participants were allowed in the control room. As much as I wanted to witness all the details, I also stayed out of the control room. But by running a video from the control center to a large screen in the auditorium, we managed to see and hear just about everything associated with the recovery, without getting in the way of those actually doing the job. It was thrilling and educational to witness the recovery. Just by setting it up in our modern comfortable auditorium and not turning anyone away, I made a lot of new friends that day.

Our most important mission, of course, was to support CINCPAC's responsibilities for command and control of nuclear war in the Pacific region. To make sure we knew our job we participated in world wide drills that simulated our war time tasks.

During these worldwide exercises, the communications and computer capabilities of the Kunia installation were taxed to the fullest. For example, we had to make sure all the different services and intelligence organizations acted in an integrated manner. That meant nine different war rooms had to be on the same page throughout the three or four day exercise.

All the differences that existed between the services seemed to evaporate when we started one of those exercises. All nine war rooms knew each other well enough to exchange information almost as though they all wore the same uniform. Our communications center, computer center, briefing and display center, and television operation all had lines into every war room. My personnel made it a point to be responsive to everything directed at them from the war rooms. That may sound simple, but it really wasn't.

Every war room had its own software support systems, as

---

the Pacific Ocean.

well as a requirement for information from the results of analysis of incoming reports from Pacific-wide sources. In addition, every one of the war rooms had to have operating information about their respective separate missions. For example, just reviewing the titles of the different commanders who had war rooms in Kunia will indicate the exceptional wide range of concerns among the war rooms. (See Figure 228.)

Of course, we had many problems and mixups, but, happily, none were serious and they became part of our learning process. There was no way anyone could design and implement a package of software systems that would be responsive to such a wide variety of commands and would work the first time. The smoothness of our overall operation was really good during the Cuban missile crisis and my whole staff got a pat on the back from Admiral Felt.

An unusual incident was connected to the magnitude 9.5 earthquake that struck Valdivia, Chile on Sunday, 22 May 1960 – still the most powerful earthquake ever recorded. In addition to the 1600 people killed in Chile, the resulting tsunami caused deaths and damage in southern Chile, Hawaii, Japan, the Philippines, eastern New Zealand, southeast Australia, and the Aleutian Islands.

Because we were a major communications center in the Pacific, we got word of the earthquake well before the tsunami hit the Hawaiian islands. It was unexpected information and we had no instructions about any role we might have in disseminating the information we received. But we didn't need anyone to tell us what to do. We notified the Commander, Hawaiian Sea Frontier, who was in touch with the media, and all the other commanders in Hawaii. We reported the time when the tsunami would reach Honolulu and what to expect on its beaches.

We also notified all our own people and cautioned them to make sure their families were taken to high ground, well away from the beaches – including famed Waikiki Beach. I remained at Kunia but sent someone to remove my family from our beachfront home.

20. Nuclear War Readiness

The first indication of the tsunami in Honolulu was when the ocean receded a considerable distance from the usual coastline. Some time later, huge waves came pouring in, passing well past Waikiki beach and the plush hotels in that area.

Sixty-one people were killed in Hilo, on the nearby Big Island, but, fortunately, the damage was limited in Honolulu. My house, fifteen miles west of Honolulu, was not damaged.

This incident gave me a solid sense of how important Kunia was to the welfare of everyone in Hawaii.

Figure 254: ***Tolovana* vs. aircraft carrier.** At 553 feet in length, the *Tolovana* was 63% the length of the aircraft carrier USS *Bennington*, shown here. The Navy classifies fleet oilers as "deep draft" commands, just like cruisers and carriers.

Chapter 21

Man Overboard

"Bridge, combat."

"Go ahead, combat," said the Officer of the deck (OOD).

"Radar contact, eight miles dead astern."

"Roger combat, thank you," said the OOD.

"Bridge, combat. The radar contact has disappeared."

"OK combat," said the OOD.

I happened to be sitting in my bridge chair enjoying the night air as we were cruising toward our next rendezvous. "How many of those disappearing radar contacts have we had tonight?" I asked the OOD.

"That's the fourth one since sunset," he replied.

I wasn't surprised. Many of the units of the Seventh Fleet were participating in an exercise against a squadron of our submarines, and the latter were searching for them. What better place to look for the carriers, cruisers, and destroyers than in the vicinity of one of their refueling ships. My ship, the Navy oiler USS *Tolovana*, was not a participant in the exercise, so we could not report these disappearing radar contacts to the main surface force.

We knew, of course, that the disappearing radar contacts were submarines following us, knowing that sooner or later our ship would meet and fuel the big surface ships.

21. MAN OVERBOARD

Figure 256: ***Tolovana* in profile.** A sturdy, powerful, dependable ship.

This was 1964 and there were no nuclear propelled surface ships in the Seventh Fleet at that time, making our presence necessary. By the end of the two week exercise we had logged eight disappearing radar contacts. I was so convinced that the submarines were following us to get to the carriers and other ships, that I wrote a letter to the Chief of Naval Operations (CNO). In that letter, which I sent via the exercise task force commander, I pointed out that, in an exercise or in actual hostilities, any smart submarine commander would just follow a fleet oiler. It didn't take a genius to figure out that sooner or later the carriers would need our fuel.

I recommended that fleet oilers like my ship be fitted with special sonar gear and weapons which would permit us to attack those submarines.

About two months later I received a reply that agreed the submarines did indeed follow the oilers to find the carriers and other surface ships. I was thanked for my recommendation and informed that the Navy Department was already investigating the feasibility of adding antisubmarine warfare capabilities to large slow ships like mine.

Fleet oiler operations were far less stressful than destroyer operations. We did have our exciting and dangerous times during replenishment operations in bad weather, but that was the exception rather than the rule.

For the most part, we proceeded independently from one refueling rendezvous to another until we were empty. Then we would go into Yokosuka, Japan or some other port, fill up our tanks, and return to the fleet operations.

Fueling for us was a breeze. All we had to do was remain on a good course, and the other ships would come alongside. Carriers would remain alongside up to five hours as we topped them off. A destroyer would be topped off in less than an hour. Many times we would have a carrier on one side and a destroyer on the other – each about 50 feet away from us as we steamed together at about 12 or 14 knots.

When the weather was good, it was easy. Nobody worked too hard. But bad weather was another matter! We would not fuel two ships at once in bad weather. It was simply too risky.

One doesn't appreciate how big aircraft carriers are until they come as close as ten feet from you while trying to maintain station in heavy weather. We really earned our pay in heavy weather refueling.

After one cycle of refueling in heavy weather, we returned to Yokuska and, during a routine inspection, learned that one of the heavy booms that held the oil lines was bent.

I had to make a decision. Do we disregard the bend in the boom and continue with our schedule? Or do we play it safe, force some other oiler to take our schedule and have the boom fixed?

You can lose brownie points by not meeting your schedule. And I was tempted to take a chance that we wouldn't have any bad weather that might bend the boom more and hurt someone.

It is easy to disregard the play it safe route, and meet the schedule. However, I had experienced enough heavy weather to respect it. So we stayed in Yokosuka and got our boom fixed.

Bad weather isn't the only problem tanker skippers have to worry about. A near tragic event occurred when my tanker had hooked up with, and was fueling, a carrier on the port side and a destroyer on the starboard side. We were part of a large formation of multiple tankers and supply ships replenishing all the ships of the Seventh Fleet in one large operation. I don't recall our exact position in this sprawling formation, but I do remem-

21. Man Overboard

ber well that we were steaming at 12 knots, 1000 yards astern of a huge supply ship that was provisioning a cruiser.

We had been fueling the carrier for about two hours and the destroyer for about twenty minutes. Everything was going just fine, when I heard simultaneous shouts from my port lookout and my signalman.

"Man overboard, man overboard – dead ahead, man overboard – dead ahead!" At the same time we saw a flashing signal light from the cargo ship dead ahead.

I quickly put my binoculars on a small disruption in the water ahead and saw a movement just astern of the port side of the *Pollux* (the supply ship dead ahead of us). Then my signalman shouted, "The *Pollux* reports three men in the water – repeat three men in the water her port side."

I immediately picked up the phone that connected us to the bridge of the carrier and destroyer that were alongside. "Get your captain on this phone."

Almost immediately I got a response from the carrier, "This is the captain go ahead." I got a similar response from the destroyer. I could tell from their voices they knew about the men in the water ahead of us.

"I am on course 290 right now. I am coming right with 5 degrees rudder and I will keep giving you my heading as we turn. Let me know if you can not stay with me."

"Roger," said both skippers

"Right five degrees rudder I ordered."

"Right five degrees rudder." Repeated the helmsman.

Then, "Rudder is right five degrees," said the helmsman

I then told both captains, "My rudder is right five degrees." Then, as my ship slowly started to swing right, I reported my gyrocompass heading for every change of two degrees. Fortunately all I heard from the two skippers was, "Roger," as all three of us, yes three huge ships, slowly but effectively turned together to the right, away from the spot where the three men could now be seen struggling in the water, as a destroyer approached them.

Because of our turn the men in the water were soon obscured by the carrier. But we could see the mast of the rescue destroyer close to the carrier's port side. "We are well clear," reported the carrier.

"Thanks, I answered, steady on course 330."

"Roger," said the carrier skipper. "Roger and goodbye," said the destroyer to starboard who had completed fueling and was now taking in his lines.

"Steady on course 330," reported my helmsman.

"Left 5 degrees rudder," I ordered. My helmsman repeated the order and reported, "Rudder is left 5 degrees."

"We will come back to base course the same way," I told the carrier skipper. "My heading is now 330. My rudder is five degrees left."

"Roger," he said.

Then after a few minutes, "My heading is passing 328, my rudder is still five degrees left."

"Roger."

And that's the way the carrier and we returned to the base course, and stayed with the formation.

We ended up a little to the right of the main formation, but we stayed there until refueling was completed about an hour later. All during this emergency maneuver we kept the fuel moving, so there was really no delay to the task force's schedule.

It may seem like a simple maneuver, but turning three different size ships steaming at twelve knots that are just 50 feet apart is not as routine as I make it sound. It is important to remember that when I initially turned right – away from the carrier – he had to speed up a little to keep from falling behind and stretching and parting our lines. As for the destroyer on my right, in addition to changing course he had to slow a little to maintain position. Then, later, when we came back left, the carrier had to change course and slow a little as I turned toward him. This maneuver is never practiced. It is not very often that three men go overboard in front of three large ships linked together by fuel and other lines.

21. Man Overboard

Imagine how the men in the water felt when they looked up and saw those ships heading right for them!

If you do the math, you will see that we had less than five minutes to change course and avoid running over those men. That may seem like a long time. But there were four delays to consider. One, the delay between the time when the men fell into the water and when I got the word. Two, the delay for my maneuver decision. Three, the delay to communicate that decision to both skippers alongside, and four, the delay in a ship's response to a rudder change. This last delay was different for all three ships, with my ship responding the slowest.

Because the key people on all three ships skipped all formalities, were alert and ready for such an emergency, there were no delays.

It may sound immodest, but it was a damn good maneuver, done without any fuss or extra words, and cleared the area so the three men, who had accidently been caught in a cargo net and dumped over the side, could be picked up safely and without injury.

I complimented my helmsman and the rest of my crew and sent a well done to the carrier and destroyer captains.

We all got a "Thank you" from the *Pollux*.

In my 32 years in the Navy this particular type of experience is the only one I ever heard or read about.

One of the biggest thrills of being a tanker skipper is to watch the hulking aircraft carriers maneuver to come alongside. As massive as they are, they still command a form of graceful speed, confidence, and sheer power that sends chills down your back. You would think that a ship that size would make some noise when it is within fifty feet of you. The noise that some make is usually that of routine flight deck announcements over their loudspeaker. But it was not unusual to have a huge carrier come alongside silently with no sounds other than that made by its bow as it cut through the water.

I remember getting that thrill when the carrier USS *Oriskany* came alongside one day. She remained alongside with fuel lines between us for about four hours before she said goodbye.

After a refueling, my supply officer normally showed up in my cabin with an outgoing message for my release, advising the refueled ship how much fuel was received.

But that didn't happen after the *Oriskany* left. I waited and waited but no supply officer. Finally I sent for him.

"Where is the fueling bill for the *Oriskany*?"

"Captain, you're not gonna believe this."

"What?"

"There is no bill. They didn't get a drop of oil or aviation gas."

"You gotta be kidding. They were alongside for four hours."

"Yes, I know. But they didn't get a drop of fuel. We have sounded (measured) our tanks three times to make sure, and they have the same content as before she came alongside. They didn't get a drop."

I was puzzled. I really didn't know what to do. If I sent the *Oriskany* a message that we didn't give them any fuel after being alongside four hours, we would both look like fools. That type of message would be the subject of fleet-wide humor.

My chief engineer, who came along with the supply officer, noted my concern.

"Captain," he said, "it wasn't us. It was them. We thought we were pumping fuel but they didn't open their valve. They didn't want anything from us." Then he added, "Sometimes they do that if they have a good supply in their tanks. They feel they always get some contaminated jet fuel and aviation gas every time they refuel."

I decided not to do anything. Then a couple days later we learned that President John F. Kennedy had visited the *Oriskany* and they had all kinds of aircraft demonstrations for him. That's when we realized it was them – not us. They didn't want to take any chances with a new batch of fuel messing up the performance of their planes.

They said nothing and I said nothing – until now – about their four hours alongside for a non-refueling.

21. Man Overboard

Replenishment operations are a critical component of the Navy's ability to remain at sea for months at a time, but they are far from routine operations.

A fleet oiler like the *Tolovana* is a workhorse type ship as are the other logistic support ships. At the same time they are ready for a shooting war, but do not spend a lot of time maneuvering with the fast carrier strike units. Nevertheless they are clearly essential to the strike force's ability to perform its mission.

One handicap is their age. Most of them, like the ponderously slow *Tolovana*, are much older than their sleek, fast-moving destroyer and carrier customers. One price they pay for this old age is that the crew isn't always up to date on what keeps the ship operating.

For example, one hot day when we were refueling a carrier, I received a report on the bridge that there was some smoke coming out of a large vent forward on our port side. Smoke is usually caused by a fire of some type, but our damage control party could not find a fire. Meanwhile the vent continued to produce smoke.

I was reluctant to declare an emergency and stop refueling the carrier. But smoke on a tanker, especially the location of this smoke – not far from our aviation fuel – is something to worry about. I left the bridge and ran to the port bow where a group of my men was looking up at a large vent leaking smoke. This particular vent was a large conduit for air that was sucked into the ship for internal ventilation.

When I joined the men standing there, it was obvious they did not know what to do. Careful searches of the vent system had revealed no heat or fire. Nevertheless, the smoke was continuing. I could add no new knowledge to the problem.

I was about to return to the bridge and terminate the refueling when a young sailor carrying a big pick and a fire extinguisher joined the group. Without a word to anyone he started swinging the pick at the smoking vent.

"What the hell are you doing?" I shouted. But he ignored me and kept chopping away. In a minute or two he had a large hole in the vent and the smoke really poured out!

Then he picked up the fire extinguisher, stuck the nozzle in the hole he had made and let the foam fly. After an even larger burst, the smoke suddenly receded and in a few minutes had almost disappeared.

He turned to me and said, "There's a motor in there and I figured that was causing the smoke." It turned out he was right. He was the only sailor on the ship who knew that a motor that helped move the air through the vent – was inside the vent! And the only way to get to it was to dismantle the vent or chop a hole in it as he did.

I thanked him profusely. Had he not figured out the problem, I am sure the motor would have caught fire and created a serious problem. I was so happy at what he had done that I awarded him a commendation. However, I failed to ask him how he knew there was a motor inside that vent.

While that incident reflected the age of the *Tolovana*, it also reflected the very high quality of my very young crew.

Spending as much time as we did in the South Pacific can get really boring, especially when you operate alone and go to the same ports to replenish cargo. There's plenty to do during the working day, and that part remains challenging and interesting,

It's a different story after working hours when the sailors go ashore in Japanese ports like Yokosuka and Sasebo. Only rarely did we have enough time there to permit the sailors to take a train to Tokyo and back. So after the first visit to those ports, there really was not much to do or see.

The 365 sailors and officers on the *Tolovana* were a responsible and well behaved group when they went ashore. But we had our exceptions.

At anchor in Sasebo one afternoon, we had just finished the working day and part of the crew was going ashore on liberty. The launch was alongside our long gangway leading down the port side, and the men were entering the launch. All of a sudden the alarm was passed "Man overboard, man overboard!" Many

21. MAN OVERBOARD

of the sailors had seen the man go into the water and he was quickly fished out, wet and bewildered!

Once I was assured the sailor was OK and could respond to questions, I ordered a Captain's mast.

With the quarterdeck watch that had been supervising the liberty party going down the gangway, along with the soaked sailor, standing before me, I told him that I wanted to find out what happened. I also told him that he didn't have to answer any of my questions or say anything that might incriminate him or get him into any kind of trouble.

When I asked what happened, the quartermaster of the watch spoke first. "Captain, everything was perfectly normal. The men were going down the ladder and getting into the launch. But when Warren here," he pointed to the soaking wet sailor, "got to the bottom of the gangway, he didn't turn and get into the launch. He just kept going straight ahead and walked off the platform into the water. And then we fished him out."

I turned to Warren. "Is that what happened?" I asked.

Looking me straight in the eyes, Warren said, "Yes sir, that's what I did."

I was dumbfounded and for a while I didn't know what to say. "Why didn't you get in the launch as the other sailors did?" I finally said,

Still looking me straight in the eyes he answered, "Captain I thought I could walk on the water."

His answer surprised us all and I didn't say anything for a minute. The Chief Master at Arms, the ship's security officer, interjected, "Warren, what have you been taking?"

Warren's forthright demeanor changed and he mumbled something none of us understood. The Chief Master at Arms then asked. "Captain, request permission to inspect Warren's locker?"

I knew right away what he was thinking, "Permission granted," I said. "Be sure to take Warren with you."

And that's how we determined that Warren and two others were taking some little white pills. I never did find out exactly what was in the pills, but we determined that it was enough to make Warren think he could walk on water.

Of course, I was disappointed and angry at the same time. It was the first time in my entire career that I had any of my sailors take something like that aboard ship. And the worse part was that the sailors involved, including Warren, all had otherwise clean records.

All three of the culprits admitted they were taking the pills, which they had purchased ashore in a previous port.

There was no way I could overlook or minimize the seriousness of what they had done. And at a formal captain's mast I awarded a lengthy restriction to the ship and a reduction in rate for all three. However, I also stated that after six months, if they maintained a clean record and had the support of their leading petty officer and department head, I would rescind the reduction in rate and remove all trace of their offense from their record.

Six months later, just before I was turning over command of the *Tolovana* to my relief, I did just that.

Figure 266: **The Pentagon.** The Pentagon is just a large office building in northern Virginia. Shown here in 2018, it was built during World War II. Famously, the Secretary of Defense's office looks onto Arlington Cemetery, which is located nearby.

Chapter 22

At The Top

You would think that duty in the Office of the Chief of Naval Operations (CNO) would be the "Nirvana" for a fired-up naval officer. And that's what I thought until I had been there about four months.

As mentioned on page 38, it was the first assignment in my career for which I was actually recruited. So I guess I had the right to have high expectations.

It was a good career decision, but I made one serious mistake. When Captain Trickey recruited me, I failed to get a commitment from his boss that I would indeed relieve Trickey as division head after he (Trickey) retired. In fact I didn't even ask Trickey if his boss was in on the agreement.

Even before my year on the *Tolovana* was up, I had been issued orders to be the branch head for electronic warfare (EW) and communications research and development on the staff of the CNO. I reported there in June of 1963 with the assumption that I would relieve my now division head, Captain Trickey, when he retired.

The work was quite interesting, especially at first. For example, I was responsible for making sure that all the Navy's research labs were treated fairly in the fight for funds. To make sure I had enough information about their projects, I visited all the labs.

Because it was also in their best interests to make sure I knew

22. At The Top

what they were doing, they withheld nothing. But I had to admit they didn't have to push me at all. The projects and programs they were working on were truly amazing. I saw so much talent and dedication focused on the Navy's operational requirements that at the end of my trip, I was convinced that those labs could solve any problem assigned to them.

Most of what I saw and heard was highly classified. Although the heads of the labs looked to me to make sure they were properly funded, I never had a problem doing that. Their projects were so timely and valuable, and the need for them so evident, they practically sold themselves.

In addition to the research labs, I was responsible for the development of a number of projects. One, called "Stand-off Jammer," was badly needed in the Vietnam war. Our aircraft were taking a terrific beating from some very effective anti-aircraft missiles that looked like telephone poles as they sped toward our planes.

Our planned stand-off jammer was to be carried in a large plane that could provide the necessary power to disrupt the electronic controls that the enemy used to guide their missiles toward our planes. Those enemy controls would be jammed at a substantial distance from the missiles themselves; hence the name "standoff".

Because it was so badly needed, the stand off jammer project was removed from R&D and made operational. My assistant for EW was tasked to accompany the jammer to Vietnam.

The jammer solved the problem and that particular missile threat subsided.

Unfortunately, my assistant was badly injured in a failed aircraft launch from a carrier, and he never returned to Washington.

I had two other projects worth mentioning. The first was an extremely low wave communication system designed to communicate with submerged submarines. It seemed that every time they tested it along the eastern seaboard, it would ring the door-bells of hundreds of houses. The adverse publicity and complaints associated with these tests forced us to find a different testing site. It took a while, but, as best I can remember, we found a site in a remote part of Washington state.

The second project was a fully automatic anti-aircraft gun for surface ships. It had a number of improvements over our existing WWII anti aircraft guns. One I liked was its ability to pick up an air target on radar, lock the guns on it when within range, and automatically start firing if the target was flying toward the ship in the wrong quadrant. I had memories of WWII where such a weapon would have done so much to protect our surface ships. But my enthusiasm for the project got me in trouble.

It happened during a budget briefing for the head of R&D, Admiral Noel Gayler, a well known fighter pilot, and Dr. Eugene Fubini, the head of R&D for the Secretary of Defense. Admiral Gayler told me he did not want a fully automatic system.

He didn't let me defend the concept.

"Don't argue with me," he said. "Eliminate the fully automatic capability. It's too dangerous for our own aircraft. We'll be shooting down our own planes!"

With WWII memories of multiple Kamikaze aircraft attacking a destroyer, I said with obvious reluctance, "Aye, aye sir," and then quietly muttered to myself that "In war-time on my ship I would wire that capability into the system."

I didn't intend for the admiral to hear my remark, but he did.

"What did you say?" he asked sharply. I was stuck and had to repeat what I said. He was visibly angry, but simply told me to carry out his orders.

"Yes sir," I responded with egg all over my face, but I did not retract what I had said.

Continued funding was approved, subject to that change.

I don't think the incident caused the admiral to pass over me for the division head job when Trickey retired in mid 1965. But that's what he did.

Of course I was pissed off. There had been no commitment that I would get the job by anyone other than Trickey, and now he was gone.

22. At The Top

The admiral brought in a senior captain he was acquainted with to be division head and, therefore, my immediate boss. This captain was an excellent naval officer with lots of sea experience, but he knew absolutely nothing about the computer-based command and control systems that were moving into the Navy's inventory of projects.

I had made the mistake of agreeing to work for Trickey without the assurance of an official commitment. In retrospect, I don't even think that Admiral Gayler was aware of that agreement.

I was more angry at myself, for not getting an official commitment, than I was with the admiral. I don't know if the latter ever considered me for the division head job and like an idiot, I never discussed it with him.

A few days after my unpleasant briefing to Admiral Gayler, I received a phone call out of the blue from an Air Force officer, Major General Bestic. Much to my surprise, he said he wanted to discuss something with me and asked if I could drop over and see him.

His office was with the Defense Communication Agency (DCA), about a 15 minute drive from my Pentagon office.

I quickly looked him up and found that he was the head of the National Military Command System Technical Support directorate within DCA. I figured he wanted to discuss one of my R&D projects. But I was wrong. Instead he told me he had a job opening that might be of interest.

It turns out that my tour at Kunia had put me in a very small group of senior officers having experience in the use of the still quite new, unknown, and intimidating use of computers in command and control for major "joint" commands.

I was still smarting from not getting the division head job and my soured relations with Admiral Gayler, so I listened carefully and with great interest to what General Bestic had to say.

Someone he thought a lot of had suggested me for a job he had open. It was a key job in his organization and a vital one in a brand new area for the Joint Chiefs of Staff (JCS). We hadn't talked for more than 20 minutes when he offered me the job.

I was very happy to say yes.

When he asked how soon I could report I told him, without being certain, that it should be very quick.

It turns out I was right.

That same day I returned to my office and wrote a short, positive letter to the CNO via Admiral Gayler, requesting a transfer. I stated that I was very happy in my job at the CNO but that the opportunity offered to me by General Bestic was a perfect match for the experience I had at Kunia. I also pointed out that I would be a senior naval officer in a vital new area for the JCS where the Navy currently had minimal representation.

The only possible obstacle to a transfer was Admiral Gayler. He called me in and indirectly stated that it's not every day that a senior captain wants out of an important CNO job. I could see that my transfer request surprised him and that he was not happy about it.

I emphasized that there was nothing about my current job that was pushing me out. It was just a golden opportunity to work in a new area in which I had been lucky enough to gain some really solid experience.

I am sure that he had no idea at all about my previous experiences, especially that I had spent three years at CINCPAC working for Admiral Felt. If he had any knowledge about the use of automation for command and control, it didn't come through during our conversation.

After answering a lot of his questions I convinced him that not only was it an outstanding professional opportunity for me, it was an opportunity for the Navy to have someone in this new and mushrooming area of automated command and control.

He finally, and I thought somewhat reluctantly, said OK and wished me the best. He endorsed my request and I departed within two weeks.

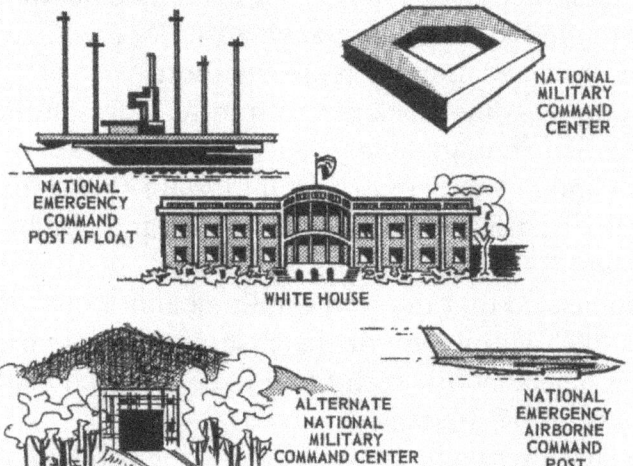

Figure 272: **National Military Command System.** The National Military Command System (NMCS) is a communications system that transmits the President's orders to his top military commanders worldwide (they are shown in Figure 276). The task is vital and must be failure-proof. It is complicated because the President may be in various locations, shown here, and because adversaries will try to disrupt communications. My organization, the NMCSTS, supported and supervised the technical parts of the NMCS. This NMCSTS diagram was developed within the NMCSTS.

Chapter 23

The Joint Chiefs of Staff

It was September 1, 1965 when I walked into Air Force Major General John Bestic's office, head of the National Military Command System Technical Support (NMCS Technical Support), whose mission was to provide technology support to the Joint Chiefs of Staff.[1]

"Good morning, General." I said cheerfully but respectfully.

"Good Morning. Have a seat. How are things going?" he responded, but not as cheerfully.

"OK sir, I'm still getting my feet wet."

"George, are you trying to fire Mitre?" Mitre Corporation was a non-profit contractor specializing in providing computer system and other support to the planning and operations mission of the national military command system.

His short, direct question really caught me off balance and I didn't answer right away.

"Well, are you trying to get rid of them?"

"No sir," I answered slowly and hesitantly. "I'm trying to shift some of their work to our own people.

"George, how many PhDs are there in the joint staff?"

Somewhat puzzled. I thought for just a minute then answered, "I don't believe they have any, sir."

---

[1] The chief of each military service, plus a chairman, comprised the Joint Chiefs of Staff (JCS) in the 1960s.

23. The Joint Chiefs of Staff

"How many PhDs do you have working for you?"

"One sir."

"How many PhDs does the Mitre Corporation have?"

That was an easy one. "I believe most of them are PhDs sir."

A short man, Bestic got up from his chair, walked around and sat on the edge of his desk right in front of me. Looking straight at me he went on. "George, anybody can fire Mitre. That doesn't take any talent. And that's not why I hired you."

He repeated, "Anybody can fire Mitre. But that's not the challenge. The challenge, the real challenge, is how to use that Mitre talent – how to use those PhDs to help the JCS." He paused as he looked directly at me to make sure I got his message. "And that, George, is one of your jobs. Do you understand?"

He really let me have it and for a few seconds I was a little shaken. He didn't expect an answer from me. He could see by my reaction that I understood him clearly.

"Now," moving back to his chair and in a more friendly voice, "let's have a cup of coffee before you go back to work."

We chatted for a few minutes about how little computer knowledge there was in the JCS staff and about my job as his assistant deputy director, responsible for the planning, design and implementation of computer systems for the JCS.

When I returned to my office I began to think. When I accepted General Bestic's offer, I had expected a well organized, smooth functioning operation that I could step into and help steer.

I was wrong.

My directorate, established just three years earlier, was one of three under General Bestic at the Defense Communications Agency. (Figure 277.) The other two were engineering and a computer center, located in the basement of the Pentagon, that operated the computers supporting the JCS. Reporting to me in two divisions were about twenty civilians with advanced technology degrees and three junior military officers. I also was the project officer for a $4,000,000 contract with the Mitre corporation to help me design systems for the JCS.

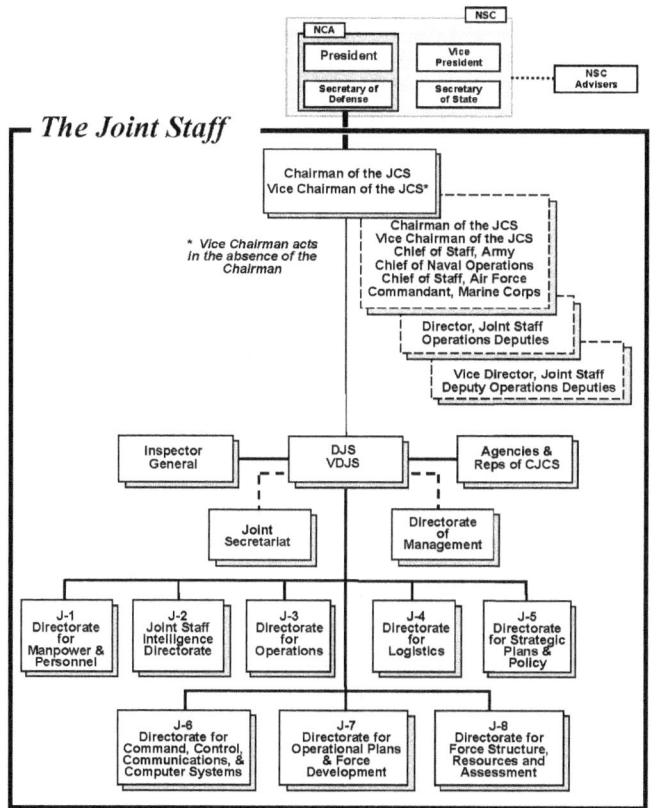

Figure 275: **Joint Staff organization.** This figure shows the organizational complexity of the Joint Chiefs of Staff, who were (and are) the users of the National Military Command System (Figure 272) and, therefore, the customer for the NMCS Technical Support services that I provided. Multiple components of the joint staff might not only use those services, but also help coordinate development of relevant systems. It is apparent from this figure and Figure 272 that developing and coordinating automated systems at the national level, as we were doing, involved extensive interaction with people at the top of the military. This was challenging in the 1965-70 era because very few in the high ranks had interest in investing heavily in the potential of automation. The NMCS Technical Support office is not on the chart because the JCS has limits on the number of staff members. But no limits apply to other agencies that can help, of which we were one. JCS = Joint Chiefs of Staff; [V]DJS = [Vice] Director of the Joint Staff.

23. THE JOINT CHIEFS OF STAFF

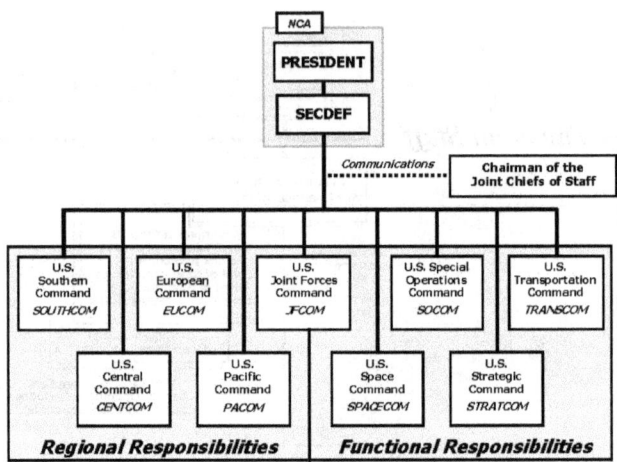

Figure 276: **Combatant Commands.** The Joint Chiefs of Staff do not command fighting forces. That is left to a handful of four-star officers called "combatant commanders" who receive their military orders directly from the President or the Secretary of Defense (SECDEF). Combatant commands may be geographical or functional. The the best known combatant commander was General Norman Schwartzkopf, who happened to be the CENTCOM commander when the 1990-1991 Gulf War erupted. The diagram shows the specific commands that existed in 2000. In 1965, the commands were: Strategic Air Command, Pacific Command, Alaskan Command, European Command, US Southern Command, Atlantic Command, Continental Air Defense Command, and US Strike Command (Cole et al, appendix 1).

I was the only one, however, who had extensive operational experience in the military. This was the opposite of Kunia where I started out with a staff consisting of naval officers with considerable operational experience and little or no knowledge of computers.

Similar to Kunia, I had flagship-type responsibilities to the Chairman of the JCS and the flag officers directing his 7 multi-service directorates: planning, operations, policies, intelligence, manpower, communications, and logistics. They translated the

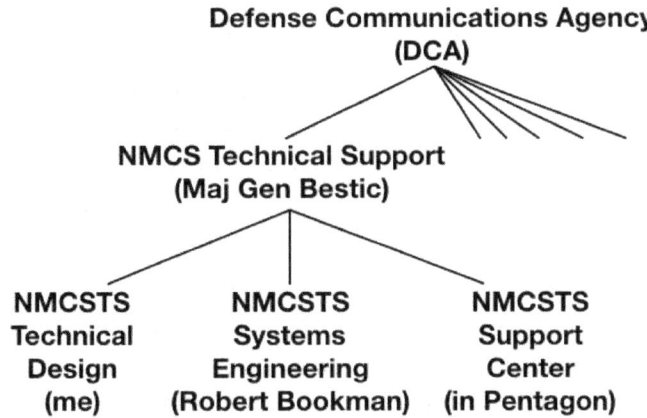

Figure 277: **Defense Communications Agency, circa 1965.** Shown is my portion of the DCA organizational chart. Because of limits to the size of the Joint Chiefs of Staff, other organizations were required to provide support in critical areas. One of these critical areas was the emerging computer technology. NMCS Technical Support (NMCSTS) was established to provide this support and was attached to DCA in Washington. DCA is today known as DISA, the Defense Information Systems Agency.

JCS's worldwide functions into action.

My big problem here was that no one on my staff, or from Mitre, had any experience or operational knowledge about the work accomplished by these JCS directorates. Without actual military experience, the only way they could acquire this information was to work closely, on a daily basis, with the military officers in the JCS who had that responsibility.

But that wasn't happening.

While the JCS officers were very interested in acquiring computer support, developing requirements for that support in terms understandable to computer systems analysts was a major obstacle. Also, it was difficult for the Mitre analysts to get into the JCS classified spaces and, when they did, security issues often got in the way.

23. THE JOINT CHIEFS OF STAFF

It took me about six months to set up a procedure that would work. That procedure consisted simply of me assigning my better staff members as permanent project officer advocates for each of the JCS directorates. In that capacity they spent all their time in their respective JCS office and acted as a right arm for the JCS officer responsible for the directorate's computer support. They were authorized to deal directly with the Mitre team leaders and other contract representatives in my name.

Their orders were to apply Mitre resources, in any way possible, to identify, develop and implement computer support for their assigned JCS office. This was not as simple as it sounds. Mitre policies required their project leaders to document all requirements, which were then reviewed by higher level Mitre officials, before work could start. All these steps had a formal paper trail that my office also reviewed.

Once the JCS officers got better acquainted with, and trusted, my staff members and the Mitre analysts, we began to get things done. This was especially true for the J3 (operations directorate) where my staff member (Dave Miquillon) made himself a very valuable and trusted addition.

In addition to reviewing and signing off on key project steps, my job focused on moving toward technical integrations as well as helping these project offices get their jobs done. They had orders to use me and my office to clear any obstacles that got in their way.

As we grew more comfortable with computers and enlarged the scope of our efforts, we encountered new problems.

For example: In May 1962, the President of South Vietnam, with the help of the joint force commander in Vietnam (General Westmoreland), began a nationwide program to convert and reorganize 16,398 existing hamlets (something like U.S. villages) into 12,000 "strategic hamlets" that were bigger, more sustainable, stronger, better fortified, better guarded, and more capable economically, socially, and politically. The objective was to improve security and reduce the influence of the communist Viet Cong, ultimately winning the war.

Clearly, it was critically important to know if this strategy was working. General Westmoreland and the Joint Staff, with the help of Mitre and our staff, initiated a large computer based effort known as the "Hamlet Evaluation Project."

The task required a steady flow of data from each of the thousands of old and new hamlets across South Vietnam, which we would then analyze. It was a large and very complex undertaking, supported by General Westmoreland's computer center in Vietnam and ours in the basement of the Pentagon.

Did the Computerized Hamlet Evaluation Project help us in that war? After about eight months it was possible to generate some answers to questions about the Hamlet strategy. Unfortunately, because there was never solid confidence in the completeness, and, especially, the reliability and accuracy of the data, there was insufficient confidence in those answers to support major decisions.

Although the U.S. finally withdrew from that war, ceding a victory to the North Vietnamese, some analysts claim that the data indicated we were actually winning the war when we withdrew.

All the data from that war is now in the National Archives. It is possible that at some time in the future, researchers will examine the Hamlet Evaluation data carefully, to determine if an automated system of that type can actually help determine a nation's progress in a major war. After all, it was probably the first time in history that an automated system was developed to help the U.S. assess the progress of a major conflict. Certainly there must be some lessons in that failed effort that would today be of value.

Using a computer system to provide critical information to the President is very risky without complete confidence in the entire system itself.

About 10 p.m. one night during the war in Vietnam, the red phone on the flag officer's watch desk in the Pentagon's National Military Command Center (NMCC) rang. The admiral on duty

23. THE JOINT CHIEFS OF STAFF

picked it up and heard, "This is the President. I want to know the correct number of casualties we have suffered in the last twenty-four hours."

"Yes, sir, I'll call you back Mr. President."

"No, I'll wait."

The source for the quickest answer to the President's question was a teletype machine about 30 feet in front of the flag officer. This machine was able to access the Vietnam database we had developed and established for the JCS. So far, so good. Unfortunately, we were all aware that the database was far from accurate. But with the President of the United States waiting on the phone, the admiral nevertheless used that teletype machine to provide a quick answer.

President Johnson probably knew almost immediately that the answer was not a reliable one. As we learned later, the President had been listening to television broadcasts that reported casualties, and that information was not consistent with the answer he received from the NMCC watch officer.

We knew the reasons for the differences in the figures. The JCS data was based on information supplied by General Westmoreland's staff. Reporters in Vietnam would use different sources and get different answers from each command they questioned – for good reason. The Navy kept track of Navy casualties, the Army kept track of Army and related casualties, and General Westmoreland's staff kept track of all casualties, including the South Vietnamese forces working with them. In addition, the term "casualties" had different meanings for different people. For some, it included the wounded as well as those killed.

The difference in time zones added to complexities in the database, as did the deep incompatibilities in the technical structures of the computer systems themselves. If any two military commands had the same hardware system or software, it was purely coincidental.

Normally, I took the heat for problems with computer systems. This time it was the operations directorate in the joint staff who took the heat.

We had additional problems. Compounding the newness of the technology, there was a shortage of knowledgable senior officers who were willing to commit and risk the resources needed to develop computer systems, as exemplified about six months after I assumed my job as the technical director for automated support to the JCS.

One of my customers, the Air Force general heading the JCS logistics directorate (J4) had, with the assistance of the Mitre Corporation, initiated a large, very comprehensive project that promised to revolutionize certain aspects of logistical planning. Specifically, it would automate a considerable portion of the work needed to identify the number and type of transport ships needed to support a planned invasion. It would also provide templates for ship loading and many other details associated with an amphibious landing in a combat area.

Loading large ships with tanks, trucks, artillery, ammunition, fuel, and massive amounts of other equipment was a time consuming, critical job that could result in a failed landing if not done well. All the equipment must be loaded so that, when off-loaded at an invasion site, the right equipment was ashore at the right time.

I had witnessed planners actually sitting at a large table placing miniature tanks, trucks, etc. in the hold of ship mockups as a way of developing their loading plans – an approach that could have been used 3000 years earlier to plan the amphibious landing at Troy!

So this was an unprecedented, far-sighted project that would never have been put together without the imaginative, technical-operational knowledge and vigorous personal leadership of the J4 himself. He was an unusually perceptive and innovative flag officer.

In spite of many problems the project proceeded on schedule and, most importantly, the concept appeared to be well ahead of any individual service's large automated logistics project. By its very leadership, it had the promise of setting logistic data reporting standards across all the services. It would have

23. THE JOINT CHIEFS OF STAFF

gone far in eliminating the complex mix of non-standard data input to automated systems that was mushrooming among the different services. This was the very problem, mentioned earlier, that prevented President Johnson from receiving accurate and reliable reports on the war casualties in Vietnam.

About three months before the project was due for a routine formal budget review to determine if it should be continued, the Air Force general's tour was up and he was transferred.

His replacement was a Navy admiral with an extensive submarine operational background, but absolutely no experience, and less affinity, for the use of computers for military matters.

At his initial briefing on the project, conducted first by his staff and then by me, we reviewed the status of the project and the uses of the proposed funds. I knew immediately that we were hitting a brick wall. It was clear that he did not in any way share the vision of his predecessor. He abruptly terminated the project.

But the two million dollars already spent on the project didn't all go down the drain. We were able to salvage some of the programs and use them in other logistic support projects. But his decision meant that the JCS abandoned its leadership role in the use of computers for logistics and the opportunity to introduce some data standards into the Department of Defense information jungle.

I have to admit we received no sympathy from anyone in the JCS. At that time, computers were a growing irritant to the operation of established procedures. Except for the operations directorate (J3) – for whom we had developed automated systems supporting target generation – damage assessment and other requirements that turned out well, computer systems were far from a proven capability.

While my office had the design responsibility for computer systems, the actual operation of the computers themselves was under a sister organization, the National Military Command System Support Center (NMCS Support Center), which was also subordinate to my boss, General Bestic.

They were in the basement of the Pentagon and operated the computers that supported the JCS and, to a degree, the offices of the Department of Defense and the White House Situation Room. It was run by an Air Force colonel, Emmet Gossnel, who preceded me in the job I had. They had a staff of programmers and performed all the day-to-day support required by the JCS, especially the J3.

Whenever my office and Mitre designed a system, we knew that the NMCS Support Center would eventually inherit the operation of that system, so they were always consulted at the beginning of and throughout systems development. I have to give Mitre credit for the way it evolved in our work with JCS. It took the JCS a while before they accepted the Mitre people into their confidence. And without really close working relations, it is very difficult to get any effective work done.

As a result of the bad experience with President Johnson, the purse strings opened somewhat for my work and we managed to increase the level of support for automated systems among all the directorates.

I can honestly say that my tour at Kunia and my five years with the NMCS Technical Support put me right at the forefront of the development of computer support for the military. These were the early days of high-level military applications of computers and so the work was not on peanut projects. It would, directly and indirectly, prove to be foundational, evolving over the years into the development of the World Wide Military Command and Control System (WWMCCS, pronounced "wimmix"), where we principally represented the interests of the JCS. We found ourselves in the middle of many changes in JCS operations and their interaction with the different services.

For example, a sister directorate under General Bestic, run by a senior executive civilian named Robert Bookman, was responsible for the engineering portion of all requirements generated by the JCS. We worked very closely with Bookman. It was his staff that hooked up the White House hot line communication system to the Kremlin, so the President and the Rus-

283

23. The Joint Chiefs of Staff

sian leader could talk over a private phone. In addition to the NMCS Support Center, Bookman's staff was involved in almost all the projects we undertook, ensuring that we were designing the computer communications part correctly.

I became good friends with the head of the White House Situation Room, Arthur J. McCafferty, as we tried to assist him. In those early days, the Situation Room was a very small operation with practically no automation capability. Art depended a lot on Bookman's staff, the J3, and the National Military Command Center in the Pentagon.

My shop, try as it did, couldn't provide Art with any significant help. Art, I know, was reluctant to commit to paper any requirements he had. The "need to know" requirement for the situation room was exceptionally tight. President Johnson was a very strict "no copies" man. This very tight security precluded any really significant projects where requirements needed to be spelled out in detail. Bookman's staff did have an ongoing assistance project with Art, but other than the Pentagon-Moscow hot line for the President and some very highly classified Mitre projects, supervised by Bookman, I was not involved in any significant support for Art.

Another interesting and challenging responsibility was the requirement to maintain compatibility with the President's alternate command site at Fort Ritchie, Maryland, also known as Site R. A deep underground relocation facility for the Department of Defense located six miles from Camp David, it is a nationally critical communications facility and serves as the Alternate National Military Command Center (schematically shown in Figure 272).

For a long time, the NMCS Support Center had difficulty ensuring that the software and data on their Pentagon computers was replicated accurately and quickly on the computers at Fort Ritchie. They were hauling magnetic tapes from the Pentagon to Fort Ritchie, an hour's ride away by helicopter. As seems natural today, the NMCS Support Center staff wanted to transmit the data electronically from the Pentagon to the Fort Ritchie computers directly. The project leader for that effort who kept at it, despite being told it could not be done, was a reserve naval officer, Jack "Bud" Hoff. I believe their first successful computer-to-computer transmission was in 1965. That was a really big breakthrough – highly classified at the time – and it occurred years before the 1969 computer linkage at the Advanced Research Projects Agency (ARPA) that is today generally recognized as first. Strangely, Bud (who now happens to be my neighbor) never received any official recognition for the accomplishment.

Not only was I up to my neck in defining and implementing automated support for the nation's highest military commands, I was in the middle of the very sensitive acquisition process for many millions of dollars worth of hardware and software systems. The latter was far less interesting, and far more exasperating and problem prone than trying to develop new software systems. It was my first brush with the very powerful forces in Washington that seek government contracts. I had no choice but to buckle down and learn all the details of that process.

One of the toughest problems was insuring that the bidding process was not only completely neutral, but that all perceptions and analyses of the process supported selections based completely on merit. It is not an easy process. The evaluation of bids is one of the most carefully disciplined procedures I have experienced, and a process I never looked forward to.

But a more significant realization on my part was the knowledge that I had been lucky enough to be involved in a big way in a major new technology that was actually changing, not only the military, but the world itself. I also came to appreciate that it would be a long time before the role of computers in the military would be optimized.

A key lesson from my 1959-1962 tour at Kunia carried over to my 1965-1970 tour at DCA. At Kunia, my staff worked with nine different war rooms. We consciously decided to develop capabilities for each of them individually, because that was what we could understand, see, and evaluate. We knew this would create some duplication, but we also knew that we did not know how

23. THE JOINT CHIEFS OF STAFF

to integrate requirements from different organizations, or even if integrated systems were technically possible. Remember, this was so early in computing that computer-to-computer communications and time-sharing did not exist.

When I was hired by General Bestic at the Defense Communications Agency in 1965, I found there the same approach: designing and and developing computer projects for single organizations, such as those in the J3 operations division of the JCS. This less-than-ideal approach, which had been proposed by Mitre, increased the number of automated systems supporting the different directorates of the Joint Staff. However, it was at least feasible given the technology of the day. The organization chart in Figure 275 clearly shows how complicated it would have been to integrate the planning for computer systems between the JCS's many directorates and other sub-organizations. The complexity would have increased still further by integrating related requirements from the combatant commanders (Figure 276). The development of on-line (computer-to-computer) capabilities in the 1970s changed the need to focus only on individual capabilities. On-line access made it possible to plan and develop systems that could be used by multiple directorates and the combatant commanders.

I mention this because some historical publications criticize the military's development of computer systems in this era. For example, in 1971 a subcommittee of the House Armed Services Committee described the Defense Communications System (a key element of WWMCCS) as "merely an association of facilities tied together and attempting to act in concert, but with no central authority to direct its action."[2] This view does not seem to understand that we started using computers from scratch in 1961, and that central authority made a conscious decision to do individual projects until and if integrated planning was feasible.

Earlier in my tour, in June 1967, I had received a call from the

---

[2]Pearson, page xviii.

captain detail officer (the officer in charge of reassigning captains in the Navy.) His name was Sam Orme and he was an old friend.

"George," he said, getting right to the point, "We have been planning your next duty station. How about a job as the senior defense attaché to Ambassador Edwin Oldfather Reischauer in Japan?"

Before I could recover from my surprise, he went on. "We've done all the background checking and the Ambassador has accepted you. We know you can hold your liquor and we checked out your wife too."

"What, you checked out my wife?"

"Yep. You know these jobs require a great deal of social skills and you have both passed with flying colors. What do you say?"

At first I was intrigued. I had always wanted a job as an attaché, but that was long before I had two young sons. I also knew that there was a certain amount of intelligence work connected with those jobs, and that might take some special training.

Then Sam continued, "I'll send you some pictures of your quarters there. They are quite large and it includes a car and some staff that go with the house. Your wife should love it. And one more thing. You will have to learn to speak Japanese. That means a year long course somewhere before you go to Japan. That's why we are contacting you now."

I knew I didn't want to learn Japanese, but I didn't say anything about it.

We talked a little more as he gave me the details. "I'll need your answer in a few days, George. We have to get this done."

I thanked Sam and told him I would call him in two days to let him know.

It didn't take Georgette long to make up her mind. In spite of all the perks, she did not want to go. I guess she could tell by my reaction that I wasn't thrilled by a tour in Japan, either. In any event we went over all the pros and cons and decided that we were just too happy in the Washington area. We didn't think it would be especially good for our sons. There were just too many

23. THE JOINT CHIEFS OF STAFF

unknowns for them. Also, I had visited Japan twice on my last ship (the *Tolovana*) and it really didn't appeal to me.

I had no idea how it would affect me professionally, so that didn't enter into my thinking. I did know that if I took the job, barring selection to admiral, it would be my last Navy job before retirement. I told Georgette that my value in the civilian job market at that time would only be high in Japan. That meant we might be tempted to stay on in Japan after I retired.

We both knew that was out of the question.

I called Sam the next day, thanked him for the offer and declined.

Georgette and I have never regretted our decision, but we have often wondered what life would have been like if we had taken the job.

ASSISTANT SECRETARY OF DEFENSE
WASHINGTON, D. C. 20301

MANPOWER AND
RESERVE AFFAIRS

6 AUG 1971

Rear Admiral R. E. Spreen
Director, Information Systems
Program Planning Office
Office of the Chief of Naval Operations
Alexandria, Virginia   22301

Dear Admiral Spreen:

Let me take this opportunity to express my appreciation for the efforts of some of the men in the Department of Defense Computer Institute who developed and presented an excellent program of computer application and management concerns over a period of some ten weeks. This program was presented to my immediate top staff and has provided for me and my staff a far broader understanding of some of the intricacies of computer operations than we had prior to that time.

In particular I should like to mention the great amount of time and attention given this effort by Captain George P. Sotos, who commands the DoD Computer Institute and Lt. Col. Frank D. Troyan who was instrumental in doing a lot of the behind-the-scenes work in preparation for the presentation of the several lectures and discussions. Additionally, I should like to express my appreciation to all of the members of the DoD Computer Institute staff who took part as resource people and as lecturers in these presentations.

To our way of thinking this has been such an outstanding effort that I have recommended to other Assistant Secretaries of Defense that they should probably find it highly rewarding to do the same thing.

Sincerely,

SIGNED
Roger T. Kelley

Figure 290: **Spreading the word about computers at the highest levels.** Personal contact with computers was still a tremendous novelty in 1971, even at the highest levels in the Pentagon.

Chapter 24

Loyalty Is a Two-Way Street

I had received another interesting call from Sam Orne in early 1968.

"You don't have a college degree, do you George?"

"No, I don't, Sam," I answered, "Why do you ask? What's up?"

"Well I don't have one either. But I'm leaving this job today and enrolling in a degree program at George Washington University. And if you're smart you'll do the same thing," he said.

"What the hell are you talking about, Sam?"

"You have just been excluded from consideration for the rank of admiral." And before I could react he went on. "The Secretary of the Navy has flat out instructed the selection board not to select any one who doesn't have a college degree." Sam's voice was bitter. "It's in his instructions to the selection board."

Both Sam and I had been promoted with or ahead of our respective groups our entire careers. And right now Sam had one of the top jobs in the Navy for a captain. Most occupants of that billet were routinely selected for admiral.

It was a death blow to any chances I had for promotion to the rank of admiral.

The Secretary's guidance to the selection board was never published outside the Pentagon. If Sam hadn't called me I would never have known.

24. LOYALTY IS A TWO-WAY STREET

Sam was right. Neither he nor I were selected for rear admiral. We both went on to acquire degrees, but we had both missed the boat! As did many others.

In better times, the Secretary's selection board instructions were more or less routine and didn't single out any group for discriminatory treatment. Yes, I thought it was a form of discrimination, but, to tell the truth, his actions were not a complete surprise.

The newspapers, especially in Washington, DC, had been on a media binge about how senior naval officers, who developed and supervised technically complex multi-million dollar projects with private contractors, were being taken advantage of by the better educated contractors. As a result, the Secretary indicated his agreement with the media by blocking our promotions.

I was called to active duty in December 1940, when I was a senior at the University of Chicago. My plan to return a year later and finish college was disrupted by the war.

Five years later, after the war, when I decided to remain in the Navy as a regular officer, I had a gut feeling that the lack of a degree would some day be a handicap in competition with my Navy peers, especially the Naval Academy graduates. But, even though I knew I would be handicapped, I felt strongly enough about a seagoing career to apply for the regular Navy.

Shortly after I was accepted into the regular Navy in 1946, I requested a year's leave of absence to obtain the college degree at my own cost. The request was denied with official assurance that lack of degree would not affect my career.

Despite that assurance, it turned out, twenty-one years later, that I was right.

The Secretary's motives were understandable. But in my view, if he actually did issue such instructions, he was disregarding the aspirations and livelihood of a large number of Navy captains who had every reason to expect a much fairer shake.

It was such an unfathomable action to be taken, without even a formal notice to those most affected, that I still find it hard to believe.

On the other hand, I knew Sam Orme well and have no reason to question what he told me.

So, did the Navy suffer from the Secretary's guidance to the selection board that excluded experienced combat veterans like Sam and myself?

In all honesty my answer has to be no. The officer quality was still there. The Navy is fortunate. It will always have a deep reservoir of excellent officers with the valuable experience and the tested judgment required for flag officer responsibilities.

In my case, even had I known what would happen, I still would have applied for a commission in the regular Navy. I was that eager.

My good fortune in assignments continued when, in June 1970, I was assigned to command the Department of Defense Computer Institute (DODCI). By then I had ten solid years of high level responsibilities that involved heavy use of computers and communications at the national command level. So I was very comfortable in my new job.

DODCI had a unique role. It was a "joint" command, meaning we had officers from all three services on the staff. They were all very bright and "into" the use of computers in the military ... despite perceptions of the old timers and most of the senior officers that it was an overblown, unproven, temporary phenomenon.

One of DODCI's jobs was to teach officers from all three services about computers and to instill in them some respect for, and appreciation of, their value.

That last sentence was easy to write, but hard to do. Notwithstanding all the good (and bad) publicity about computers in the military, the technology simply was not on the front burner when it came to officer qualifications.

Of the three services, the Air Force had made it the most important to their officers' careers. But neither the Navy nor, I believe, the Army, had.

24. Loyalty Is a Two-Way Street

DODCI had three-week, two-week, and one-week courses which we taught locally and all over the country with traveling teams.

One of the first things I did upon assuming command was to review in detail what we were teaching. I learned that we were doing a good job, that my instructors were first class, and the students were giving us excellent evaluations.

But to my surprise, we were not teaching how the computers were actually being used nor what the plans were for the use of computers in the military. I had just spent the last five years in a job where my primary mission was to provide computer support to the directorates of the Joint Chiefs of Staff. So I was certainly up to date on computer use in the military.

There was a good reason why the DODCI curriculum was not up to date. None of my instructors or even my civilian advisors had much experience with the actual use of computers for military purposes. Yes, they knew a great deal about the theories associated with computers and how they operated, but that was as far as it went.

And that's what we were teaching. The theory was interesting and the potential was exciting, but teaching their growing, actual military use was missing.

I immediately set in motion a plan to include in our curriculum information about the current use of computers.

This turned out to be easy since I had friends in all the Joint Chiefs of Staff directorates. They were happy to allow my instructors to shadow them for weeks at a time. Each instructor I sent there had to return with material that we could insert into our curriculum.

After about six months, my staff had completely rewritten our curriculum. We were finally teaching the nuts and bolts of how the JCS was currently using computers, and what their plans were.

The senior civilian computer advisor for the JCS, Herb Goertzel, encouraged our efforts and greased the skids for us in the Pentagon. He helped us in so many ways. At the same time, we helped him by sending our traveling teaching teams to sites he was working with the JCS.

In this way, my instructors learned a great deal about the JCS computer operations and the computer operations of many different commands that interacted with the JCS. It was a good solid "win win" arrangement, and our students benefitted greatly from it.

The Institute did so well that several years after I left it was made a part of the National War College.

Strangely, my eagerness to spread our computer knowledge paid unexpected, very valuable dividends for me personally.

In response to a request from Carl Clewlow, a senior official in the DOD human resources office, I established an after-hours introductory computer course for senior personnel from that office. For three evenings a week, over a period of about ten weeks, we carried our teletype machines and other equipment into the Pentagon and taught ten or so of the most senior officials in that office. We were happy to teach the course and we met some very dedicated officials who recognized the potential value of computers and wanted to learn more (see Figure 290).

When I was approaching retirement Mr. Clewlow called and asked if it was OK to drop to the head of the General Accounting Office (GAO) a note that I was retiring and might be of some use to the GAO. Of course, I said yes and thanked him. About ten months later, I was recruited by the GAO for a very responsible position to head up computer training for the GAO staff. That led to 12 years at the GAO conducting computer system audits of major federal agencies like the Veterans Administration and the Air Force Global Weather Command.

Even more strangely, after I was at GAO for twelve years, I was contacted by an official of the Department of Education. He invited me to apply for a position as the head of their information resources department. Equivalent to flag rank in the Navy and with a substantial increase in salary, I was pleasantly surprised at the invitation. However, at the time I was 65 years old and quite happy at the GAO as a GS 15 civil servant, a grade comparable to

24. Loyalty Is a Two-Way Street

that of a Navy Captain.

Convinced that the purpose of the invitation was merely to increase the applicant field and improve the appearance of a competitive selection, I decided not to apply.

A month later the same person called me again and urged me in very strong terms to apply. So I did.

Much to my surprise I was selected and that led to 13 years in a very challenging leadership role at the Department of Education.

At a reunion of the DODCI staff about two years after my selection, I learned that the official who persuaded me to apply had attended a DODCI course. He sought out the instructors and asked if they could recommend someone for the position he was trying to fill. The dominant requirement for that individual was that he could institute and manage major changes in their computers systems operation. Apparently I was their unanimous recommendation and that's when he called the second time.

My work at DODCI was very stimulating. So much so that I qualified as an instructor in my own school and was soon teaching. If that sounds easy, it was not. We had a procedure that all instructors would be evaluated by a three man board before being certified as qualified.

I had a very tough time getting qualified. At my first evaluation, reluctant to tell me in detail how poorly I had done, the evaluation board simply handed me the diagram shown in Figure 297.

The diagram was very effective and I got the message. Apparently they thought I was a pretty good boss, but were recommending I stay out of the classroom. Three months later, after four more trial runs with the board, they certified me and I started teaching on a regular basis.

After two years at DODCI I had completed thirty-two and a half years in the Navy and it was over! (Figure 298)

There is no way I could have designed a career with a mix of jobs that were more varied, challenging, interesting, and satis-

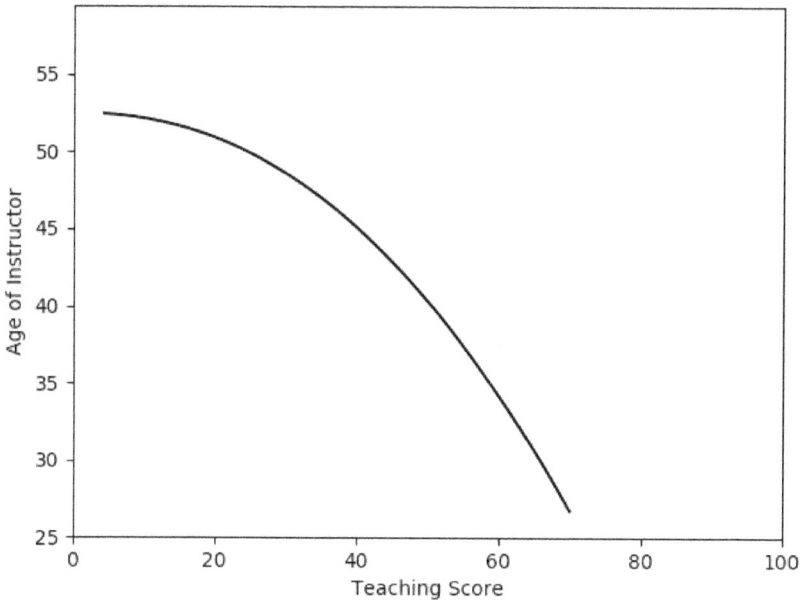

Figure 297: **Age vs. teaching.** A not-very-encouraging evaluation from a instructor-evaluation board at the Department of Defense Computer Institute. "Poor" was 0-60. "Acceptable" was 60-70. "Average" was 70-80. "Excellent" was 90-100, and was our required level. I was by far the oldest teacher.

---

fying. None of them were dull and it was always fun. It seemed that every single day I was confronted with, and had to learn something, new.

Like most naval officers who survived three hot wars and a long cold war, I consider myself damn lucky.

For 30 years the turmoil caused by those wars kept pushing me into responsible command-type jobs where I received a minimum of orders, very little guidance, and learned pretty much on my own.

None of my numerous mistakes, including a 1942 grounding

24. LOYALTY IS A TWO-WAY STREET

Figure 298: **A goodbye from DODCI and the Navy.** Rear Admiral Roger Spreen, my boss (left), says goodbye to me and my family as we retire from the U.S. Navy in June 1972, after my $32\,^1/_2$ years of service. Our younger son, George, now an oncologist, is on my right. Georgette, my lovely wife, is on my left and our older son, John, now a cardiologist and Air National Guard colonel, is on Georgette's left.

---

at the entrance to the Miami Ship Channel when I was the executive officer and navigator of the *PC 476*, ever resulted in an official action. Our bosses, remote and busy with other more important issues, didn't bother to look into my transgressions.

I also managed to find and marry Georgette, a naturally beautiful girl whose quiet intellect, love of the arts, common sense, and good humor rubbed off on me. Yes, I was damn lucky. A terrific mother to our two sons, she turned all our Navy moves into mini-vacations and family adventures. The one girl that really made life complete!

And my good fortune continued as John and George, our two curious, handsome, personable, now-physician sons, kept tackling challenges that erased the word boring from our lives.

I was 52 years old when I retired from the Navy. I worked 25 more years in computer systems as a civil servant and retired at age 77 in 1997. As I write this I am 101 years old. And for both Georgette and myself, these 49-and-still-counting post-Navy years remain exciting and full of challenges!

Appendix A

Photo Credits

Boxes contain the figure numbers, each of which matches the page number where the figure appears. The credit appears after the figure number.

Images for which formal permission is not acknowledged below are either historical artifacts now in the public domain or are used by the author for purposes of comment, criticism, and scholarship pursuant to the Fair Use Doctrine of the U.S. Copyright Act.

[2] cryptome.org. [12] Microsoft Virtual Earth via cryptome.org. [16] Microsoft Virtual Earth via cryptome.org. [21] US Navy photograph via United States Naval Institute [24] National Security Archive (public domain) [30] California State Military Museum. https://bit.ly/35UKZby or http://www.militarymuseum.org/CommStaDavis.html [31] California State Military Museum. http://www.militarymuseum.org/CommStaDavis.html [36] Royal Canadian Air Force. Downloaded from: https://bit.ly/3qcrm6W [54] http://www.navsource.org/archives/06/326.htm [56] Consult this web page: http://www.desausa.org/ [61] Left: Erich Utecht 1968-1970 via navsource.org. Right: National Archives 7573650 [66] US Navy photograph [71] US Navy. [72] Royal Navy photograph via Wikipedia. [76] USAF photo 070119-F-0000R-101 via Wikimedia Commons [78] Author's collection [81] [Left] Allied Photographers via navsource.org. [Right] Paul Regarding via navsource.org. [82] Georgette C. Sotos, 1999 [92] [Top] Wikimedia [Middle-Left] Wikimedia [Middle-Right] US Navy [Bottom-Left] US Navy [Bottom-Right] US Navy [94] Wikipedia "USS Rankin" [95] Author [97] Author [104] US Navy photo via Wikimedia [120] US Navy photograph [123] US Navy photgraph [124] US Navy photgraph [140] US Navy photograph [156] Wikimedia Commons [166] National Archives 24743045 [176] US Navy photo [181] Author. [184] Author's collection [187] US Navy photo, reprinted in newspaper. [198] US Navy [204]

US Naval War College [209] *Proceedings* Magazine - September 2014 Vol. 140/9. [212] http://www.willyvictor.com/Pacific_Barrier/PacBar_1.html [220] U.S. Navy photograph [226] National Security Archive (public domain) [228] Author. [235] Honolulu Star-Bulletin. [238] Hawaii Visitors Bureau [244] Author [254] US Navy photo, reprinted from: www.navsource.org/archives/09/19/19064.htm [256] National Archives 7573652 [266] Wikimedia Commons: Touch Of Light, under the Creative Commons Attribution-Share Alike 4.0 International license. The license is at: https://bit.ly/1SrbRBk [272] Public domain [275] Joint Staff Officer's Guide, chapter 1. [276] Joint Staff Officer's Guide, chapter 1. [277] Author. [290] Author's collection [297] Author. [298] Author's collection.

Appendix B

Bibliography

Note: Some long internet URLs have been shortened with the bit.ly service.

Bamford, James. *The Shadow Factory*. New York: Doubleday, 2008.

Clift, A. Denis. "Ringside at the Missile Crisis." usni.org October 25, 2012. https://news.usni.org/2012/10/25/ringside-missile-crisis

Cole, Ronald H.; Poole, Walter S.; Schnabel, James F.; Watson, Robert J.; Webb, Willard J. *The History of the Unified Command Plan, 1946-1993*. Washington, DC: Joint History Office, Joint Chiefs of Staff, 1995. Available on-line at: https://bit.ly/2JCImhY

Cunningham CM; Watson DW. "Suppression of antibody response by group A streptococcal pyrogenic exotoxin and characterization of the cells involved." *Infection and Immunity*. 1978; 19: 470-476.

Galinsky, Victor. "On Tickling The Dragon's Tail." *Bulletin of the Atomic Scientists*. Feb 28, 2016.

GlobalSecurity.com. "Tunisia – Navy." https://bit.ly/2VFXh0R (Accessed Jan. 9, 2019)

Graff, Garret M. *Raven Rock: the Story of the Government's Secret Plan to Save Itself While the Rest of Us Die*. New York: Simon and Schuster, 2017.

Gregory, Eric. "Pearl Harbor: 16 Days To Die – Trapped By The Memories – Few Knew The Secret Of The Sunken Battleship; Families Weren't Told Of Sailors' Lingering Deaths." Seattle *Times*. December 7, 1995. https://bit.ly/1HRLIe7

Joint Staff Officer's Guide 2000 (Joint Forces Staff College Publication 1). Norfolk, VA: National Defense University, 2000. Available on-line at: `https://bit.ly/2GNvGH7`

Khrushchev, Nikita S. (Translated and edited by Strobe Talbott.) *Khrushchev Remembers*. Boston: Little, Brown, 1970.

Kile, Shannon N.; Kristensen, Hans M. "Fact sheet: Trends in world nuclear forces, 2017." SIPRI (Stockholm International Peace Research Institute), 2017. Available on-line at: `https://bit.ly/2go6is3`

LaVerde, Rene. navsource.org. https://bit.ly/2RpXgj9 (Accessed Jan. 9, 2019.)

Pearson, David E. *The World Wide Military Command and Control System: Evolution and Effectiveness*. Maxwell Air Force Base, AL: Air University Press, 2000. Available on-line at: `https://bit.ly/2GPWC1q`

Rust, William J. *Before the Quagmire: American Intervention in Laos, 1954-1961*. Lexington, KY: University Press of Kentucky, 2012.

Schlosser, Eric. *Command and Control: Nuclear Weapons, the Damascus Accident, and the Illusion of Safety*. New York: Penguin, 2013.

Sorenson, Theodore. Memo, Oct. 18, 1962. *jfklibrary.org*. https://bit.ly/2sl3P7F

sputniknews.com. "Cuban Missile Crisis: 14 days when the world was on the brink of nuclear war." October 14, 2017. https://bit.ly/2FhQHbN

Walker, Martin. *The Cold War: A History*. New York: Henry Holt/Owl, 1995. Pages 170-171.

Watson, Leon; Duell, Mark. "The man who saved the world: The Soviet submariner who single-handedly averted WWIII at height of the Cuban Missile Crisis." *DailyMail.com*. September 25, 2012. https://dailym.ai/2FlitnQ

Index

The index is restricted to ship names.

Antietam, 156
Arizona, 218, 219
Arkansas, 80
B-59, 44
Bennington, 254
Catamount, 102, 108, 112, 113
Colonial, 69–72, 74, 77–87, 90, 93, 94, 97, 99–102, 104–108, 110–112, 117–119, 170
Epperson, 220
Falgout, 219
Fitzgerald, 13
Franklin, 118
Gary, 54, 56–58, 60, 62, 63, 93, 94, 220
Harlan R. Dickson, 154, 157, 162, 164, 166, 167, 171, 176–178, 180, 181, 183, 188, 191, 193, 194, 196
Haverfield, 63
Henderson, 163, 164
Highway, 72
Jenkins, 220
McCain, 13
Nancy Moran, 58
Newell, 220
Nicholas, 220
O'Bannon, 220
Oak Hill, 104
Oriskany, 260, 261

PC 476, 170, 298
Philadelphia, 186
Philip, 220
Pollux, 114, 258, 260
Portland, 82
President Bourgiba, 63
Randolph, 179
Rankin, 94
Renshaw, 220
Shelton, 156
Sigma 7, 249
Squalus, 145
Sturtevant, 213
Taylor, 220
Tolovana, 37, 38, 60, 61, 156, 162, 254–256, 262, 263, 265, 267, 288
Truxton, 114
Walker, 220
West Virginia, 219
Whetstone, 92
Wilhoite, 220
Wilkes, 114
Willis, 87, 170, 304
Yellowstone, 194–196
Yorktown, 167

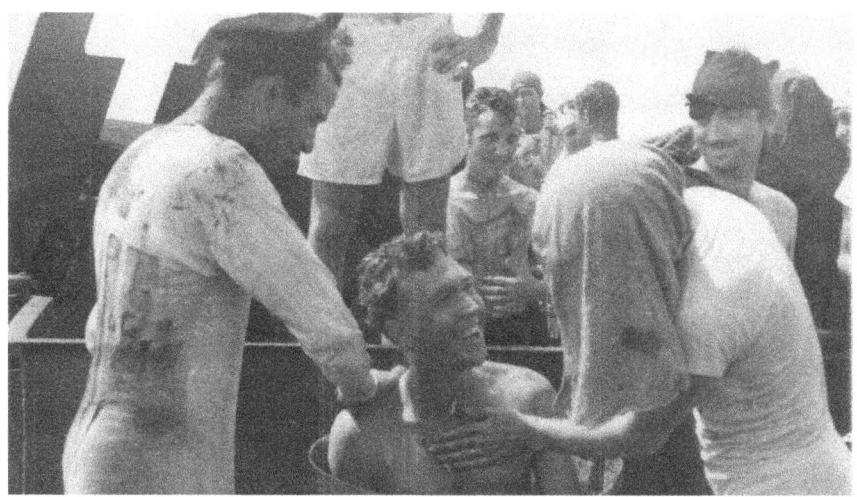

Figure 305: **About the author.** George P. Sotos, a Chicago native, retired as a Captain from the US Navy in 1972 after having six commands at sea over a career of more than 32 years. Above, he is shown on the left, participating in the ancient "crossing the line" ceremony in 1945. Below, he is conning the USS *Willis* into its berth alongside another ship in Guam.

www.ingramcontent.com/pod-product-compliance
Lightning Source LLC
Chambersburg PA
CBHW071736150426
43191CB00010B/1594